HONDURAS

&

BAY ISLANDS GUIDE

YOUR PASSPORT TO GREAT TRAVEL!

CRITICAL ACCLAIM FOR OPEN ROAD PUBLISHING'S CENTRAL AMERICA TRAVEL GUIDES

"First of its kind, **Honduras and the Bay Islands** includes Honduran history, the people, accommodations, restaurants, transportation, recreational facilities, maps, health concerns, money, climate ... and much more."

Travel Books & Language Center

"If you have to choose one guidebook, Paul Glassman's **Costa Rica Guide** provides a wealth of practical information, with a sharp eye and a sense of humor."

Travel and Leisure

"Belize Guide is *the* book you need. Don't leave home without it. Invaluable."

International Travel News

"... full of well-researched information on hotels, restaurants, sightseeing, history, and culture ... Selections for lodging and food cover a wide range of prices with plenty of inexpensive and moderate choices. Glassman's practical information tips are worth the price of the book alone ... definitely recommended." -

Series Reviews (Reviews of Travel Guide Series)

Guatemala Guide is "filled with useful information ... thoroughly explores the territory and subject."

Booklist

ABOUT THE AUTHORS

Jean-Pierre Panet is a travel writer who has bicycled and hiked through North America, Central America, South America, and Europe. He makes his home in Montreal, Canada.

Paul Glassman is the foremost authority on Central America travel, and has been writing the best-selling travel guides to the area since 1975. His **Costa Rica Guide**, **Belize Guide**, **Guatemala Guide**, and **Honduras Guide** (co-author) are the best sources for accurate, comprehensive, inside travel information to these beautiful and exciting lands. His research and attention to detail is unsurpassed, his style lively and literate.

Glassman's books are widely considered to be the classic guides to Central America.

ACKNOWLEDGMENTS

Many thanks to Jean-Pierre Panet, who prepared the original edition of *Honduras and the Bay Islands*, of which this is an update. As much as possible, I have tried to keep J.P.'s friendly, off-beat view of Honduras while bringing in new material about all the exciting happenings in this developing destination.

To Mario Gutiérrez Minera, who provided back issues of *Honduras This Week*, which were a gold mine of leads. You can obtain the latest information for yourself by subscribing to this excellent publication (at P. O. Box 1312, Tegucigalpa).

To Judith Shaffer of the *Honduras This Week* staff, who provided last-minute fact-checking as my deadline hovered ominously. Aside from her welcome assistance, Ms. Shaffer is the author of many detailed and sensitive articles about the countryside of Honduras.

To Arnold Greissle of Sahsa Airlines, who has aided my travels in Central America.

To numerous business owners in Honduras who, without knowing exactly what I was up to, chatted to a curious non-customer about their hotels and restaurants and travel agencies and their plans and prospects, and did so graciously and with apparent pleasure. Honduras is that kind of place.

To these and many others I am grateful, and I think you will be too, once you visit Honduras.

HONDURAS

&
BAY ISLANDS GUIDE

YOUR PASSPORT TO GREAT TRAVEL!

JEAN-PIERRE PANET
with
LEAH HART & PAUL GLASSMAN

OPEN ROAD PUBLISHING
PASSPORT PRESS

Second Edition

Library of Congress Catalog Number 93–87289
ISBN 1-883323-05-3

Back cover (scuba diving), front cover, and interior photos pages 11, 14, 254 and 255 courtesy of Frederick J. Dodd, International Zoological Expeditions
Photos on pages 31, 34, 75, 89, and 215 courtesy of the Embassy of Honduras
Back cover photo (macaw) by Mark W. Russell

CONTENTS

MAPS & SIDEBARS

MAPS

Regional Map 11
Honduras 17
Central Tegucigalpa 84
Metropolitan Tegucigalpa 91
Comayagua 121
Lake Yojoa 129
The Bay Islands 175
Roatán 189
The Ruins of Copán 217

SIDEBARS

Holidays in Honduras 50
Airlines with Direct Service to Tegucigalpa 55
Airlines with Direct Service to San Pedro Sula 55
Airlines with Direct Service to La Ceiba & Roatán 55
Prices in US Dollars 66
National Parks 76
Driving in Tegucigalpa 87
Emergency Service Numbers from Tegucigalpa 110
AIDS Warning 137
Driving High Points 179
Driving Low Points 179

1. INTRODUCTION

What does Honduras have in store for you? There are hundreds of miles of pristine, unspoiled, practically deserted beaches. You've got diving wrecks and walls within a swim of shore, along an extension of the longest barrier reef in the hemisphere.

You'll also find the ancient city where the Maya achieved their greatest artistic expression; cloud forest peaks where the elusive *quetzal* can be sighted; remote rivers lined by impenetrable tropical forest; and remains of pirate forts and Spanish forts and English forts that tell of the struggle for dominion and booty along the Spanish Main.

Honduras has it all, and more. And yet, for reasons of politics and economics and bad luck, it has never developed as a tourist destination – which is good luck for you.

Some day, before too long, the all-inclusive resorts will be in place, the gift shops will be everywhere, the charter flights will disgorge their hordes, the tour buses will shepherd groups to the accompaniment of canned patter, and you will have the privilege of putting down your money in order to get away from home and be a cipher.

But for now, you can go to Honduras and be part of the extraordinary. It's an opportunity not to be missed.

YOUR PASSPORT TO GREAT TRAVEL!

Editor's Note

Jean-Pierre Panet (pa-NAY) is one of those Montrealers who can get around and along in English, Spanish, Italian, and several other languages, not to mention French. But more importantly, in his role as the author of this book, he is skilled in the ways and language of travel.

J. P. is intrepid. He has bicycled and hiked through North America, Central America, South America, and Europe. He is a fastidious planner. His trips are preceded not just by perusals of guidebooks (sometimes there *are* no guidebooks to his destinations), but by research into details most people wouldn't think of, such as prevailing winds. He is persistent, but not to a fault. He will intrude himself gently into a hotel, a restaurant, an official agency, and not depart until he has all the facts. He is fussy. He will sleep in basic rooms, but he prefers moderate accommodations that offer value for money. He likes good food. A cyclist travels on his stomach.

In this book, you will have the benefits of J. P.'s extensive travel by plane, bus, foot, and, most of all, bicycle, and of his extensive research into what makes up Honduras, and what makes it a worthwhile travel experience for you. J. P. was accompanied on his travels by his wife, Natalie Rivest, M.D., and her contributions, while many, are especially notable in the section of health advice. Leah Hart worked with J. P. to gather background and introductory information, and to produce the final text and maps.

Honduras was discovered thousands of years ago by its original Amerindian inhabitants. It was "discovered" once again in 1502 by Christopher Columbus. Now, with *Honduras and Bay Islands Guide*, it becomes accessible to you as an off-beat, affordable, and fascinating destination.

Paul Glassman
Travel Editor

IN THIS BOOK, PRICES ARE EXPRESSED IN US DOLLARS.

REGIONAL MAP

HONDURAS IS FAMOUS FOR ITS GREAT DIVING

2. EXCITING HONDURAS!
- OVERVIEW

What do you think of when you think of — if you ever have thought
of — Honduras?
- A banana republic?
- Wars and revolutions, dictators and despots?
- A comic-opera country, the far-off land depicted by O. Henry in *Of
  Cabbages and Kings*?
- A place that nobody goes to, except, perhaps, to cut another notch in
  their travel belts?

Let me tell you that if you think of Honduras in any of these ways, you
are perfectly correct, at least to some degree. Honduras *has* largely lived
from the export of bananas. Honduras certainly *has* had an awful lot of
presidents and chiefs of state and influential generals since the Spanish
were expelled 170 years ago. There *are* quaint and funny aspects to the
country.

But if you think that you might go to Honduras just for the sake of
going, let me disabuse you of that notion.

Honduras has:
- **Jungly ruins**, where the artistic expression of the ancient, mysterious
  Maya reached its greatest development.
- Dozens of towns with gems of **colonial churches and monuments**, and
  a full-fledged Spanish fortress.
- **Pine-clad highlands**, and virtually untouched and unpopulated lowland
  forests alive with jaguar and tapir.
- Hundreds of miles of **deserted Caribbean beach**.
- **Excellent bird-watching**; a unique tropical botanical garden; swim-
  ming, fishing, tennis, golf and all the outdoor sports of a mild climate.

To a greater or lesser degree, other countries in Central America have
comparable, little-known attractions that have for well-known reasons of

politics and turmoil been ignored or avoided by vacationers and intrepid travelers until fairly recently, and which are now just being discovered and widely publicized.

But Honduras also has the **Bay Islands**, where hamlets barely changed since buccaneer times line the shores, where uninhabited jungled mountains extend inland, where diving along the barrier reef is as good as anywhere in the hemisphere, and where, oddly, the inhabitants speak English.

Personally, I enjoy cycling on roads not too heavily trafficked, with new scenes, new surprises, around every bend. Honduras fits the bill perfectly.

One of the best aspects of Honduras is that it is not yet heavily traveled. Yet the facilities are there: good, if not luxurious hotels, a road system that connects most points of interest, well-developed air transport, tour operators, and acceptable conditions of sanitation and health. The inhabitants are ready to greet and help the visitor from abroad, who is still something of a rarity.

And, maybe best of all, the prices for what you get can be very reasonable, even downright cheap, when you compare with other destinations in the Caribbean.

If you go to Honduras now, you will have the satisfaction of having been there before the boom, before the international hotel chains arrived and drove up prices and infringed on some of the charm. I think that will happen, but not soon. The touristic development that is now going on is being carried out by families and small companies, and most of the hotels and resorts, especially in the Bay Islands, are wonderfully idiosyncratic, some with pet exotic birds, and mini-zoos, and resident ghosts, and private wrecks for diving. Eating places are sometimes basic, usually wholesome, and sometimes gourmet quality. This is not yet Holiday Inn country, and it won't be, I think, for quite some time.

Here's a quick preview of what Honduras has in store for you:

TEGUCIGALPA

Central Tegucigalpa, still somewhat colonial-flavored, is small enough that you can get a sense of the city during a walk of just a few hours. There are some fine old examples of colonial and nineteenth century architecture, city squares in which to linger, and pedestrian streets for shopping and observing the flow of city life.

TO THE NORTH

There is much majestic countryside to be seen during a journey along the major highway, along with **Comayagua**, the old capital where colonial churches still stand; small and little-visited towns where old ways and a

HONDURAS AWAITS YOU!

slow pace of life still hold sway; and Lake Yojoa, as pleasant a stopping point and vacation area as will be found on the mainland. At the end of the route is **San Pedro Sula**, the metropolis of the north, and of modern Honduras; beyond are the coastal cities, beaches, and the special world of the **Bay Islands**.

THE NORTH COAST

The northwestern lowlands of Honduras — a strip about 50 kilometers wide, backed by mountain ridges for almost 200 kilometers — are the banana republic of Honduras. I don't mean this in any demeaning, stereotyping way. It's just that banana cultivation and commerce in bananas have made this area what it is today.

For the visitor interested in peoples, this is where you'll find the **Garífunas**, or Black Caribs, near Trujillo and Tela, and the **Miskito**, **Sumo**, and **Paya Indians** along the eastern stretches of coast.

The main attraction of the north coast, however, is **beaches**. There are miles and miles and miles of sandy strip, bordered by palms, as idyllic as any. The most accessible parts, near the ports, have some hotels, and even a few rather good resorts. And if it's isolation that you're after, you do not have to travel very far from any coastal town to find a stretch, away from major roads, where hardly anybody has gone before you.

THE BAY ISLANDS

More than a stretch of water separates mainland from islands. Mainlanders speak Spanish, while Bay Islanders speak English (sort of). Mainlanders are farmers. Islanders are fishermen and mariners and boatbuilders. Mainlanders are mostly *mestizos*, descended from Spaniards and native Americans. Bay Islanders are largely descended from Africans and Englishmen, from slaves and buccaneers and pirates.

For the visitor, the Bay Islands are a world removed not only from the mainland, but from everywhere else in the universe, a paradise of beach and rain-forested peaks in the sea, with few telephones, clocks, or cares, and some of the best fishing and diving in the hemisphere.

Located about 60 kilometers offshore, the islands, running in a 125-kilometer arc, are the tips of undersea mountains that extend out from the mainland's Omoa ridge. Their peaks, rising as high as 400 meters (1300 feet), are covered with oak and pine and cedar and dense, broad-leafed undergrowth, and studded with caves and cliffs. Coral reefs, often within swimming distance of shore, virtually surround most of the islands, forming natural breakwaters, and creating ideal, calm pools for diving, fishing, swimming and sailing.

Roatán is the largest of the Bay Islands, with the major towns, though there are also settlements on **Utila** and **Guanaja**. The smaller islands are **Morat**, **Helene** (Santa Elena) and **Barbaret** (or Barbareta). With more than 60 smaller cays offshore, the Bay Islands cover about 92 square miles.

WESTERN HONDURAS

Western Honduras is a mountainous region, curving along the borders of Guatemala and El Salvador. It is fairly densely populated for Honduras (though it doesn't seem so), with the highest concentration of Indian inhabitants, some living in villages virtually isolated from modern life.

You'll find the **Copán Ruins** in western Honduras. Copán was the Athens of the Mayan world, where art and astronomy flourished. There were larger Mayan cities to the north, in present-day Mexico and Guatemala, and the structures at Copán are relatively modest compared to those at Tikal and Palenque and Chichén-Itzá. But there are more carved monuments at Copán then elsewhere, and the intricate, swirling, decorative art surpasses not only that of other Mayan cities, but of any other civilization in the Western Hemisphere before the arrival of Europeans.

SOUTHERN AND EASTERN HONDURAS

In southern and eastern Honduras, there are good views of high plateaus. The vegetation changes to pines, and it is fresh and windy as you gain altitude. From the heights, before long, you can see the Gulf of

Fonseca in the distance, as you begin to wind down through hilly and broken terrain toward the Pacific Ocean.

ADVENTURE IN THE RAIN FOREST

Honduras is the last frontier of travel in Central America, where an adventuring soul can still be one of the few outsiders to drift along a lazy river bordered by centenary trees, listen to the roar of howler monkeys trooping through the jungle canopy, spot a limpkin wading in the shallows, and wonder at petroglyphs carved by mysterious ancient civilizations.

DIVING

Diving is what the Bay Islands are most known for. The sea is calm within the fringing reefs, and there are practically no drift currents along the south side of the islands. And if you like **coral reefs**, you'll find the corals around the Bay Islands spectacular, intact, and very much alive.

The underwater landscape features wandering clefts and caverns, sheer walls, cracks, tunnels, caves and ledges, reverse ledges, and dropoffs of 100 to 200 feet. Walls start as little as twenty feet under the surface, which affords more natural light than is usually available in wall diving.

FISHING

For the most part, sport fishing is something you'll participate in from resorts in the Bay Islands. On the mainland of Honduras, the most famous fishing hole is **Lake Yojoa**, known for bass weighing in at about ten pounds on the average.

NATIONAL PARKS

In just a few years, Honduras has moved into the forefront of Latin America in protecting and preserving its natural treasures. And treasures there are aplenty — over 700 species of birds, 500 piscine species, and flora that includes scores of species of orchids alone.

The **Mosquitia** region along the border of Nicaragua is one of the last largely undisturbed lowland forests in Central America. And there are pockets of highland cloud forest that the magnificent resplendent quetzal, the holy grail of birders, still calls home.

RAFT AND KAYAK THE JUNGLE RIVERS

Honduras has white water! It's rapid, it's exhilarating, it's ecological, it's adventurous, it's off-beat, it's inexpensive, but best of all, it's warm. There are major rivers throughout Honduras, but rafting operators mainly use those on the north coast, where water levels are most reliable during the rainy season from October to May.

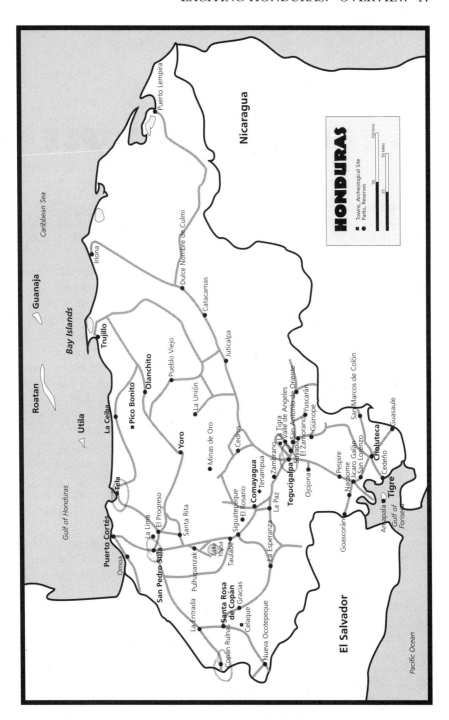

3. THE LAND & PEOPLE

INTRODUCTION

As Central America goes, Honduras is a large country, with few people. It has lots of resources, mineral and agricultural and scenic. It has, you might say, limitless possibilities.

But Honduras is a country that has never arrived, or "taken off." For its size, it has few people. Most of the suitable land is unused for agriculture. Minerals are unmined. Forests are cut and not replanted.

In colonial times, parts of Honduras were ruled from different imperial outposts, leaving no sense of nationality, and no tradition of self-rule. Dictatorships and frequent changes in government and competing regimes and foreign intervention have been the norm for most of the nation's independent history, making Honduras, in effect, a country without a government. Boundaries have changed, and part of the country has been controlled by foreigners.

In bare statistical terms, Honduras ranks somewhere near Bolivia and above Haiti in terms of national income and wealth per person.

This is all pretty dismal stuff, and yet it would be wrong to put Honduras in the category of national basket cases and depict it as a terrible place. Dictatorships there have been, but in the context of the times, they have never been as severe or sanguinary as in neighboring states. Poverty is a national condition, but there has never been the extreme divide between rich and poor, nor the large-scale exploitation of the masses, that has characterized countries elsewhere in the region. You'd never guess it, but it was Honduran banana workers who took the lead in the region in improving their conditions. Racial tensions have been few. There has been some land reform, and land is available to those who want to till it. The press has been relatively free, and in the absence of stable and far-reaching national governments, Hondurans haven't done badly at managing their affairs at the local level.

I don't want to make excuses. There *have* been cases of human rights abuses for which the government has been internationally condemned. Honduras *has* been the major base for the Contra War against Nicaragua.

But in recent years, the government has been constitutional, elections have been free and fair, and the Central American conflicts that have spilled over the borders of Honduras are receding. The outlook for Honduras is a fairly happy one. And it is a happy place to visit.

THE LAND

Honduras is a fertile country. It rains enough almost everywhere. There are many valleys, with expanses of flat land, there is plenty of sun and rich soil. Everything grows here, from apples and wheat and peaches at the higher altitudes to pineapples down in the wet, hot lowlands.

But Honduras does not have a simple landscape, anything but. It's a bit disordered, even messy. There are mountains here and there, spots of desert, jungle, with no continuation of anything. Nevertheless, it is possible to make something intelligible out of the ensemble.

Honduras covers 112,088 square kilometers (43,644 square miles), about the size of the state of Tennessee, or the country of Bulgaria in Europe. By Central American standards, Honduras is big, second in size after Nicaragua. But this is a sparsely populated land, with just under 5 million inhabitants. El Salvador, next door, has about four times the population density of Honduras.

Honduras stretches between 13 and 16 degrees north latitude, and from 83°15' to 89°30' west latitude. Though its peaks do not reach dramatic heights, it is the most mountainous country in Central America, and most of the land is more than a thousand feet above sea level. Roughly, very roughly, the country is shaped like a triangle bulging on one side. Along the north is the 800-kilometer (500-mile) Caribbean coastline. On the east, an 870-kilometer (545-mile) border with Nicaragua runs south and west from the Caribbean to the Pacific. The distance along the west side of the country is almost as long — 339 kilometers (211 miles) southwest with Guatemala, then 341 kilometers (212 miles) to the southeast with El Salvador, ending at the 145-kilometer (90-mile) Pacific coastline along the Gulf of Fonseca. Apart from this huge chunk of mainland, there are also the Bay Islands off the north coast, and farther out in Caribbean waters, the Swan Islands, or Islas del Cisne.

Mountains cover more than two-thirds of the land thus enclosed. Spread almost haphazardly, they create numerous valleys with small expanses of arable land, mostly isolated one from another. Some valleys, north and east of Tegucigalpa, are broader than the others, covered with savannas. Major ranges are the Merendón and Celaque, running roughly from southwest to northeast, with peaks as high as 2800 meters (over 9000 feet). The Nombre de Dios range, with peaks up to 8000 feet, lies just back from the Caribbean shore, forming the spectacular southern boundary of the department of Atlántida. The Entre Ríos range parallels the Nicaraguan border in the sparsely populated northeast region. The Bay Islands are just a short above-water expression of an undersea continuation of the Merendón mountains.

Mountains not only dominate the topography, they have dominated the history of Honduras as well. In this landscape, with few or no roads for most of the life of the country, regional rivalries flourished, and national unity suffered. Revolts and plots could be repeatedly hatched in the countryside out of earshot of and communication with the capital.

Within the many valleys of Honduras, you can select the climate you desire, for each has its own pattern of rainfall, and temperature, and typical vegetation, depending on altitude, and prevailing winds, and where it is in relation to the coasts, and to what extent mountains can block the passage of clouds. There are some general patterns that apply to the country as a whole, however. The central, southern and western parts of Honduras have a well-defined rainy season, from May though October or November, when prevailing winds bring clouds inland from the coast with great regularity, to shed their water over the mountainous interior. For the remainder of the year, when the winds shift, there is hardly any rain at all. Along the northern coast, where winds blow off the sea throughout the year, rains are more constant, and much, much heavier.

Most settlement was originally attracted to the basin that run from San Pedro Sula south to Comayagua and Tegucigalpa and the Gulf of Fonseca, actually a series of valleys, with mountain passes in between. This area still has the greatest concentration of population. The bottom lands of valleys and sometimes the slopes are planted to corn, and sometimes to coffee, beans, and sorghum. At the lower altitudes, sugar, rice, tobacco and vegetables are grown. Some of the high plateaus are still forested in pine and oak. Much of the farmland is exhausted, while fertile land elsewhere goes unused. By some estimates, only a fifth of arable land is used for farming.

Eastward and to the north of mountainous Honduras are the great savannas, grasslands where rainfall is limited by the mountain ranges along the coast. Settled sparsely in colonial times, and off the beaten track for many years, they are now home to large cattle ranches.

The two lowland areas of Honduras are around the Gulf of Fonseca in the south, and along the Caribbean, in an irregular strip enclosed by meandering mountains running 40 to 100 kilometers inland. Along the Gulf of Fonseca are settlements that date from well before the arrival of the Spanish conquerors. The natural, seasonally dry landscape of savanna and acacia has given way to fields of cotton and irrigated rice, and cattle ranches. On the other side of the country, the Caribbean coast was virtually uninhabited until the end of the nineteenth century. There, initial Spanish settlements were lost to the dread diseases of malaria and yellow fever, insects, torrential rains, wild animals, endless heat, and impenetrable jungles. Only in the last hundred years has this area been exploited, with the development of banana cultivation, and it is now, in its western reaches, the fastest-growing and most industrialized part of Honduras. Natural vegetation here is as abundant and varied as in almost any other place.

But the economy is still dominated by just a few crops: bananas, and the African oil palm, cacao, pineapple, and other fruit products promoted and exported by American companies. Farther east, the landscape is a waterlogged terrain of mangrove and swamps and lazy rivers, of hardwood and rubber trees and palms and wide sandy bars near the sea, and stretches of scrub Caribbean pine on sandy soil inland, and a few settlements along the rivers. Honduras mahogany of renowned quality, growing sparsely, is cut and shipped out, but few other uses are made of the land.

Honduras is rich in minerals: gold and silver that first attracted avaricious Spanish adventurers; and lead, zinc, tin, iron, copper, coal and antimony. Some of these have been exploited for centuries. There are deposits of gypsum, strata of marble, and limestone, used since Mayan times to make a durable mortar.

Dozens of rivers drain the mountains of Honduras, combining and renaming with their flow as they near the oceans. Major waterways are the Goascorán, Nacaome and Choluteca in the south, and the Ulúa and Chamelecón in the north. Farther east along the Caribbean, the Coco and Patuca were once highways for pirates and English adventurers, and are still major routes in an area where few roads penetrate.

FLORA

Tropical countries have a diversity of vegetation that astounds people from the temperate latitudes, and Honduras is no exception. Here you'll find many of the plants you're familiar with from home, along with "exotica" that you thought could only survive in hothouses.

In your travels around Honduras, you'll mainly see the crops that Hondurans commonly farm for home use and for sale. These include corn, beans, and sorghum at the temperate altitudes toward the center of the country; coffee on mountains slopes; tobacco in warm valleys; and in the hot lowlands, sugar, coconut, manila hemp (*Abacá*), pineapple, cotton, African oil palm, and that signature crop, bananas. Garden crops and fruits include cassava, common vegetables such as tomato and cabbage, cacao, and tropical fruits such as mangoes, avocados, *zapote*, *anona*, tamarind, guava, papaya, *nance*, and *jocote*.

Outside cultivated areas, Honduras' forests are a treasure trove of tropical variety that has only recently been set aside, in part, as national parks and biological reserves. Atop mountain peaks and along the crests of ridges are cloud forests, the "weeping woods" where abundant moisture allows ferns and vines and orchids and broadleaf plants to thrive at every level, from the rich humus of decaying matter at ground level, up to the crooks of tree branches, where bromeliads take their nourishment from passing detritus blown on the wind, and capture the moisture in the air. Live oaks and wild avocados are common in most cloud forest areas; the exact plant variety varies according to particular moisture conditions.

Practically beside some of these wonderlands are patches of desert, starved of moisture by nearby peaks that catch the clouds on the prevailing winds. Pines and firs cover vast stretches of highland Honduras below the peaks, and toward the wetter lowlands, mahogany, *ceiba* (silk-cotton), Spanish cedar, and rosewood are typical, with palms along the beaches, and mangroves in the water-soaked coastal areas. Acacias and even cactus are typical of the savannas of the northeast.

FAUNA

Assorted common forest animals typical of Honduras: anteater, armadillo, coyote, deer (white-tailed and brocket), raccoon, kinkajou, coati, turkey, cats (puma, ocelot, jaguarundi, margay, jaguar), opossum, white-lipped and collared peccary, monkeys (howler, spider, capuchin, marmoset), gray fox, gopher, porcupine, tapir, turtles, lizards (iguana, skinks, gecko, etc), snakes (boa, worm, coral, bushmaster, rattlesnake, fer de lance), sloths, cottontail rabbits, rodents (flying squirrel, mice, rats, porcupines, agoutis, paca [*tepezcuintle*]), skunk, river otter, bats).

Near and in the water are assorted crocodiles, caymans, turtles (leatherback, Ridley, loggerhead, hawksbill, green), manatees, salamanders, and frogs and toads.

Fish, aside from game species mentioned in connection with the Bay Islands, include catfish, minnow, cichlid, gar-pike, mud-eel, sea catfish, sharks, guapote (a bass-like river fish), mojarras (cichlids), top minnows (mollies), and black bass introduced in Lake Yojoa; and there are such mollusks as snails, lobster and fresh-water crabs.

For coral and fish watchers, a good reference is *Guide to Corals and Fishes of Florida, the Bahamas and the Caribbean*, by Idaz and Jerry Greenberg (Miami: Seahawk Press, 6840 S.W. 92 Street, Miami, FL 33156), available in a waterproof edition. Natalie's fish-sighting list includes: green moray, spotted moray, barracuda, sand diver, trumpet fish, squirrel fish, fairy basslet, tiger grouper, yellowtail snapper, French and Spanish grunt, porkfish, banded butterflyfish, reef butterflyfish, queen angelfish, rock beauty, French angelfish, yellowtail damselfish, blue and brown chromis, parrotfish, black durgon, blue tang, ocean surgeon, white spotted filefish, hawksbill turtle, coral crab, spiny lobster, spotfin butterflyfish, moon jellyfish, octopus and urchin.

Birdwatchers, take along your bird books. A comprehensive checklist of Honduran birds, mentioning over 700 species, is available for about $2 from Natural History Tours, P. O. Box 1089, Lake Helen, FL 32744. *Field Guide to Mexican Birds*, by Roger Tory Peterson and Edward L. Chalif (Boston: Houghton, Mifflin) includes about 93 percent of known Honduran species. The most notable locale for birding is the Lancetilla Botanical Garden near Tela. But there are many others, some of them mentioned in passing in this book.

Among typical or notable species (and these are mentioned just to indicate the range of species in Honduras):

The quetzal, an elusive cloud forest trogon in iridescent red and green, with an arc of tail feathers several feet long, which every Central American country claims as its own; nightingale thrush (*jilguero*), black robin (*sinzontle*), wood hewer, clorospinga, hummingbirds (more than twelve varieties), motmots, curassows (*pavones*), chachalacas (wild hen), tinamou, quail, parrots and macaws, toucans, partridge, wrens, grebes, cormorants, pelicans, hawks, falcons, ospreys, vultures, herons, ibises, ducks, swallows, flycatchers, warblers, dippers, orioles, jays, blackbirds, cuckoos, rails, plovers, gulls, terns, pigeons, owls, kingfishers, swifts, mockingbirds, jacana, storks, flamingos, guans, limpkins, sun bitterns, potoos, puff-birds, manakins, honey creepers, finches, sparrows, frigatebirds, boobies, anhingas, egrets, spoonbill, doves, roadrunners, woodpeckers, tanagers, cardinals, turkeys, chickadees.

THE PEOPLE

What do you notice first about the people of Honduras? They are friendly and they are helpful. They are easy-going. They are approachable. They are not at all hard to get along with.

To me, this is slightly surprising. For Honduras is a poor country, indeed. Yet in this place, you do not feel the inequalities, the seething social tensions that form a backdrop to a visit to so many other places that are far better off. There are rich people, indeed, in Honduras, but the out-and-out exploitation of the masses that has characterized the history of neighboring countries has been in Honduras less pronounced, if not totally absent.

Nobody in Honduras runs after you on the street to badger you into buying something. Violent crime is not a major problem, and you can feel safe everywhere. Aggressiveness is at level zero. People are quite relaxed, but when you need something, as a visitor, service is not bad at all. There are no lineups and kowtowing to officials as in some other Latin American countries.

There are some odd statistics that illustrate that while Hondurans are poor, they are not desperately off. For example, there are more domestic animals—pigs, horses and mules—than elsewhere in the region. Honduran farmers use animals to work the earth, a luxury for, say, a rural Salvadoran. And they have land to grow the forage to feed their animals.

Another indication of the relatively benign nature of Honduras is that it has attracted immigration, and not just the immigration of slaves and displaced persons and avaricious Spaniards of colonial times. In the last century, freed slaves took up residence in the Bay Islands, and in this century, many Syrians and Lebanese have found opportunity in the developing areas along the north coast.

Hondurans comprise many of the races of the earth. Whites, blacks, Amerindians, Orientals, Lebanese, and every mixture thereof can be found, either as part of the national culture, or as a group maintaining its own separate ways. Spanish is the national language, but American Indian tongues and English dialects are also spoken. Hondurans, as are many of the peoples of poorer countries, are mostly young, mostly country people, and mostly farmers. But there are notable differences between the different groups.

Ladinos

Most of the five million Hondurans, those you typically think of as Hondurans, and who think of themselves as Hondurans, are Mestizos, or **Ladinos**, people who have both European and American Indian ancestors. About 88 percent of Hondurans fall into this category. Native Americans are the next largest group, as much as ten percent of the population. Blacks, whites, and assorted other groups and mixtures make up the rest.

Ladinos live everywhere in Honduras, but mostly in the more heavily populated west-central corridor of the country, running from San Pedro Sula to Comayagua to Tegucigalpa to the Gulf of Fonseca. Other groups reside in specific areas, mainly near the perimeter of Honduras.

The Ladinos of Honduras have a heritage similar to that of other Spanish-speaking nations of America. They are overwhelmingly Catholic. They have until recent times been tied closely to the land. Where educational opportunities have presented themselves or been sought after, it has been in the law and arts and literature. The Church, in the absence of other, secular influences, has largely controlled education, officially or otherwise, and sometimes the only way to advance has been to join the clergy. Administrative and governmental skills have been neglected, and commerce was often left in the hands of immigrants from other countries.

Personalismo, the valuation of individuals over ideology and society in general, is a common heritage. Leaders are popular for what they're like, rather than for what they stand for. People are inclined to save their own skins, and those of their loved ones, and euphemistic sacrifice for the good of the nation and society is less of a fact than in some other countries. In Honduran society, family counts for everything. At home, the head of the family is the father, whose word is generally unopposed. Men dominate outside the family as well, still taking the best jobs, and determining which roles are suitable for women. A man's man, a *macho*, is an admired ideal. Extended to politics, strongman rulers who decide rather than consult have been the norm.

Family connections are everything in determining who gets a job, and who gets promoted, and who marries whom. Cronyism is the norm, in business and politics. Who you're descended from, how old your money is, and what your education is determine where you stand on the social ladder. In business, operations can be family-like, and this is not without advantages for workers, who are looked after and helped in difficult times. Family alliances are made through godparent relationships, and endure throughout life in a country where people do not move around from place to place and job to job. Social welfare is an individual, not a governmental, responsibility. Ladino society is difficult for immigrants to penetrate, which is one reason that newcomers such as the Lebanese remain apart, no matter how rich some of them might be.

Overwhelmingly, Ladinos are Catholics, though strict Catholicism is not the norm. This is somewhat odd, for it was the Church that tried to conquer the soul of Honduras for imperial Spain. But, far removed from Spain, colonial Honduras never had enough priests, or money, and even today, much of the clergy is foreign. Pilgrimages to the Basilica of Suyapa near Tegucigalpa and to Esquipulas in Guatemala are made faithfully, but these, as well as village fiestas and exchanges of saints between neighboring towns, are as much social as religious occasions. With a history of Church involvement in politics, sometimes on the losing conservative side, the church and state have been kept separate, and at times, church orders have been legally forbidden.

If Honduras has remained largely Catholic, it may well be from a lack of interest by other religions. This has changed in this century. Methodists have gained converts on the north coast, and more recently, Protestant missions have made gains throughout Honduras. Nevertheless, Catholic holidays, and lip service to Catholic ways, are part of the national culture.

Though families are strong, half of marriages are common-law, due to the lack of priests and the expense of a church wedding. It's understood that people marry within their social class, though beyond this, there's little in the way of formal courtship. In poor families, children by necessity take a role in earning the family living. But when the kids don't have to work, upbringing is permissive, and the kids are spoiled. The late teens are a suitable age for marriage for women. Legal marriages usually endure, at least on paper. When a marriage breaks down, and even when it doesn't, it's accepted that company will be sought elsewhere.

Like other Latins, in fact, like native American Hondurans and like most people in traditional societies, Ladinos are fatalistic. There's a limit as to how much you can do to change your lot in life. So you don't lose out on some of the pleasures, like conversation and passing the time with family, that you might ignore if you were too occupied with trying to get ahead.

Blacks

Blacks have been present in Honduras since the arrival of the Spanish, who soon brought African slaves. Most of these early immigrants, however, blended into the general population, and slavery was abolished with independence.

Blacks who migrated later to Honduras did so as part of distinct groups. Escaped slaves of the British landed on the coast and, in some cases, married natives. Others came from the West Indies to work on banana plantations established by American companies toward the end of the nineteenth century. Gradually, some of these have lost their English language, and blended into Ladino society.

Blacks who came to the Bay Islands, however, have maintained their West Indian ways. Some originally arrived as slaves of British buccaneers, who were intermittently expelled. More permanent settlement started in the 1830s and afterward, as freed blacks, mainly from Grand Cayman but also from other English Islands and from Belize, sought opportunity elsewhere in the Caribbean. On the Bay Islands, they have managed to maintain their own ways, speaking English and holding to their Protestant, largely Methodist religion. Blacks and their former white masters generally live in different communities on the islands. Many make their living as fishermen, boat builders and merchant seamen.

Black Caribs

Black Caribs, also called **Garífunas**, or **Morenos**, are an ethnic group with both American Indian and African roots, now living mainly along the north coast of Honduras in the vicinity of Trujillo and La Ceiba, as well as in adjacent parts of Guatemala and Belize. The Black Caribs are descended from the Carib Indians who lived in the Lesser Antilles and on the South American mainland, and from escaped and shipwrecked slaves who found shelter among the Caribs, especially those on the island of St. Vincent.

Rebellious Caribs were deported by the British in 1796 from St.

Vincent to Roatán, and in turn were encouraged by the Spanish to leave the islands and settle on the mainland.

Modern Caribs speak their original Antillean language, with ample Spanish and English words thrown in. Many travel regularly to Carib settlements up and down the coast in Guatemala and Belize, and are perfectly fluent in English and Spanish, and some can speak the tongues of their Indian neighbors. Though they are mainly African in racial origin, their customs are a mixture of American Indian and British West Indian ways. Formally Catholic, they have many practices that are African in origin. Celebrations of special importance are held on Christmas day and at New Year's, when masked men dance the traditional Yankunu (or John-Canoe) all night. Dancing and mass processions accompany funerals, which are especially important, for the dead can have an important influence on the living. Many other ceremonies are kept shielded from the eyes of outsiders.

Most Caribs live in seaside villages of huts with steep thatched roofs, and cultivate root crops, such as manioc, yams and taro. Many are boat builders and fishermen.

Whites

Whites have been present in Honduras since the Spanish conquest. More whites arrived in the nineteenth century from the British West Indies, and still others from the Middle East. With their varied backgrounds, whites as such do not form an ethnic group in Honduras, but, rather, are components of other groups.

Most of the colonial Spanish settlers intermarried with natives of Honduras, and their descendants form the majority Ladino class, in shadings from white to brown. It is hard for a foreigner not to notice that light-skinned people are generally at the upper end of the social and political ladder.

Whites with quite a different background have inhabited the Bay Islands off and on for hundreds of years. Some of the original settlers were pirates and shipwrecked sailors and British merchants, who were intermittently expelled by the Spaniards, only to return later. Others arrived in the nineteenth century from the Cayman Islands, and for decades kept themselves apart from other, black Cayman Islanders who immigrated to Honduras following emancipation. They have kept their archaic dialect of English even to this day.

Immigrants from the Middle East, or "Turks," as Hondurans call them, constitute a third group of whites. These are mostly Arabic-speaking Christians from Lebanon, though, to the broad class of Hondurans, Jews, too, count as Turks. Many are involved in small businesses and trade, especially along the north coast.

Other whites of European and American descent constitute a class apart as in other Latin American nations. Some are Americans and Europeans in Honduras temporarily on aid missions, as volunteers or paid advisors, or as executives with multinational companies. Though the faces change through transfers, they constitute a permanent and highly visible fixture on the Honduran scene.

Indians

The term "**Indian**," or "*indígena*," generally refers to Hondurans descended from the peoples who inhabited the land when the Spanish arrived. There have been blood mixtures to some degree among all the Indian peoples of Honduras, and the ways of the Spanish and British have had an influence on their customs. Still, after 500 years of domination by Spain and by independent Ladino governments, many Hondurans maintain ways of life readily identified as Indian, and quite apart from the national culture.

There are several broad groups of Indians in Honduras. Those who inhabited the western parts of the country, the **Lencas** and the **Chortís**, were descended from and related to the Mayas, who had built a great empire in Mesoamerica while Europe was still in the dark ages; and to migrants who came from what is now Mexico. They were largely a settled people, who cultivated corn and squash and beans. As such, they were relatively easy for the Spanish to control, once initial resistance was crushed. The Spanish relocated them to villages built like the towns they knew from Spain, made them worship in churches, and allowed them to go out and work communal lands and Spanish estates. The Indians continued in many cases to perform the daily tasks to which they were accustomed, but for new Spanish masters who substituted for the former Indian nobility.

The conversion of Indians to Catholicism was allegedly what the Spanish conquest of America was all about, and religion remains stronger today among Indians than among the broader class of Hondurans. Partly, this could be because the natives already had a well-developed religious structure, and Catholicism was overlaid upon it, rather than substituted for it. Instead of worshipping in caves and at shrines, newly converted Indians worshipped in churches. They honored saints, with attributes roughly similar to those of their old gods and idols. Processions of idols became processions of saints, and images honored in basilicas had a familiar brown cast. If Indians in Honduras, especially in the west, appear to be more religious than their Ladino countrymen, it's partly because it's not, for them, quite the same religion.

In modern Honduras, many Indians have merged into the Ladino, Hispanic, national culture. Sometimes the dividing lines between the two groups are unclear. Different generations of the same family may be more or less fluent in Spanish or an Indian language, or dress in the kind of clothing typical of Indians, or prefer western wear. But even in Ladino culture, Indian heritage is present. Many place names are derived from Nahuatl, the language of the Mexican Indian allies of the Spanish conquerors, and slang words often have an Indian origin.

Of those Hondurans who remain identifiably Indian, more than half are Lencas, who live in the southwestern part of the nation, to the west of Comayagua, roughly north of the border with El Salvador. Their largest concentration is around Intibucá, the only town in Honduras with an Indian majority. After the conquest, the Lencas, like other western Indians, were resettled in towns. Their language broke down into local dialects, which are spoken by fewer and fewer people today. But old ways remain. Some Lencas still work communal lands, allotted for lifetime use, instead of owning private property. Some belong to *cofradías*, or religious brotherhoods, devoted to a particular saint. Fiestas in honor of a patron saint have a more serious religious significance than in Ladino towns, and exchanges of saints — *guancascos* — are practiced. Women wear a long skirt and short blouse similar to those worn by Spanish women in colonial days.

Other characteristics that set the Lenca apart are their festival dances, a few remaining handicrafts, such as basket-making and pottery, and the home brewing of *chicha* liquor. While many rural Hondurans use plows and pack animals, Lencas more typically use a digging stick and carry loads on their backs. Unusually, the women as well as men work in the fields. They are said to choose their leaders through consultations of elders, which choices are then confirmed routinely in obligatory elections.

Chortí Indians, another group with a Mayan heritage, live for the most part near the town of Copán Ruinas. Other members of this ethnic group live in nearby mountainous parts of Guatemala. Chortí men are easily recognized by their white shirts and trousers, similar to those worn by Indians in parts of Mexico. Another remnant group is the **Pipil**, a few of whom live near the border with El Salvador. The Pipil speak a language related to Nahuatl, and it is thought that their ancestors migrated from Mexico to the lowlands of what are now Guatemala and El Salvador. Many of the Pipils who maintained their identity into modern times were massacred in El Salvador in the 1930s.

Indian groups living along the Caribbean shore when the Spaniards arrived were far less settled than those who lived in the highlands of the west and south. Heavy rainfall and soggy lands subject to flooding discouraged the practice of settled agriculture. Abundant game and waterways allowed them to rely on hunting and fishing.

One northern group, the **Jicaque**, possibly of Mexican or South

American origin, once inhabited the Caribbean coast, but moved inland to the department of Yoro in the nineteenth century as their lands were taken up by others, especially Black Caribs. Under the influence of missionaries, they settled in villages and began to cultivate corn, much like Indians in the west. Only a few hundred still maintain their language and traditions, such as dress in old-style tunic, and distinctive style of house made of planks tied with vines and roofed with thatch, and old food-gathering ways, such as hunting with blowguns.

Miskitos (or *Táwaira*, as they call themselves) and **Sumos** are two related groups of Indians living in isolated groups along the north coast. They share a heritage of hunting and fishing, and cultivation of root crops in shifting agriculture; and languages related to those spoken by Indians in South America. But racially, the Miskitos are a mixed group, having intermarried with blacks who found their way to the coast as servants and slaves or escapees from the British who once held sway over the area. Another group, the **Paya**, or **Pech**, living in the same area, is thought to have a different heritage.

Without wealth or cultivable lands, the Indians of the coast were ignored by the Spaniards, and it was the English who traded with them, and finally established a protectorate over the so-called Kingdom of Mosquitia. After the region reverted to Honduras, it was largely ignored by the central government.

Miskitos, Sumos and Payas still live mostly in small, self-sufficient settlements, burning and clearing plots for root crops, and moving on when the land is exhausted. Miskitos generally live along the coast, the Sumos upriver. Water transportation is, of course, important in a land mostly without roads, and these tribes have their characteristic *cayucas*, or dugouts, and *pipantes*, boats with flat bottoms. Some fish by stunning their quarry with an extract of jungle vines, and dress in clothing made from bark.

Other small groups of Indians live in scattered groups. Some, isolated in mountains near the Nicaraguan border, are probably of **Matagalpa** heritage, while others in the northwest near Santa Bárbara are probably of mixed background.

Arts and Letters

With a limited potential audience, arts and letters have never been historically developed in Honduras, though there have been some notable figures. Poet and dramatist José Trinidad Reyes founded the predecessor of the University of Honduras early in the nineteenth century, and brought the first piano to Tegucigalpa. Modern formal painters include Carlos Garay, Miguel Angel Ruiz Matute, and Alvaro Canales, the last of whom made his reputation in Mexico. Just as appreciated by visitors are the primitive landscape artists of El Zamorano, near Tegucigalpa, such as José Antonio Velásquez.

Noted poets of this century include Froylán Turcios, a revolutionary as well as writer; Juan Ramón Molina, a follower of Nicaraguan modernist Rubén Darío; and, more recently, Rafael Heliodoro Valle and Clementina Suárez.

MUSEUM OF MODERN ART OF LATIN AMERICA

4. A SHORT HISTORY

INTRODUCTION

Honduran history can read like the enumeration of generations in the Bible. From the time the Spanish left until the present, there have been more than 100 presidents, chiefs of state, military rulers, and similarly designated persons-in-charge. Regional chieftain has been succeeded by national savior to be succeeded by a puppet for the country next door. The person at the top has generally ruled without significant limits on his powers by any legislature or courts, and always with an eye to who might want to take his seat. Buccaneers and English traders held sway for years in parts of the country, and the capital shifted back and forth, in colonial times and after independence, until a hundred years ago.

As in other former colonies, much of Honduran history has been an uphill battle to bring together parts of a geographical expression made up of diverse peoples, and swatches of vastly different and uncommunicating territory.

Instability, however, should not be read as necessarily meaning harshness or oppression. Far from it. Generally, nobody has ruled for long enough in Honduras to set up efficient machinery of exploitation and cruelty. Few great riches have led to the advent of avaricious exploiters or enslavement or reduction of natives to serfdom. Honduras throughout its history has been poor, by modern, western standards, but it has not been miserable. Its central government has continued to perform limited functions despite the musical chairs at the top, somewhat in the fashion of Italy.

HONDURAS BEFORE THE SPANISH

Central America is a meeting ground for North America and South America, for the inhabitants and cultural traditions that have crossed back and forth on this land bridge. Before Europeans reached Honduras, the land was populated by groups of people who spoke differing and unrelated languages, and whose ways differed significantly one from another.

It was 10,000 years ago, more or less, that people first came to Honduras. Those early settlers might have been descendants of migrants from Asia across the Bering Strait, or of Polynesians who crossed the Pacific on rafts. The first settlers were probably hunters who lived in simple, perishable dwellings, and in caves. Thousands of years later came people who knew how to plant and harvest root crops, such as cassava, or this knowledge was absorbed from peoples of neighboring lands.

Gradually, in Central America and to the north and south, information and ways were shared by neighboring settlements, or carried to subject peoples on waves of conquest. Cultures, similar ways of doing things, began to develop, and these different ways traveled to and through Honduras. Farming developed, based first on root crops, such as cassava. Pottery-making and other early technologies were discovered.

Those who inhabited the Caribbean coastal areas of Honduras lived in small settlements. When they cultivated crops, it was in shifting areas, burning and clearing and moving as the land was exhausted, which it quickly was, given the torrential rains, and the thin layer of soil that underlay the exuberant rain forest. These inhabitants are thought, by modern studies of the language of their descendants, and of their agriculture, to have been related to Indian tribes of northern South American forests, not least because they practiced head-hunting. The spread of such customs to Honduras might have resulted from migration, or from conquest by distant tribes. No ancient villages or monuments remain from those early inhabitants, but pottery fragments found near the Caribbean coast have been dated as far back as 2000 B.C.

More is known about the native inhabitants of central, western and southern Honduras of pre-Hispanic times, for many were living in settled communities when the Spanish arrived, and others, the ancestors of some of these peoples, erected monumental cities that can still be visited.

In the west and south, geography and politics created more stable and stratified societies than those on the northern coast. Land, more elevated and seasonally dry, was suited to continuing cultivation. At some point, thousands of years ago, some of the peoples of ancient Mesoamerica domesticated wild plants into crops that were regularly sown and harvested. The most important of these was corn, a plant that reliably produced abundant harvests.

With the development of agriculture, all the accoutrements of settled society became possible, and even necessary. When more food was produced than all workers could consume, it became possible for some of the population to become craftsmen, and builders, and administrators. Writing and mathematics were by-products of a society that had time to devote to thinking, and not just surviving. In time, administrative systems had to develop to supervise the division of labor, and the production of food for all the non-farming hands. Hunting and fishing continued, of course, but they were not essential to the survival of the society.

Eventually, the inhabitants learned how to turn clay not just into simple tools and vessels, but into objects of beauty. Their huts evolved into temples. Through war and conquest and trade, the characteristics of different cultures and peoples began to spread across wider areas.

Of the early inhabitants, the Maya were the most powerful and advanced. The Maya dominated what is now western Honduras for at least a thousand years, made numerous significant discoveries and advances, and then faded mysteriously, though their descendants are still present in Honduras and neighboring countries.

People readily identifiable as Mayan, by their pottery and other artifacts that have been found by modern archeologists, began to appear as far back as 1000 B.C. in an area that today includes southern Mexico, Guatemala, and Honduras. Soon after the time of Christ, Mayan settlements began to contain not just houses, but ceremonial structures at their centers. Temples were erected on great platforms throughout the Early Classic period, from 300 to 600 A. D. Some were the tallest buildings in the hemisphere until this century.

Mayan cities, such as **Copán**, in Western Honduras, contained numerous plazas surrounded by temples, multi-roomed structures, ball courts, and what might have been specialized buildings such as sweat baths. The cities were built with the most simple, back-breaking techniques, of rubble carried to the construction site without the aid of wheels or machines, piled into platforms behind retaining walls faced with limestone blocks and plastered over with lime mortar. Limestone was easily worked, and occurs everywhere in Mayan territory. The landscape was also remade as necessary: hilltops were cut off, cisterns constructed, streams diverted, swamps cut by canals for transport and drainage, and built up to create raised gardens. Corn and cassava and yams were planted, and nuts were harvested from the forests.

In the city centers, stelae, or carved stones, were erected in the plazas to record important events, especially those in the lives of royalty. Those at Copán were the most beautiful works of art of any pre-Columbian people. Probably only the nobility and priests could be accommodated in the few, small rooms that could be created under the primitive Mayan arch, or corbel — a single capstone over two walls protruding inward toward each other. Nobility were buried in tombs under temples, which were decorated with painted friezes, and hieroglyphic writing. Games, with death for the losers, took place on ball courts, and captives were sacrificed, at times by decapitation. The different Mayan cities communicated and traded with each other: limestone highways were built through the jungle, inscriptions record the names of far-off cities, and jade from Guatemala and gold from far-off Panama have been found in tombs at Copán. The money of the Maya was probably cacao, or chocolate, still a local product.

The greatest achievement of the Maya was their calendar and arithmetical system, used at first as a guide to planting and harvesting, and eventually, with continuing refinement, as part of a great cosmic and religious system. The Maya understood the concept of zero before it was used in Europe and the Islamic world. They counted using a system of twenty digits, from zero to nineteen, each represented by a series of dots, for units, and bars, for fives.

The basic counting unit of the Maya was the day, twenty of which made up a month. Eighteen months made up a year, with an extra five-day period. There were further units of twenty years, and twenty twenty-year periods. A separate, ceremonial year, or *tzolkin*, consisted of twenty day names combined with thirteen day numbers, making a 260-day year of each of the possible pairs. The combination of any tzolkin day name and a solar day name occurred every 52 solar years. The 52-year cycle, or calendar round, was shared with many other peoples of Central America.

A third time calculation, however, set the Maya apart. This was the **long count**, which tracked the number of days from the beginning of Mayan time, approximately equivalent to 3113 B.C. Long-count dates interpreted by modern scholars are a major aid in deciphering the history of the Maya. Other sophisticated Mayan calculation concerned the solar system. Most notably, Mayan astronomers of the Post Classic period, in Yucatan, calculated that Venus crosses between the earth and sun every 584 days, a fraction of a day off the period calculated by today's astronomers.

Mayan writing, like numbers, gives details about the lives of their cities and rulers. Much of the information that is just now being deciphered comes from places and names and dates inscribed as single glyphs or numbers at Mayan cities. Phonetic syllables that "spell" additional words are currently being decoded, and yielding new information about Mayan genealogy.

For reasons that are still little understood, Mayan cities in Honduras, Guatemala and southern Mexico underwent a sudden and swift decline, starting in about 850 A.D. Temples and stelae were left uncompleted, population declined, and scientific advances halted in the central part of the empire. But in Yucatan, to the north, Mayan civilization continued, influenced by the Toltecs of the central part of Mexico.

In Honduras, the descendants of the Maya survived as separate, remnant nations, alongside groups that migrated from the lands to the north, and others that were either conquered by migrants from Mexico or largely succumbed to foreign influences and rule. Major Maya-related groups are the Chortí and Lenca peoples. The Pipil, of Nahuatl descent, lived along the southwestern mountain slopes, toward the Pacific.

By the time the Spanish arrived, the natives of western Honduras had declined from the levels of achievement of the Maya. There was no central authority ruling over a large area, and interregional trade was limited. Without knowledge of outsiders of other races, there was no solidarity, and warfare occasionally raged not only between nations, but sometimes among people speaking a common language. It was by subduing and subsequently allying themselves with different native groups that the Spanish were able to conquer.

THE CONQUEST

The first encounters between natives and Spaniards in what is now Honduras were peaceful. Christopher Columbus himself sailed along the Caribbean coast in 1502, and in July of that year landed on the island of Guanaja, which he called *Isla de los Pinos* (Pine Island). Contemporary accounts describe a visit by Indian nobility in a long canoe, bearing cacao beans. Columbus continued his journey, and on August 14 went ashore on the mainland at Punta Caxinas.

Nearby, where present-day Trujillo stands, Bartholomew Columbus celebrated the first Catholic mass on the mainland of America. Continuing along the coast, Columbus gave the name Gracias a Dios to the cape at the extreme tip of present-day Honduras, in thanksgiving for delivery from frightful storms.

It was at the time of this first European visit that Honduras received its modern name, though there are several versions of just whence the name comes. Some say that *Honduras* — literally, "depths" — was applied to describe either the deep seas or low-lying lands of the adjacent coast.

Others say that *hibueras*, the native word for floating gourds, was corrupted into *higueras*, Spanish for fig tree, and later into *Honduras*; or that the aboriginal name was Ondure. The land was also called the Coast of the Ears, after native ear-plugs; and Guaymura, after a tribe thought to be so named; but Honduras is the name that stuck.

The coast was further explored by Vicente Yáñez Pinzón and Juan Díaz de Solís in 1508, but the land remained largely untouched by the Spanish for a number of years.

Rivalries among various Spanish military leaders led to thrusts into Honduras, finally, from different directions. Gil González Dávila, exploring from Panama, sailed as far as the Gulf of Fonseca, on the Pacific Coast, in 1522. In 1524, González Dávila returned to exert Spanish authority. The Spanish governor of Panama sent another expedition from a base in Nicaragua. Not wanting to lose the initiative to a rival, Hernán Cortés in Mexico authorized an expedition, and when the leader resigned, sent still another force.

It was this last force, led by Cristóbal de Olid, that first conquered Honduran territory for Europeans. After outfitting himself and his 370 soldiers and 100 archers in Havana, and buying 22 horses, he landed on the coast on May 3, 1524, and established a settlement that he named El Triunfo de la Cruz (Triumph of the Cross).

Things did not go well for Olid. He fought with the leaders of the other Spanish groups, and was accused of trying to usurp authority for himself. The internecine struggle ended with the trial, conviction and beheading of Olid. Leadership passed to Francisco de las Casas, a relative of Cortés, who established Trujillo as the head town to replace El Triunfo de la Cruz. This struggle of factional leaders, and the relocation of the capital, was to be a repeating pattern throughout Honduran history.

Distraught at the disorder in his fiefdom, Cortés himself undertook to lead still another expedition to Honduras, this time going overland, through jungles in the Petén region of Guatemala, which hundred of years later would still be largely unexplored. With several hundred Spaniards, and thousands of Mexican Indian allies, Cortés suffered terrible losses, mainly from floods, hunger and disease. The remnants of his force encountered Spanish stragglers at Nito in the spring of 1525, and moved them farther along the coast to the mouth of the Ulúa River. At Trujillo, Cortés managed to enforce a truce between the warring Spanish captains, and exert his own authority. Satisfied with the state of affairs, he departed in 1526 to deal with other headaches in Mexico. In the same year, a governor, Diego López de Salcedo, was first named.

The boundaries of Honduras were shifting and never clearly defined. A vast territory claimed by the Spaniards lay to the interior, populated by assorted Indian nations, to whom the machinations and rivalries of the Spaniards made no sense. By 1532, Pedro de Alvarado, who had brought the native nations of Guatemala to their knees, was authorized to establish effective Spanish control in Honduras. After dealing with assorted rebellions elsewhere, and widely accused of having ignored his conquistorial duties, Alvarado finally got around to the task in 1536. He and men acting under his orders founded San Pedro Sula and several other outposts. Alvarado's successor, Francisco de Montejo, turned his attention inland, and ordered a lieutenant, Alonso de Cáceres, to establish a headquarters between the two seas. This was Santa María de Comayagua, founded in 1537, which was to be the capital of Honduras for much of the colonial period.

The Spaniards had battled each other, and disease and rain and hunger, but the native inhabitants of the north coast, isolated in small groups, and evasive, had posed no problems. Now things changed. Spanish penetration of the highlands was brought to a halt and effectively repelled by the Lenca Indian nation, under their chieftain, Lempira. For two years, battles raged between the Spaniards and their Mexican allies, on one hand, and the warriors of Lempira, estimated to have numbered as many as 30,000.

Unable to conquer by force, the Spaniards turned to an old and familiar weapon: treachery. Offering to negotiate a truce, they entered the impregnable fortress of Lempira, and there murdered the native leader, and overpowered the garrison. Within months, the invaders took control of Lenca territory.

Once pacified, Honduras resumed its pattern of administrative indecision and division of authority. For a time, the Audiencia de los Confines, the Spanish colonial authority, was based in Honduras. In turn, the colony was ruled as part of Guatemala, then from Mexico, or Santo Domingo, or Panama, or even directly from Comayagua by a governor sent from Spain. The coastal area was sometimes ruled separately from the highlands, called Higueras. Finally, authority was placed in Guatemala, and Honduras, roughly encompassing the territory of today's nation, became part of the Kingdom and Captaincy-General of Guatemala, which covered the stretch of isthmus from modern southern Mexico to southern Costa Rica.

Honduras was settled in the colonial period, but never to the extent of Guatemala or other Spanish colonies in the isthmus. Discoveries of silver led to the founding of Tegucigalpa as a mining center. And there was some settlement of Spaniards along the land route from Guatemala in the southwest, which already was highly populated by Indians. There was also interest in Honduras as an overland route between the oceans, though that role was to fall to Panama.

The government and society that the Spanish set up in Honduras were based on life in Spain, modified to suit local conditions, with the twin aims of converting the natives and enriching their new Spanish overlords. Spanish-style towns were created: a church and administrative buildings went up around a central square and market. Mercedarians and then Franciscans were authorized to bring the natives into the Christian fold. Local labor was used to build and decorate, under the instruction of master craftsmen from Spain. Indians were forced to settle in the new towns. At first they were apportioned as slaves to Spanish landholders under the *repartimiento* system. Later, under the *encomienda* arrangement, they were tenants on their former land, paying their new Spanish masters through required labor.

Conquered in war, reduced to servitude, ravaged by smallpox, venereal disease, and other ailments brought by the Spaniards, the natives of Honduras suffered a holocaust comparable to the worst of modern times. By one estimate, more than 90 percent were wiped out in the first twenty years of effective Spanish settlement. All this was afflicted by just a few hundred Spaniards, and a few thousand Mexican Indian allies. Occasionally, a voice cried out among the Spaniards, protesting ill-treatment of the natives, such as that of Cristóbal de Pedraza, in the mid-sixteenth century. New laws attempted to protect Indians, as much to preserve the economic base of the empire as from altruism, but avarice and ill-treatment continued as facts of colonial life.

The colony of Honduras remained a backwater. Some cattle were raised and traded, mainly to the mining areas of Honduras; but indigo, cochineal and cacao, the major export crops of the captaincy general, were grown only on a limited scale. Silver, sugar, lumber and tobacco were also exported, along with mules. And slaves went to the West Indies, to replace natives who had perished in the first years of Spanish dominion. Spanish mercantile policy limited trade outside the empire.

It was the early importance of mining that helped to determine the character of Honduras as a society distinct from neighboring colonies, where the Indians stayed on or near their ancestral lands. Those Indians who were forced to work in the mines came from different villages. They spoke different dialects or languages. They were forced to communicate with each other and their masters in Spanish, the common colonial language. In the filth and abuse and violence and dangerous conditions of those early mines, the new Ladino culture was born from the mix and remnants of the old ways, overlain with the new ways of the Spanish.

Far from the mother country, with a small garrison, sparsely settled, vast Honduras was only tenuously held by Spain. As pirate attacks on Spanish convoys increased in the Caribbean, Spain reinforced Puerto Caballos (today's Puerto Cortés), but the long coastline was impossible to defend. Caballos was intermittently taken by pirates, in 1602 and 1639 and 1660, and sacked and burned. Trujillo was captured in 1639, and San Pedro Sula in 1660.

Dutch and British buccaneers sheltered in the Bay Islands, behind the protection of reefs that kept out the larger boats of the Spaniards. British buccaneers, planters, loggers and sailors landed in and occupied parts of Mosquitia in the early seventeenth century. Spain at times tried to dislodge the English, and at other times, admitting its lack of police powers, tolerated their presence, in return for British promises to control piracy, promises which were rarely kept. Only hundreds of persons were involved, just scores at times, but in the business of establishing sovereignty by presence and effective control, the fates of great empires hung in the balance.

By the opening of the eighteenth century, the British had a firm grip on Belize, and protectorates over the Bay Islands and the Miskito Indians on the Honduran coast. Provided with guns and liquor by the English, the Miskito and Sumos attacked any Spanish ships that dared to enter their territory. British forces repeated occupied and lost Omoa and Trujillo, and were more firmly established eastward along the coast at Black River (Río Tinto) and Brus.

By the end of the century, as part of the settlement of the American Revolutionary War, the British had mostly been pushed off the mainland, though Spanish control remained weak. Hampered by Spanish mercantile policy, residents of the colony traded illegally, but willingly, through English intermediaries, moving lumber and sugar and gold and silver to and through the Bay Islands and Belize, in exchange for cloth and manufactured goods. At times in the colonial period, most of the trade of Honduras involved smuggling.

INDEPENDENCE

Honduras at the turn of the nineteenth century was a highly stratified society, with a broad base of Indians with few rights. Above them were a few blacks, and the mixed bloods who dwelled in the towns. Those who worked as craftsmen and artisans and provided European-style services had the most prestige.

At the top of the social structure were government officials sent from Spain, and the hierarchy of the Church, who controlled not just the religious life of the people, but also their education, and, through landholdings, a significant portion of the agricultural economy. Below the Spanish officials were Creoles, persons of pure Spanish descent born in the new world. As colonials, they were barred from the highest governmental positions, which were filled by officials sent from Madrid, and could gain lesser positions of prestige only through bribery. Merchants, Creoles and Ladinos, likewise were a class with limited prestige and much dissatisfaction, obliged by Spanish policies to sell and buy goods through illegal channels.

When independence was declared in Guatemala on September 15,

1821, the Creoles and merchants of Honduras went along, and when the forces of the newly independent Mexico under Agustín de Iturbide marched into Central America, influential people in Comayagua acceded to the new union as well, though Tegucigalpa wavered. José Cecilio del Valle, a Honduran who had been educated in Guatemala, went off to Mexico as a representative for Central America.

When Iturbide fell from power, a Central American assembly in Guatemala City proclaimed independence again, and Honduras became part of the United Provinces of Central America, a loose federation with no taxation powers of its own, and a constitution that notably emancipated all slaves and provided for limited voting rights. Honduras was an odd member. Unable to choose between joining as one state or two, it became a single member, with its capital alternating between Tegucigalpa and Comayagua. Dionisio de Herrera became the first Honduran president.

In Honduras, as elsewhere in Central America, conservatives favored privileges for the Church and a strong central government. Liberals, who included those who originally favored independence, wanted a loose federation, and were somewhat anti-clerical. The two factions competed not just in the Honduran and federal legislatures, but on the battlefield as well. Conservatives from the Central American government invaded Honduras in 1826, joining local partisans. Francisco Morazán, a prominent Honduran liberal, led the forces that repelled the invasion, and eventually took over the Central American administration in Guatemala. Morazán promulgated laws that cut church tithes and restricted church orders. The result was a series of revolts against his power.

Short of funds, with conservative rebellions flaring in Honduras, and opponents gaining strength in Guatemala, Morazán moved his government to El Salvador in 1833 as the union weakened. By 1838, the states of Central America decided each to go its own way.

The latest stage of "independence" meant little for Honduras. Honduras promulgated a new constitution in 1839, but there was little or no sense of nationhood or nationality. Guatemala and to some degree Nicaragua continued to meddle in national politics and impose and depose presidents. Meanwhile, in a primitive economy that was regionally self-sufficient and traded little with the outside world, where most were farmers, where local plantation owners were the only effective law, the installations of successive regimes meant little. Francisco Ferrera, first president under the independence constitution, went to war against regional leaders, and ruled even after his term of office expired. Juan Lindo ruled from 1847 until the Guatemalans sent him running in 1850. José Trinidad Cabañas succeeded peacefully and legally to the presidency in 1852 — a notable event — but was deposed by the Guatemalans in 1855.

José Santos Guardiola, at least, scored foreign-policy advances against the English. It was Honduras' weakness and disorganization that had allowed Britain to maintain and expand its claim to disputed territories during the early independence period. British subjects from Belize and the Cayman Islands settled the Bay Islands after Spain was no longer a threat, and even threw out the Central American garrison in 1838. Since Britain dominated trade with Central America, taking strong action against the interlopers was a chancy matter.

Financial claims against Honduras led to Britain's short-lived seizure of Tigre Island in the Gulf of Fonseca in 1849. Britain's actions stirred the interest and alarm of the United States, and in the 1850 Clayton-Bulwer treaty, both nations agreed to keep their hands off the Central American mainland. Britain soon violated the spirit of the agreement by declaring the Bay Islands a crown colony in 1852. The Wyke-Cruz treaty with Britain in 1859, during the presidency of José Santos Guardiola, provided for British withdrawal from the Bay Islands, with guarantees for the religious freedom of the islanders. British influence along the coast of Honduras gradually came to an end over succeeding decades.

Unlike most heads of the government, Guardiola was distinguished outside of Honduras as well, for helping to oust the American adventurer William Walker, who for a time had taken control of Nicaragua. When Walker attempted a comeback, using the Bay Islands as a base, he was captured by the British, and turned over to the Hondurans, who placed him on trial and executed him in Trujillo.

Guardiola was murdered in 1862, to be succeeded by twenty leaders in ten years, some of them installed or removed by various Guatemalan governments. Constitutions were promulgated in 1865, 1873, 1880, 1894, 1906, and 1924. A country with so many constitutions and governments was, in effect, a country without a government.

Other presidents were only local heroes, particularly Marco Aurelio Soto, who had broad support. Soto allowed secular marriages and separated church and state, expanded the school system, and generally improved public services. Tegucigalpa became the permanent capital of Honduras in 1880, after high society in Comayagua snubbed President Soto's Guatemalan Indian wife.

While British influence was on the wane, that of the United States was increasing. A promoter named Ephriam George Squier, who had once served as U.S.consul, attempted to start up a railroad across Honduras in 1853. No track was constructed until 1871 — money intended for the railroad had a way of going to arms purchases instead — and the railroad never operated. In the process, though, various American business interests learned of and invested in Honduras. Mining was the key attraction at first, and later, banana plantations on the north coast.

Under President Luis Bográn, from 1883 to 1890, Honduras was once again influenced by Guatemala. The last of a string of three conservative presidents was deposed just three years later by Policarpo Bonilla, a liberal, with Nicaraguan aid. Bonilla oversaw the revision of many laws to streamline administration and encourage foreign investment, and signed Honduras to a union with El Salvador and Nicaragua that never came about. Bonilla was backed by a more formal political party structure than Honduras had previously known.

Succeeding presidents were generals Terencio Sierra and Manuel Bonilla, the latter using a show of force as well as votes to get into office in 1903. Guatemala invaded in 1906, and when Bonilla made peace, Nicaragua invaded the following year and kicked Bonilla out. Bonilla staged a revolt against his successor, Gen. Miguel Dávila, and the presidency was settled on yet another person, Francisco Bertrand, through U.S.-sponsored negotiations.

BANANAS

While an elite of politicians and generals from Honduras, Nicaragua, and Guatemala were playing out their power games in Tegucigalpa and regional capitals, it was in the north of the country that the real changes were unfolding, as Honduras was converted into a banana republic.

Around the turn of the century, banana traders in New Orleans began to look into Honduras as a reliable supplier of commercially grown bananas, which were being exported principally from Costa Rica. The predecessor of the Standard Fruit Company made the first shipments. In 1911, the Cuyamel Fruit Company, organized by Sam Zemurray, began operations, followed in 1913 by the United Fruit Company. Honduras soon became the leading exporter of bananas in the world, and bananas were to remain the mainstay of the modern sector of the economy for many years. The banana companies, through their assorted commercial ventures and worker welfare system, were to be, in effect, more important than the government for many Hondurans.

In Tegucigalpa, central authority remained shaky. Bertrand assumed the vice-presidency after an election, succeeded to the presidency, and fled in 1919 after a revolt. New revolts broke out repeatedly under Bertrand's successor.

The elections of 1923 produced no majority for any candidate. With the country on the brink of a new civil war, and Augusto Sandino harassing the U.S. Marines in Nicaragua next door, the United States once again brokered a political solution. New elections were won by Miguel Paz Baraona of the National Party whose leader, Gen. Tiburcio Carías Andino, had gained the most votes in 1923, but, to everyone's surprise, had refused to take power by force.

Carías was a Renaissance man of the times, an intellectual who for a while held his party above his personal ambitions. Carías himself came to power in the 1932 elections. His party allegedly stood for good management, reconciliation, and free elections, but Carías managed to stay in office until 1948, through constitutional amendments. Revolts and opposition flourished at the beginning of his term, but the nation eventually became resigned to his authoritarian rule. Political exiles were encouraged to return home, but those who continued to speak out were subject to arrest.

Early in the Carías regime, Panama disease caused the banana industry to go into a tailspin, and world war cut off trade. During Carías' tenure, the economy diversified somewhat, into mining and ranching and timber exports, and coffee production. Carías selected his successor, Juan Manuel Gálvez, who took office in 1949, his Liberal opponent having conveniently withdrawn. Gálvez cooperated with the Central Intelligence Agency in promoting the overthrow of the populist Arbenz government in Guatemala and restoring the position of the United Fruit Company in that country. After another election which produced no majority, Vice President Lozano seized the government.

While Honduran leaders were helping to meddle in Guatemala, in their own country, banana workers became increasingly dissatisfied and went on strike, and unrest spread throughout the small sector of the economy where people labored for wages. The strike ended with significant increases in benefits for United Fruit and Standard Fruit workers, and recognition for the first time of their right to bargain.

Lozano exiled one of his political opponents, Ramón Villeda Morales, allegedly for helping to foment the "leftist" United Fruit Company strike — certainly not the last time the specter of labor unrest and communism would be used against an opponent. In the end, the army seized power and sent Lozano packing.

MODERN HONDURAS

A constituent assembly brought in a new constitution in 1957, and selected Ramón Villeda Morales of the Liberal Party as president. During Villeda's term in office, the Central American Common Market took shape. Import restrictions were removed, and many products that formerly were imported into Central America began to be manufactured in the region. But most of the new factories went up in Guatemala, El Salvador and Costa Rica, where there were more roads, more shipping facilities, and more sophisticated investors, and Honduras was left behind, in many cases helping to finance the development of its neighbors.

Under Villeda, schools were built and labor rights were strengthened, though unrest continued in the realm of the United Fruit Company. As elsewhere in Central America, a social security system was installed to take care of the medical needs and pensions of a limited number of workers. The border with Nicaragua was finally determined through arbitration, after the neighboring country threatened to invade the newly delineated and sparsely populated Gracias a Dios department. Villeda was turned out of office in 1963 on the eve of new elections by Air Force Col. Osvaldo López Arellano, whose accession was handily "confirmed" by a constituent assembly.

Over the preceding decades, many Salvadorans, crowded by a coffee-plantation economy, had come to settle in Honduras, crossing an ill-defined border and squatting on uncultivated lands. As the numbers of Salvadorans grew, they faced increasing discrimination, and with no documentation, were subject to arbitrary actions by both government and ordinary Hondurans. In 1969, the situation came to a head with the expulsions of many Salvadorans, and exploded after a soccer match between the two countries. In five days of bitter fighting, El Salvador, then called "the Israel of Central America," drove into Honduras along the Pan American Highway and around Nueva Ocotepeque. The air force of Honduras managed to damage a refinery in El Salvador, but the country was rescued from disaster only by a cease-fire declared by the Organization of American States. A sullen Honduras refused to cooperate further with the Central American Common Market, and despite a peace treaty signed in 1980, hard feelings from the war continue.

López turned the government over to civilians in 1971, but took power again in 1972, this time spouting the reformist populism that was the rage among the military in parts of Latin America. In 1978, a new junta, lead by Policarpo Paz García, seized the government.

Military rule began to wind down once again in 1980, with the convening of a constituent assembly. Still another constitution was implemented in 1982, and Roberto Suazo Córdoba became president. Military buildups in Honduras were significant under Suazo, as the United States poured in weapons in response to the Sandinista victory in Nicaragua. "Contra" opponents of the Sandinistas found refuge and set up bases with American support and Honduran connivance, and American troops staged maneuvers on a near-permanent basis.

Following a traditionally inconclusive election in 1985, José Azcona Hoyo became president, after the various factions of his party, though not Azcona himself, together gained more votes than the leading Liberal, Rafael Leonardo Callejas Romero. Callejas ran again in 1989. This time he scored a clear victory, and was sworn into office in January 1990.

Callejas came to office facing severe economic problems. The wind-down of the unofficial Contra war with Nicaragua meant a decrease in the flow of military spending from the United States. Export earnings had been stagnant for years, as the price of coffee and other relatively new export crops stayed low, while prices for imported industrial goods went just one way — up. The projected savings in oil imports from the completion of the El Cajón hydroelectric project soon went to pay interest on the international debt.

In recent years, there has not even been enough money available to buy fertilizer. The uneven balance of trade and waffling about paying a large foreign debt led to an overvalued currency, and, in turn, a decrease in foreign investment.

Other problems faced by the government were continuing ones: poor agricultural management and a lack of infrastructure; inadequate schools, poor technical education, and deficient health care; a population growing almost as fast as production; a lack of roads and railroads, except in the banana country of the north; limited port facilities. But Honduras has many material and human resources, it is near potential markets, and its weather and attractions make it a prime candidate for touristic development. With stability returning to the region, the prospects for the nation are promising.

GOVERNMENT AND ADMINISTRATION

Honduras is divided into 18 *departamentos* (departments, or provinces), each with its *cabecera* (administrative center, or capital). The departments (and their cabeceras) are: Atlántida (La Ceiba); Colón (Trujillo); Comayagua (Comayagua); Copán (Santa Rosa de Copán); Cortés (San Pedro Sula); Choluteca (Choluteca); Paraíso (Yuscarán); Francisco Morazán (Tegucigalpa and Comayagüela, Distrito Central); Gracias a Dios (Puerto Lempira); Intibucá (La Esperanza); Islas de la Bahía/Bay Islands (Roatán [Coxen's Hole]); La Paz (La Paz); Lempira (Gracias); Ocotepeque (Ocotepeque); Olancho (Juticalpa); Santa Bárbara (Santa Bárbara); Valle (Nacaome); and Yoro (Yoro).

Departamentos are further divided into a total of 289 *municipios* (municipalities, or townships), each consisting of one or several *aldeas* and *caseríos* (villages and hamlets).

Under the current constitution, municipal officials are elected every two years.

The judiciary consists of a supreme court, lower courts, and courts with special jurisdictions, such as labor courts.

The legislature consists of one chamber, with parties represented in proportion to their electoral support. The president is elected by popular vote every four years, and prohibited from succeeding himself.

The major parties are the Liberal and the National, which represent the traditional liberal-conservative split in Central American politics.

There are smaller parties as well, such as the Christian Democrats. The president governs in consultation with the council of ministers, or cabinet. The military continues to have a significant influence on politics and policies, beyond that of any party.

5. PLANNING YOUR TRIP

An eighteenth-century Englishwoman, Mary Lester, wrote a famous (in its time) memoir of travels alone in Honduras, under the pseudonym María Soltera. She commented about the scarcity of food for travelers, the trials of getting around, the difficulty of finding a place to sleep. She brought her own hammock, of course.

Is it all that different now?

I'm happy to say that it is. You can find comfortable lodging and good meals in many parts of Honduras, and not just in the few places on the beaten track for tourists. But you can also end up where there is no decent place to sleep, and no good food to eat, and if you just follow the logical routes on a map, you could easily miss the very best that Honduras has to offer.

Before you go, then, read through this book. Consider a few possible travel strategies:

- Go right to the Bay Islands, and spend your vacation diving or fishing in a tropical hideaway.
- Discover unexplored beaches and colonial fortresses along the Caribbean mainland.
- Travel the overland routes, to Mayan ruins and bass fishing and a tropical botanical garden.
- Stay a while, and experience the pace of life in a Central American capital.

Once you think you know what you're going to do, make any reservations you think are necessary. Consult a travel agent, if you wish, to find a package that suits your plans. In general, resorts in the Bay Islands are accustomed to offering hotel/diving/meal packages; those on the mainland are not. In any case you can perfectly well make reservations yourself, through hotels and resorts directly, or through their agents in the United States.

CLIMATE AND WEATHER

- Temperatures are warm all year, and you can get good weather somewhere in Honduras in every season. But some months are better than others. Or, to put it another way, you can decide what weather you like, and go to the appropriate area of Honduras at the appropriate time.

- Tegucigalpa, along with most of Honduras, has moderate, spring-like temperatures throughout the year. In central Honduras, temperatures get cooler the higher you go. May is the warmest month, but it is rarely uncomfortably hot in the capital.

- It rains for six months of the year in Tegucigalpa and most of central Honduras, from May through October, for a few hours a day, and it is dry on most days during the rest of the year (*verano*, or "summer"). But even in the rainy season (*invierno*, or "winter"), precipitation isn't too high. You can visit Tegucigalpa at any time of year without concern for the weather.

- The south coast along the Pacific has a rainy season, just like Tegucigalpa, but the wet is wetter, and the temperatures are generally hotter. But half of the year is very dry.

- The Caribbean coast on the north, and the Bay Islands, get rain throughout the year. The trade winds that blow from the northeast bump up against the Nombre de Dios mountains that lie just inland from the shore, causing clouds to dump their moisture. Tela and La Ceiba get more than three meters (ten feet!) of rain in a year. Montreal, Houston, and New York get about one meter in an average year. While October through November is the rainiest time, you always have to expect some rain along the coast. But you can expect sunny periods on every day as well. There are occasional hurricanes during the rainiest times along the coast.

- Temperatures throughout the lowlands are hot all year. But right along the water, there is usually a breeze, especially from October through April. Along the Caribbean coast, it is always very humid, so you might need air conditioning for sleeping. Nothing dries, and everything is a little bit rotten.

- Out on the Bay Islands, away from the mountain ridge, rainfall is lower than right along the coast, and though the chart doesn't show it, humidity is lower. January through September are considered good months to visit the Bay Islands. But if you can stand some rain mixed with your sunshine, the rest of the year is okay as well.

HOLIDAYS IN HONDURAS

Here are the holidays, both familiar and unfamiliar, to watch out for in Honduras. Banks and businesses will be closed, and you won't be able to make a plane reservation or book a tour, on these days.

January 1	New Year's Day
Moveable	Holy Thursday
Moveable	GoodFriday
	(Many businesses close all week)
April 14	Day of Americas
May 1	Labor Day
September 15	Independence Day
October 3	Day of Francisco Morazán
October 12	Columbus Day (Día de la Raza)
October 21	Armed Forces Day
December 24-25	Christmas Eve and Christmas
December 31	New Year's Eve

In addition to national holidays, every town has its own local celebration day. Some will be worth looking at and participating in. For a complete fiesta calendar, see the miscellany section at the back of this book.

ENTRANCE AND EXIT REQUIREMENTS

I have to tell you to re-check with your airline or a Honduran consulate before you leave on your trip. Entry requirements are subject to change, and vary by nationality.

U.S. and Canadian citizens currently require only a passport to enter Honduras. U.S. citizens may also enter with a tourist card.

As of recently, no visa is required of citizens of: Argentina, Australia, Belgium, Chile, Costa Rica, Denmark, Ecuador, El Salvador, Finland, Germany, Guatemala, Iceland, Italy, Japan, Netherlands, New Zealand, Nicaragua, Norway, Panama, Peru, Spain, Sweden, Switzerland, United Kingdom, and Uruguay.

Citizens of the above countries are initially granted permission to stay in Honduras *for 30 days*. After that period, they must request an extension to remain in the country, just as if they held an expired visa.

Visas

Visas are not required of transit passengers.

When required, visas are issued by Honduran consulates. A visa will usually allow an initial stay of 30 days. To remain longer, you'll have to apply to the immigration department.

Tourist Cards, which can be used in place of a visa by nationals of certain countries, are sold for $2 at the check-in counter by airlines serving Honduras, and by some travel agencies. You can also buy a tourist card upon arrival at an airport in Honduras, but it's safer to have one beforehand. To get a tourist card, you need to show a passport, a birth certificate, or some other convincing evidence of your citizenship. A tourist card is initially valid for 30 days, and can be extended by the immigration department in Tegucigalpa, La Ceiba, or San Pedro Sula.

Special **investors' visas** are issued at no charge to businessmen and technicians for three months and one month respectively, with renewals available to a total stay of six months. Documentation of the purpose of the trip is required.

When you arrive in Honduras, whether by land or air, you *could* be required to show that you have either a return ticket, sufficient funds to cover your expenses, or both.

Entry points along the borders with neighboring countries are generally open "officially" from 8 a.m. to 5 p.m. weekdays, but you can cross outside these hours for an extra fee (see below).

Vaccinations

No vaccination is required unless you're arriving from an area where there is currently an outbreak of some dread disease, such as yellow fever.

Entry and Exit Fees

There's an arrival tax of about $2 per person to pay when you enter Honduras, and fees totalling about $10 to pay when you leave by air. Children are exempt. In addition, there are fees of several dollars to pay for cars, for crossing land borders outside regular business hours, and for assorted other reasons.

In addition, and aside from any official increase in charges, there are *unofficial welcome and goodbye fees* that can range up to $10 per person. Call them tips, bribes, or what you wish. You'll find that they can be negotiated downward if one person in your group is in charge of paying for everyone, and even eliminated entirely sometimes if you ask for a receipt, or to speak to a supervisor (who may acknowledge that a slight mistake was made by the man at the point of public contact).

You may be asked to identify yourself at any time, usually near borders. *Carry your passport* or tourist card with you at all times, and if lost, contact your embassy immediately to obtain new travel documents.

The *exit tax* when departing Honduras by air is a hefty 95 lempiras — almost $19 at the current exchange rate!

Staying On

Most visitors are granted an initial stay of 30 days, though this may be shorter, especially if you enter overland and are short of funds. Extensions of permission to stay are processed at immigration offices in major towns: Comayagua, San Pedro Sula, La Ceiba, Tela, Santa Rosa de Copán, and other departmental capitals. With more difficulty and delay, they may be processed in Tegucigalpa, at *Migración,* 6 Calle, 11/12 Avenidas.

CUSTOMS - ENTERING HONDURAS

You're allowed to bring in anything reasonable for a vacation trip to Honduras, along with gifts and new personal items up to a value of U.S. $1000. For children, the limit is $500. You're limited to two liters of liquor, and 200 cigarettes or 100 cigars or about a pound of tobacco. Firearms require a permit, and fresh fruits and vegetables should not be carried.

For questions and clarifications about customs, contact the Dirección General de Aduanas, Avenida Juan Lindo, Colonia Palmira, Tegucigalpa, tel. 382566 (tel. 331290 at the airport, 562154 at the San Pedro Sula airport, 420013 in La Ceiba).

CUSTOMS - RETURNING HOME

If you're going back to the States, you have an exemption of $400 for goods purchased in Honduras, which can include up to a quart of alcoholic beverages and 200 cigarettes. Many handicraft products that you might buy in Honduras are totally exempt from U.S. customs duty.

Canadians can use their yearly $300 exemption, or $100 quarterly exemption, with a cap of 200 cigarettes and 1.1 liters (40 ounces) of liquor.

Whatever you take home, don't include pre-Columbian articles or yaba-ding-dings; coral; fish; or shells. These could be confiscated on your way out of Honduras or into your home country and/or land you in jail or delayed with a court case.

USING TRAVEL SPECIALISTS

I think that you're best off using the services of a travel agency near your home with which you've dealt before. However, it's perfectly possible that the folks near home won't have much to offer. Among agencies with some familiarity with Honduras are:

• **Roatan Charter**, Box 877, San Antonio, FL 33576, tel. 800-282-8932, fax 904-588-4158. Helpful people, with a line on everything new in the Bay Islands and the rest of Honduras.

• **Great Trips**, P. O. Box 1320, Detroit Lakes, MN 56501, tel. 800-552-3419 or 218-847-4441, fax 218-847-4442. The folks at Great Trips know a lot about both the mainland of Honduras and the Bay Islands, and make reliable arrangements.

- **Triton Tours**, 1111 Veterans Blvd., Kenner, LA 70062, tel. 800-426-0226 or 504-464-7964, fax 504-464-7965. Triton is one of the original travel agencies serving the Bay Islands.
- **Bahia Tours**, 1385 Coral Way, Miami, FL 33145, tel. 800-443-0717 or 305-858-5129, fax 305-858-5020. Represents Anthony's Key and other dive resorts and live-aboard boats.
- **Elegant Vacations**, 1760 The Exchange, Suite 150, Atlanta, GA 30339, tel. 800-451-4398, fax 404-859-0250. Represents several hotels, and arranges inland tours.
- **Maya World Tours**, 9846 Highway 441, Leesburg, FL 34788-3918, tel. 800-392-6292 or 904-360-0200.
- **Journeys**, 4011 Jackson Rd., Ann Arbor, MI 48103, tel. 313-665-4407, fax 313-665-2945. Operates monthly tours that emphasize the marine life of the Bay Islands, and a family tour.
- **Laughing Bird Adventures**, P. O. Box 131, Olga, WA 98279, tel. 800-238-4467. A small adventure travel company, offering sea kayaking in the Bay Islands, mountain hikes at Pico Bonito, and river kayaking.
- **Landfall Productions**, 39189 Cedar Blvd., Newark, CA 94560, tel. 800-525-3833 or 510-794-1599. Specialists in dive vacations, offering especially detailed information about the resorts they represent.
- **Americas Tours and Travel**, 1402 Third Avenue, Seattle, WA 98101, tel. 206-623-8850, 800-553-2513, fax 206-467-0454. Founded by Mr. Javier Pinel, a Honduran who is now back home and looking after things at that end. Mr. Pinel runs a week-and running week-long package tours of Honduras throughout the year. These folks claim to be able to get lower rates than other agencies at certain resorts in the Bay Islands..
- **South American Fiesta**, 910 W. Mercury Blvd., Hampton, VA 23666, tel. 800-334-3782, fax 804-826-1747.

Travel agencies *in* Honduras are mentioned in various parts of this book. But here are a few that you might want to consult from home, in case the above agencies are unable to give you the service you require.
- **Explore Honduras**, P O Box 336, Med-Cast Bldg., Blvd. Morazán, tel. 311003, fax 329800 in Tegucigalpa; tel. 526242, fax 526239 in San Pedro Sula. Explore Honduras has a superb reputation for reliability, and is the ground operator for many U.S. agencies offering Honduras travel.
- **Cambio C.A.**, P. O. Box 2666, San Pedro Sula, tel. 527274, fax 520523. Specializes in low-impact, sustainable, ecologically oriented excursions, including canoe trips in Mosquitia, quetzal and manatee watching, hiking in cloud forest, and rafting on the Chamelecón River near San Pedro Sula and the Cangrejal River near La Ceiba.

One week-long adventure trip includes camping, trekking with pack mules, and floating down the Cuyamel and Patuca rivers through the remote northeast, with opportunity to observe endangered wildlife and visit remote Indian villages. Services in English, German and Spanish. Cambio C.A.'s services are available through most of the U.S. agencies that specialize in Honduras, or they can be contacted directly.

· **La Mosquitia Ecoaventuras**, a younger company than Cambio C.A., specializes in ten- to fourteen-day low-impact adventures in the vast forests of Mosquitia, including the Río Plátano Biosphere Reserve, with emphasis on birding, wildlife viewing, and non-intrusive contacts with native peoples. Information is available from La Mosquitia Ecoaventuras, P. O. Box 3577, Tegucigalpa, tel. 370593, fax 379398.

Also, consult the hotel listings in this book for U.S. representative agencies with toll-free telephone numbers. Some will handle not only hotel bookings, but air arrangements as well.

GETTING TO HONDURAS
Arriving By Air
For a country that almost nobody knows about, Honduras is amazingly easy to get to.

To start with, most little countries have only one point of entry by air. Honduras has three. You can land in Tegucigalpa, the capital. Or, if you're just visiting the Caribbean area, you can fly into San Pedro Sula or La Ceiba. A short connecting flight takes you from La Ceiba to Roatán in the Bay Islands.

Then there are extensive route choices to Honduras. Honduras' national carrier, Sahsa, has flights from New York, Houston, New Orleans and Miami to San Pedro Sula, La Ceiba and Tegucigalpa. Some flights land in Belize on the way south, and connections are available in Tegucigalpa for every Central American capital, as well as San Andrés Island.

Fares and route structures offer endless possibilities, and some bargains that are hard to refuse. Sahsa Airlines offers a Maya World fare that allows stops in Belize, San Pedro Sula, Tegucigalpa, Guatemala and Roatán for just $399, with a 21-day maximum stay, half price for children. In effect, you can see virtually all of Central America for the price of an excursion ticket to one city. So your options for a trip to Honduras can include: a few days for diving in Belize on the way down . . . a jaunt to Guatemala, for Mayan ruins, colonial monuments, and unsurpassed handicrafts . . . white-water rafting in Costa Rica.

In the case of a group put together by a travel agent, even a group of just two people, the fare will be somewhat lower. Excursion fares are also available from cities not served by Sahsa, in conjunction with U.S. carriers. For details, see your travel agent. Or call Sahsa at 800-327-1225. Aside from Sahsa, Tegucigalpa is currently served by American, Aviateca, and Taca airlines; and San Pedro Sula by Lacsa and Continental. Each company has its own peculiar fare structure, offering reductions in some cases in combination with pre-arranged hotel stays or tours. Some travel agents will give you better prices than those quoted directly by the airlines.

AIRLINES WITH DIRECT SERVICE TO TEGUCIGALPA

Sahsa	*Miami via Belize*
800-327-1225	*Houston via San Pedro Sula*
	San Andrés Island
	New Orleans
	Guatemala, Managua, San José
American	*Miami*
800-433-7300	
Taca	*Belize, Guatemala, San Salvador*
800-535-8780	

AIRLINES WITH DIRECT SERVICE TO SAN PEDRO SULA

Sahsa	*Houston, New Orleans; Miami via Belize*
800-327-1225	
Continental	*Houston, Belize*
800-231-0856	
Lacsa Airlines	*New Orleans, New York, Cancun, Guatemala*
800-225-2272	*Los Angeles, Mexico City, San José*
American	*Miami, New York*
Taca	*Miami, Guatemala, San Salvador*
Iberia	*Miami*
Aero Costa Rica	*Orlando*
Copa	*Mexico City, San José, Panama*

AIRLINES WITH DIRECT SERVICE TO LA CEIBA AND ROATAN

Sahsa	*Miami*
800-327-1225	

Cancun Connections

If you can get to Cancun, Mexico, on an inexpensive charter, you can also get to Honduras cheaply. Lacsa Airlines, among others, flies daily between Cancun and San Pedro Sula, at a round-trip fare of only $200. Not only is this a low-cost way to get to Honduras, it also saves many of the landings, takeoffs and changes of plane often involved in taking scheduled carriers all the way.

For the moment, charters operate to Cancun mainly from major Canadian cities.

Always try to buy a round-trip ticket before you leave home. You'll usually get a better price, and there are significant taxes to pay if you buy your return ticket in Honduras.

Arriving By Car

I was tempted not to include this section. After all, for most visitors with just a few weeks of vacation, there's no reason to spend up to a week to get to Honduras from home. But if you have extended time, and want to see the sights along the way, and if you love your car, go ahead and start your engine.

But first, drive off to your mechanic for a good inspection and some preventive maintenance. Tune it up, grease it, and replace those bald tires and anything else that's about to go.

Many roads along the way to Honduras are bumpy, and some roads in Honduras are unpaved. Accordingly, you might want to install heavy-duty shock absorbers, and take more than one spare tire. Also useful: a gasoline can, a water container, extra spark plugs, belts, basic tools, electrical tape, and wire. If you plan extensive travel off paved highways, extra inner tubes, air and gas filters, and wiper blades could be useful, along with screens to protect your headlights and windshield.

Unleaded gasoline is not available in Honduras, so you'll have to disconnect your catalytic converter after crossing through Mexico. Gasoline prices are slightly higher than those in the United States, lower than in Canada. In general, it's wise to drive during daylight hours, and to look for a gasoline station when your tank is half full.

While labor for auto repairs is inexpensive in Honduras, parts always cost more — sometimes double the price in the country of manufacture — and sometimes they're not available for your make of car. Don't drive anything too exotic, or in bad condition. Volkswagens, Toyotas, Datsuns and U.S. pickup trucks are good choices.

Tourists may enter their vehicles for an initial period of 30 days. Renewals are available through customs offices to extend your stay for up to six months. I recommend that you enter Honduras through Guatemala, rather than via El Salvador.

Arriving By Bus

Here's another feat that's possible, though I wouldn't want to go non-stop by bus from North America to Honduras. As part of a measured overland journey, though, it can be fun, and the fare is about $100 from the U.S. border.

Basically, you have to take a first-class bus to Mexico City. This will take from ten hours to two days, depending on where you cross the Mexican border. In Mexico City, catch a Cristóbal Colón bus for the Guatemalan border. There are at least two each day, and the trip takes sixteen hours. Connecting buses take you to Guatemala City, where you catch the Rutas Orientales bus for Esquipulas, then a mini-bus to Agua Caliente on the Honduran border. From this point, it's easiest to travel to San Pedro Sula, or to the ruins of Copán. You can also travel from Guatemala via San Salvador and the Pan American Highway to Tegucigalpa, but you should verify current conditions in El Salvador before doing so.

WHAT TO TAKE

Before you pack for your trip to Honduras, consider what your trip will be like, and look at the checklist below. You don't want to take anything but what you'll need. On the other hand, you don't want to leave behind any essentials.

If you'll be at one hotel, take as many changes of clothes as you feel you'll need (as long as it all fits in a couple of suitcases), and do the laundry when you get home.

The other extreme is incessant travel, a single change of clothes in a carry-on bag, and laundry in the hotel sink every night.

Also consider where you'll be. Casual clothes are the norm for visitors, but there are differences in local standards. If you're just going to the Caribbean coast or the Bay Islands, summer clothing will do. You can wear shorts everywhere along the north coast, but they look out of place — even downright silly — in Tegucigalpa and the highlands.

A visit that includes Tegucigalpa, will require some extra packing. You'll need a heavier sweater for cool nights and some mornings. Dressing in layers is suitable. You can peel off your sweater and outer shirt as the day warms. You'll need long slacks, and a plain shirt or blouse. You don't have to dress in a tie and jacket or formal dress for dinner, though you won't be out of place in these items.

Essentials

- passport
- travelers checks
- tickets
- some U.S. cash in small-denomination bills.

Which Clothes?
Take lightweight all-cotton clothing, or loose-fitting, easy-care cotton blends. T-shirts and beach wear are available at reasonable prices in Honduras, but the selection may be limited.
Include:
- hat with ample brim
- a bathing suit
- a few shirts or blouses
- shorts
- comfortable walking shoes. Running shoes will suffice for most purposes, even for jungle walks. Non-slip shoes are helpful on boats.
- socks, underclothes
- sandals or surf shoes
- at least one lightweight, long-sleeved top and slacks, in case you overexpose yourself to the sun, and for evenings, when mosquitoes might lurk.
- a light sweater or jacket for cool mornings and evenings, though a heavier one or a jacket will do if you're going to spend much time around Tegucigalpa and at higher elevations.
- a raincoat or umbrella if you travel during the rainy months, which vary according to where you're going.

The Business Traveler
Take a light suit or jacket, though a *guayabera* — a light shirt worn outside the pants, and without a tie — is the more usual "formal" attire along the north coast.

Fishing and Diving
Fishing and diving equipment are available, but the selection is sometimes limited, so you're often better off with your own gear.
If you have them, take:
- mask, snorkel and fins
- regulator, buoyancy compensator, certification card, wet suit (optional), underwater light (optional)
- preferred fishing equipment.

Packing for Other Sports
Take equipment for other sports that you practice, as it is unlikely to be found easily in the country:
- a day bag for carrying purchases, sunscreen, whatever. I prefer a see-through mesh bag — it shows that you have nothing worth stealing. Fanny packs are insecure and undesirable in towns, but fine for the countryside.

• A pen or two, including a felt-tip pen (ballpoints clog up) and paper.

Personal Items

Bring your cosmetics, toiletries, and small personal items, including:
• sunglasses
• your favorite personal kit of aspirin or substitute, sunscreen, sunburn cream, malaria pills, spare prescription glasses, mosquito repellent (most convenient in stick form), etc.

Habits, Hobbies, and Vices

According to your habits, hobbies and vices, take your:
• camera and waterproof bag, film (more than you think you'll need), batteries
• camping equipment and flashlights
• personal stereo
• duty-free cigarettes and liquor
• snacks (especially if traveling with children).

For a vacation at the beach or on the Bay Islands bring reading material. Keep your luggage as light as practical, tag your bags inside and out, and pack your indispensable items in your carry-on. And remember that if you don't take it, you might not find it, or you might not want to pay the price.

GETTING AROUND HONDURAS

Getting Around By Air

Honduras has a well-developed domestic air transport network. You can't go everywhere, but you can fly the long distances, and continue by bus, taxi, or boat.

Sahsa, the major carrier, has several flights daily between Tegucigalpa, San Pedro Sula, La Ceiba, and the Bay Islands. Smaller airlines, such as **Isleña** and **Sosa**, also connect with the Bay Islands and operate along the north coast to Mosquitia. For details, see coverage in later chapters.

Fares in all cases are reasonable. The top tariff is about $150 round trip from Tegucigalpa to the Bay Islands. A one-way hop from La Ceiba to Roatán costs from $25 to $40.

Getting Around By Bus

They're not Greyhounds, but on major routes in Honduras, buses are comfortable enough. You'll get a padded seat on something that looks on the outside like a school bus. Standards for leg and hip room might be lower than what you would desire, but for a ride of a few hours from Tegucigalpa to San Pedro Sula, the bus will be tolerable.

As you venture off the main routes, the level of service becomes less desirable. Minibuses and microbuses — vans — serve the less-travelled, bumpier routes, for example, from San Pedro Sula to La Entrada and the ruins of Copán. Seats are small and stiff and crowded together to provide no knee room. Buses may be underpowered, and whine along in low gear at low speed, turning short trips into ordeals. Sometimes, out of greed, or sympathy for passengers who have no other way to travel, the passenger load is beyond reasonable safety limits.

To increase your comfort, wherever you're going by bus, try to start your trip at the terminal point. Line up early to get a reserved seat. Generally, you'll have more leg room, and less bouncing, at the front of the bus, near the driver. Buses usually leave the terminal fully loaded; if you flag one down along the road, you could be obliged to stand.

Bus stops along roads are never marked. Ask the driver to let you off where you want to get off, and flag down a bus when you want to get on.

In all cases, bus fares are low. For example, you'll pay about $3 to travel from Tegucigalpa to San Pedro Sula, a distance of 250 kilometers.

Getting Around By Car

What's it like to drive in Honduras? Well, you have a good chance of getting lost if you're not careful, if you don't ask questions, and if you don't have a good sense of direction. Road signs hardly exist. You'll see some kilometer posts, stop signs, and arrows to indicate the flow of traffic and one-way streets. But directional signs that tell you where to turn to get to a village or town are practically unknown. Always follow your map carefully, and when you reach a junction, stop and ask for the way to your destination. It's the only way.

The major paved highways in Honduras are the Pan American Highway crossing from El Salvador to Nicaragua in the south; the highway through Tegucigalpa to the north coast; part of the route along the north coast; and the western highway that roughly parallels the border with Guatemala. There are some other paved stretches, but travel off these main routes will often involve unpaved roads either dusty or muddy, according to the season, over winding, unbanked routes that are the descendants of the mule trails that once snaked through the mountains of Honduras.

But look on the bright side. Only 25 years ago, there were fewer than 100 kilometers of paved road in Honduras, out of a total of 1000 kilometers of roads. There are now more than 2000 kilometers of pavement, almost 10,000 kilometers of all-weather unpaved road, and 7000 kilometers of seasonably passable road. The network is expanding, with paving and construction, and chances are, you *can* get there from here.

When driving in Honduras, take the same precautions you would in any unfamiliar area. Never drive at night, and take it easy when travelling a road for the first time. You never know what's around the curve and just beyond your line of sight: a horse, a cow, a parked truck, a cyclist, an oncoming vehicle passing on a blind curve, or a pedestrian on the wrong side, sober or otherwise. Potholes occur in the most unexpected places on the nicest of roads. Fill your gasoline tank before you turn off any major, paved highway. Sound your horn when approaching a curve, and be prepared to back up when you encounter an oncoming vehicle on a narrow stretch.

Repairs can be accomplished in Tegucigalpa and San Pedro Sula on most familiar passenger cars and pickup trucks. Outside of major centers, you'll probably have to send for parts. Sports cars, turbos, and similar unusual vehicles (for Honduras, anyway) should stay home, rather than face servicing by unfamiliar hands, or a lack of parts.

Automobile Rental

Cars are available for rent in Tegucigalpa, San Pedro Sula, La Ceiba and Roatán. I think that taxis are a better way to go (see below), especially in Tegucigalpa. In addition, you can obtain only limited insurance protection in Honduras.

For more comments on car rental, see page 87.

Taxi

Getting around by taxi is cheap — if there's two of you, it's cheaper than taking a bus in North America. For a five-kilometer ride, you might pay as little as $3. Or you can hire a taxi by the hour for $7 or so.

By all means, take a taxi! Just make sure that you agree on the fare with the driver before you start out. And on any out-of-town trip, give the vehicle a once-over to make sure that you'll make it to where you're going.

HOTEL RATES

In the United States, you often pay for a hotel according to season, with discounts sometimes available if you're an AAA member or have some other affiliation, or if your employer has negotiated a corporate.

In Honduras, *what you pay depends on who you are.*

The highest rate is the **rack rate**, which is generally what you'll be charged as a foreigner, whether you make your reservation through a travel agency, a toll-free telephone reservation service, or directly with the hotel from abroad. Usually, the rack rate is the rate I've quoted in this book. The 7 percent tax is included, unless otherwise mentioned.

At some resorts in the Bay Islands, you'll pay an additional 10 percent service charge, but this is not the practice throughout Honduras.

Since Honduras is a poor country, and many rooms are empty outside the high season, **resident rates** are often available to Hondurans, resident foreigners, military personnel, peace corps volunteers, and Central Americans. If you feel that you qualify for a discount under any category, by all means *ask for it*. Sometimes it takes a little forwardness, sometimes it takes a little fluency in Spanish, but you can often cut your hotel bill just by asking.

In addition, some travel agencies (very few, actually) claim that they can get the Honduran rate for foreigners. Do some price comparisons to check out any such claims.

Note that this double-rate structure applies only at the high-end hotels. You'll look pretty silly if you ask for a resident's discount at a budget hotel that has mostly Hondurans among its clientele.

6. BASIC INFORMATION

BUSINESS HOURS

Hondurans are early risers. In a country where many do not have electricity, people get up at sunrise, and don't go out much after dark.

Businesses are generally open from 8 a.m. to 11:30 a.m. or noon, and from 1:30 or 2 p.m. to 5 or 6 p.m. Along the hot coast in the north, businesses may open even earlier. On Saturday, businesses keep morning hours only.

Exceptions: Banks are generally open from 9 a.m.–3 p.m. Monday–Friday. Government offices are open from 7:30 or 8 a.m. until 3:30 p.m.

COST OF LIVING AND TRAVEL

It costs less to live in Honduras than in North America, and it also costs more. Everything depends on what kinds of goods and services you're buying. For most travellers, though, Honduras will turn out to be a *very* inexpensive destination.

If you take a look at prices mentioned in this book, you'll see that hotels are generally inexpensive. The top hotel in Tegucigalpa has a rate of about $125 double, but modern, comfortable lodgings, usually with a pool, are $50 double or less, tax included. You can usually get a decent meal for $4, though fancy food, when available, will cost more, and imported wine will raise the cost considerably. Locally produced liquors — mostly rums — are inexpensive, at about $3 per bottle. If you ever shop for an occasional picnic, you'll find prices for local produce quite low in season.

Some hotels, especially those in the Bay Islands, have a **two-tier price system**, with one rate for foreigners, and another for Hondurans. In a way, this is fair, and in another way, it's discriminatory. You can sometimes get the lower rate during slow periods simply by requesting it. And a few travel agencies in the States are authorized to charge the lower rate to their clients. Shop around.

Public transport is inexpensive. You can cross from the Caribbean to the Pacific by bus for $6. Taxis are cheaper than rental cars. A hop across the Caribbean to the Bay Islands by airplane costs about $25.

In the Bay Islands, all costs are somewhat higher than on the mainland. Some hotels charge an inclusive rate of more than $100 per person for lodging, meals and diving. But this is an incredible bargain compared to every other Caribbean locale with near-comparable amenities. And there are clean, modest lodging places that charge much, much less.

It's only if you're going to stay for longer than a vacation that you might find some things expensive in Honduras. Imported food, appliances, cars, and anything not produced or processed in Honduras (or elsewhere in Central America) generally costs double the U.S. price, with a few exceptions. It can also be surprisingly expensive to rent an apartment or house with the appliances and amenities you might be used to – $1000 or more per month for a three-bedroom house or apartment in Tegucigalpa. Outside of the capital, housing costs are lower, and if you can do without built-in closets and American-style bathrooms and kitchen, costs will drop. Household workers earn low salaries, and there are no fuel bills for heating.

The moral: rely on local goods and services, and your costs in Honduras will generally be low.

ELECTRICITY

Most electricity is supplied at 110 volts, 60 cycles, just as in the U.S. However, some locales operate only on 220 volts, so inquire before you plug anything in.

Sockets take standard American-type plugs with parallel blades and no grounding prongs.

I should mention here that Honduras is undergoing an energy crisis, reminiscent of the one that hit the world in 1973. Cards in all hotels request that you turn out the lights when not needed, and close the hot water taps (though they all leak). There are no blackouts, but cooperate anyway.

HEALTH CONCERNS

According to my wife Natalie, a few preparations and precautions are in order for travel to Honduras.

Before You Go

If you are taking any medications regularly, pack twice the quantity you think you'll need. Brand names in Honduras might be different from the ones you're familiar with. Also prepare a small emergency kit (see below).

It's important to be current with your routine vaccinations, such as tetanus, diphtheria, and polio. Vaccination against typhoid, and gamma globulin as a precaution against hepatitis, are also recommended. There is some malaria in rural areas. Antimalarial pills, such as Aralen (chloroquine), are taken once a week, beginning two weeks before and ending six weeks after your trip.

In Honduras

If you don't drink the water, and watch what you eat, you shouldn't have any health problems.

In general, you should stick to foods that have been well cooked, and are still hot when served. Fruits and vegetables are okay if they have a peel, or are cooked. But avoid salads, and sandwiches that are decorated with fresh vegetables. Don't hesitate to leave anything doubtful sitting on your plate. Water is not safe to drink from the tap in *any* city in Honduras. Stick to bottled beverages, or take along Halazone tablets or laundry bleach (two drops to a quart, allow to stand 30 minutes).

Your medical kit should include: a sunscreen containing PABA (sunburn can be a problem if you're not used to being outdoors); insect repellent (the best brands, such as Cutter's or Muskol, contain methyl toluamide); condoms (if there is any chance of a new sexual relationship); personal medications; anti-malarial tablets; Halazone or bleach for drinking water; sterile pads, bandages, antiseptic soap, and analgesic pills.

For longer stays, consult a public health or travellers' clinic before you go. Useful publications include *Health Information for International Travel* (Department of Health and Human Services), available from the U.S. Government Printing Office, Washington, D.C. 20402; and *Health Guide for Travellers to Warm Climates*, available from the Canadian Public Health Association, 1335 Carling Avenue, Suite 210, Ottawa, Ontario, Canada K1Z 8N8. The International Association for Medical Assistance to Travellers may be able to provide a list of English-speaking doctors, in Honduras and other countries, for a small fee. Write to **IAMAT**, 736 Center St., Lewiston, NY 14092.

In Tegucigalpa and San Pedro Sula, and in any town of any size, there's *always* a pharmacy open at night. Look for a lighted "*de turno*" sign on the outside. "*De turno*" pharmacies are also listed in many newspapers.

LEARNING SPANISH

The **Escuela de Español Ixbalanque** ("Ish-ba-lan-keh" Spanish school) in Copán Ruinas (site of the greatest Mayan city in Honduras) offers one-on-one instruction in Spanish for four hours a day, five days a week. Students board with local Spanish-speaking families, or have the option of staying at a hotel. For more information, see page 212.

Contact Darla Brown, Escuela Ixbalanque, Copán Ruinas, Honduras, tel. 983432, fax 576215.

MONEY AND BANKING

You pay for goods and services in Honduras in *lempiras*, the coin of the realm, named after the native chief who died fighting the Spanish invaders. The exception is the Bay Islands, where, in some resorts, everything is priced in dollars, and lempiras may not even be welcome.

Lempiras come in bills, and in coins of 1 lempira, 50 *centavos*, 20 centavos, 10 centavos, 5 centavos, 2 centavos, and 1 centavo. Once upon a time, U.S. coins were in circulation here, leaving *daime* ("dime") as the nickname for the 20-centavo coin of the same size, and *búfalo* as the name for the 10-centavo coin, after the buffalo on the American nickel. A 50-centavo piece is a *tostón*, and sometimes you'll hear of, but never see, a *real* (ray-AL), or "bit." Two *reales* are 25 centavos.

> *In this book, prices are expressed in U.S. dollars, based on the current exchange rate of about 6 lempiras to the U.S. dollar. In the case of hotels, especially in the Bay Islands, that quote prices only in U.S. dollars, I give the actual rate in dollars charged by the hotel.*

Black Market, Gray Market, Free Market

Honduras has a black market, but it's so open and tolerated, that you might as well call it the gray market, or, even better, the free market.

How do you change money on the free market? Generally, you don't have to look for it, it will find you. Taxi drivers, hotel clerks, owners of stores that sell imported goods will all offer their exchange services, or can direct you to somebody looking for dollars. Money changers speak enough English to consummate the deal — more than bank clerks. They'll take travelers checks without much ado, and their hours are certainly flexible. Street money changers generally don't hold more than the equivalent of $100 or $200 in local currency. To change more than that amount, try a store.

Of course, this information is subject to change. Verify the current official and free-market rates as soon as you arrive.

Exchanging Money

Then there are the *casas de cambio* (exchange houses), which, for the moment, are legal, and offer a quicker exchange service than that provided by banks, with more security than you'll get with street changers. Some are said to launder money for the drug trade, and some have minimums of $200. Their numbers are growing, and you should spot one near your hotel; if you don't see one, look for ads in *Honduras This Week*.

Exchange houses will handle the currencies of other Central American countries, which can be difficult otherwise to exchange.

Banks

Banks will give you a *less advantageous* exchange rate, generally about five percent less than what you'll get at an exchange house, and you'll often face discouraging lineups. And hotels and other services catering to tourists usually give you even less for your foreign money. Wherever you end up changing money, at a bank or on the free market, you'll find that only U.S. dollars, in cash or travelers checks, have any value. Currencies of neighboring countries can be exchanged at the border, or sometimes at exchange houses, but Canadian dollars, sterling, German marks and other solid currencies might just as well be play money in Honduras.

Credit Cards

Visa, Master Card and American Express are widely accepted at middle- and upper-range hotels in Honduras. Your charge slip will be processed at the bank rate of exchange – certainly no advantage.

For **cash advances** on a Visa card, try any bank that displays the Honducard-Visa symbol. Bancahsa and Bancahorro are authorized to make cash advances throughout the country. Otherwise, for Visa or Master Card cash advances, contact Credomatic, second floor, Interamericana de Seguros building, Tegucigalpa, tel. 326030; or Ficensa building, San Pedro Sula, tel. 532404; or try any bank with a Credomatic, Ficensa or Futuro sign.

Investment Information

For investment information, one source is **FIDE** (Foundation for Investment and Development of Exports), P. O. Box 1858, San Pedro Sula, tel. 527616, fax 572162; tel. 329345, fax 311808 in Tegucigalpa; 170 Hamilton Ave., Suite 211, White Plains, NY 10601, tel. 914-761-4233, fax 914-761-4389; or Airport Corporate Center, 7200 19th St NW, Miami, FL 33126, tel. 305-592-3166, fax 305-592-3969.

POST OFFICE AND COURIER SERVICES

Post offices are generally open from 7 a.m. to 6 p.m. during the week, from 8 a.m. to noon on Saturday. There could be some variation in small towns. I should tell you that everything that I've ever mailed from Honduras has arrived safely in Canada.

Alternative Mail Services provide express air shipment of urgent letters out of Honduras, avoiding delays and other possible contretemps in the local mail system. One company offering quick delivery of letters and packages is EMS, tel. 224971 in Tegucigalpa, 570707 in San Pedro Sula.

From North America, you can find express service to Honduras from some cities with Hispanic communities. Check the yellow pages under Courier Service for a company with a Spanish-sounding name. Express letter services charge more than the post office, but a fraction of what large courier companies collect.

If nothing else is available in your area, DHL and some other courier companies will deliver letters and documents to Honduras at a minimum charge of about $40 from North America.

RETIRING IN HONDURAS

Honduras, like several other Central American countries, provides an immigration status for foreigners who would like to live in the country as retirees. And retirement status is one of the easier ways for a foreigner to attain residence.

Benefits

Among the benefits of retirement in Honduras are low-cost medical care, where available; inexpensive liquor, household help, and many other products and services; a benign climate; low construction costs; cable t.v. with U.S. programming in population centers; and small expatriate communities in several towns with clubs and activities.

Under the Honduran law, pensioners (*pensionados*), usually of retirement age, must have a stable monthly income of $600. Annuitants (*rentistas*) require a monthly income of $1000.

Spouses and children under 18 (and children up to 25 who are students) may also qualify as residents, without additional income requirements.

The major statutory benefit under the retirement law is that household goods and furniture, as well as a car, may be entered into Honduras free of duty. The car may be replaced, again duty free, every five years, but household goods may enter one time only.

In addition, retirees' income from abroad is not taxed in Honduras.

Restrictions

Retired residents generally may not work in Honduras, but there are many exceptions and loopholes. Anybody, whether a resident or not, may own an incorporated business. And retirees may be specifically allowed to work if they invest in tourism, housing, industry or agriculture.

Retirees usually must live in Honduras for at least four months a year, but they can stay out of the country if their funds continue to be deposited every month in a Honduran bank, or if they invest a minimum of $50,000 in Honduras.

Leaving the country is more complicated for retirees than for tourists. The Honduras Tourism Institute must certify that the retiree has complied with all conditions of the law. An official identification card, or *carnet*, must be renewed every two years.

Applying for Retirement

Among the documents required by applicants for retirement status are: birth certificate, passport, medical certification, good-conduct certification by local police, attestation that one is not a Communist, affidavit of willingness to abide by the laws of Honduras, six photographs, and proof of income.

Information on the retirement law is available through Honduran consulates. Within Honduras, the retirement law is administered by the Honduran Tourism Institute (Instituto Hondureño de Turismo).

Lifestyle Explorations, 101 Federal St., Suite 1900, Boston MA 02110, tel. 508-371-4814, fax 369-9192, specializes in familiarization trips for prospective retirees and investors. Their program includes sessions with resident foreigners

SHOPPING

Honduras isn't famous for its shopping, but there are some products that are rather typical of the country, and of special quality.

What you'll see everywhere in Honduras, in gift shops and hotels and markets, is hardwood, especially mahogany, made up into assorted useful and decorative items: bookends, sculptures, oversized salad servers, and lamps.

Straw hats from Santa Bárbara are of especially good quality, come in many sizes and colors, and are useful during your travels, as well as making attractive souvenirs.

Wicker work is intricate and of excellent quality, especially near and along the north coast, where, along the highways, you will find animals, suspended chairs, rockers, and all kinds of utilitarian and decorative items, many of them, unfortunately, too large to take home easily.

Leatherwork, jewelry, baskets, t-shirts and beachwear and embroidery are also available, along with primitive paintings, which are a special favorite of mine, and of many other people as well.

Honduran crafts are supplemented by crafts from neighboring countries. You can buy fine weaving from Guatemala, and textiles from El Salvador. You should also keep an eye out for more mundane bargains that are offered in *pulperías* (corner stores) and larger outlets: ground coffee, tropical fruit jams, rum, and assorted sauces.

Bargaining is common in Honduras, but you won't get the big discounts you'll find in some other countries. (Or, to put it another way, asking prices aren't as inflated as in places where tourists abound.) The "right" price in a market may be about 20% less than the first price. In any case, if you walk away and the price doesn't move as a result, you've probably gone as far as you can go.

TAXES

A 7% tax is added to all room and meal bills. On beverages, the tax is 10%.

Departure taxes at airports total about $19.

Indirectly, you'll be paying import duties on anything you buy. Much of government funding in Honduras comes from taxes on both imports and exports, rather than from income taxes. Innocent items like film and tape cassettes, as a result, sell for double what they would cost in the United States or Canada.

TELEPHONES

The national telephone system, operated by Hondutel, serves only a few of the major towns of Honduras.

Calls within Honduras can be made conveniently from hotel phones, or from pay phones where they are available.

You'll find coin telephones – they work with ten-centavo pieces – on the main streets of Tegucigalpa and San Pedro Sula, but nowhere else, for the moment, as most of the country lacks direct-dial service.

Calling Hone

Rates to the States and Canada are approximately $2.50 per minute during the day, less at night. Collect calls may be placed to the United States, Canada, Mexico, the Bahamas, and all Central American countries except El Salvador.

For international calls, try to use a private line if possible. Direct-dial service to foreign countries is *only* available from Tegucigalpa, San Pedro Sula (phones beginning with 53), La Ceiba, the Bay Islands, and a few other locales. Hotels can arrange foreign calls – it's not so expensive, and easy to get a line. Or you can go to an office of Hondutel, the telephone company, but you'll often face a long lineup and confusing procedures.

USA Direct is available from many public phones (coin deposit required) in Tegucigalpa, and from USA Direct phones at Toncontín airport and certain Hondutel offices. From public phones, dial 123 to reach an English-speaking AT&T operator.

TIME

Honduras is on Central Standard Time, equivalent to Greenwich Mean Time less six hours.

TIPPING

Generally, you can leave a ten-percent tip in any restaurant, and be considered generous. Many local people will leave less, or nothing at all, especially in small, informal eating places. You can give one lempira (about 25¢ U.S.) to anyone who carries your bag, more in fancier hotels. Taxi drivers don't get anything on top of the negotiated fare.

Some hotel restaurants add a ten-percent service charge to your bill, in which case there's no need to leave an additional tip, except for exceptional service.

WATER

In general, do not trust the tap water for drinking, anywhere in Honduras. There are exceptions to this rule of thumb. You may find clean spring water flowing from the tap in the Bay Islands. But unless you're assured that the tap water is safe, don't drink it.

In most places on the mainland of Honduras, the water is hard — it has a high mineral content. It's not easy to take a shower, and you'll need plenty of shampoo.

WHERE TO FIND INFORMATION ABOUT HONDURAS
The Tourist Office

For a map of Honduras, and assorted pamphlets, try writing to the Honduras Tourist Bureau (Instituto Hondureño de Turismo), P. O. Box 3261, Tegucigalpa, D.C., Honduras. They take up to six months to respond — sometimes they don't respond at all — and don't answer specific questions, so try other sources of information as well.

All the News

Honduras This Week is a gold mine of information about Honduras, and the indispensable tool for keeping up with the latest developments. This weekly paper covers local happenings, profiles villages in the countryside, runs in-depth investigative reports on everything from Tegucigalpa's street children to ecological conflicts to the struggles of indigenous communities to maintain their integrity, serves as an exchange for commercial opportunities in Honduras, and has selective regional and international coverage. New hotels, restaurants and travel services are profiled, and at least one page is devoted to ads for diving services, hotels, restaurants, and other facilities of interest to visitors.

In addition, *Honduras This Week* carries many press-service stories from the States that concern the interests of lesser-developed countries, and are not carried by most U.S. papers. *Honduras This Week* is available in major towns in Honduras, mainly through hotels. You can often find a copy in a Honduran consulate. To subscribe (for $40 annually in the

United States), write to Apartado Postal 1312, Tegucigalpa, D.C., Honduras, or call 315821, fax 322300.

Books and Maps
Books and Maps published in Honduras can be hard to obtain if you're out of the country, but *Honduras This Week* has a reading club, with an order form printed in the back of most issues. Listings included maps, and books on Honduran history, archaeology, ethnology, and folklore. Most are in Spanish, but some are illustrated and of interest even if your knowledge of the language is limited. They can even arrange to send you the Honduran phone book.

Maps of Honduras and Central America may be available from your automobile club. One excellent detailed map (ISBN 0921463170) is published by **ITMB**, P. O. Box 2290, Vancouver, B.C. V6B 3W5, Canada, and is available at many travel bookstores for $8.95 Canadian or $7.95 U.S. funds.

In Tegucigalpa, good maps are available at the **Instituto Geográfico Nacional** (see pages 108-109).

Consulates & Embassies
Honduran consulates and embassies generally handle trade matters, but in some cases might be able to answer questions about the retirement law or travel in the country.

In **New York**, the **consulate** is at 80 Wall St., New York, NY, 10005.

In **Washington, D.C.**, the **embassy** is at 3007 Tilden St., NW, Washington, DC, 20008 (tel. 202/966-7702).

7. SPORTS & RECREATION

CRUISE THE ISLANDS AND THE COAST

Sail Down in Your Own Boat

The definitive handbook for these waters is *Cruising Guide to the Honduras Bay Islands*, available from Wescott Cove Publishing Co., P O Box 130, Stamford CT 06904. This book includes numerous maps, charts, and customs information that will get you safely to, through, and out of the Caribbean waters of Honduras.

Charter a Sailboat

To have a sailboat waiting for you, contact a travel agency that specializes in Honduras, such as **Roatán Charter**, Box 877, San Antonio, FL 33576, tel. 800-282-8932, fax 904-588-4158.

For more details, see the chapter on the Bay Islands.

Take a Cruise

The Ukrainian-registered *Gruziya* ("Georgia") sails regularly from St. Petersburg, Florida, to Cozumel, Belize, and onward to Puerto Cortés, Honduras. The five-deck vessel has two restaurants, a casino, pool, disco, and a crew offering an unusual Russian and Ukrainian experience in the Caribbean. Rates for a one-week cruise range from about $1000 to $2000 per person, with deep discounts for the third and fourth person sharing a cabin. Contact **Odessa America Cruise Company**, 170 Old Country Rd., Mineola, NY 11501, tel. 800-221-3254.

To arrange diving in conjuction with the cruise, contact **Maya World** Tours, 9846 Highway 441, Leesburg, FL 34788-3918, tel. 800-392-6292 or 904-360-0200. The folks at Maya World plan a cruise package that includes diving in Mexico, Belize and off Roatan for a package price of under $1000 per person.

Charter a Boat

Motor vessels without sails can also be secured through **Roatán Charter**, and through many of the hotels in the Bay Islands.

DIVING

Here's an activity that you will enjoy exclusively in the Bay Islands, so see "The Bay Islands" chapter for more details.

Skin Diver magazine regularly publishes articles covering diving and accommodations in the Bay Islands, and classified and display advertisements for hotels and diving packages. Available at newsstands, or by subscription from *Skin Diver*, P. O. Box 3295, Los Angeles, CA 90078.

FISHING

For the most part, sport fishing is something you'll participate in from resorts in the Bay Islands. See "The Bay Islands" chapter for further information.

On the mainland of Honduras, the most famous fishing hole is **Lake Yojoa**, known for bass weighing in at about ten pounds on the average. The few hotels along the lake have limited equipment available for rent. If you own your own gear, it's advisable to bring it along.

A fishing license is required, and is usually obtained in advance through a travel agency.

HUNTING

Southern Honduras, around the city of Choluteca, is known as the dove-hunting capital of the world. The season is from November 1 to March 15, and a daily limit of 50 doves is imposed.

Hunting, of course, requires a license, and the details are best handled through a travel agency. One company familiar with procedures is **Dockside Tours**, 339 Hickory Ave., Harahan, LA 70123, tel. 800-235-3625, fax 504-737-2998.

Within Honduras, contact the **Departamento de Caza y Pesca** (Department of Hunting and Fishing).

NATIONAL PARKS

Here's another of the surprises of Honduras. In just a few years, Honduras has moved into the forefront of Latin America in protecting and preserving its natural treasures. And treasures there are aplenty — over 700 species of birds, 500 piscine species, and flora that includes scores of species of orchids alone.

Paradoxically, the backwardness of Honduras has left this ecological bonus intact. Few roads — and poor ones at that— underpopulation, and limited industrial agriculture, except in bananas, have left nature alone in much of the country. The Mosquitia region along the border of Nicaragua is one of the last largely undisturbed lowland forests in Central America. And there are pockets of highland cloud forest that the magnificent resplendent quetzal, the holy grail of birders, still calls home.

But the remaining untouched forests of Honduras are now in danger. Multinational companies are turning envious eyes toward stands of pine and deposits of minerals. Farmers from the exhausted soil of the central part of the country are seeking new lands to clear and plant.

Over a dozen treasure troves of nature are now protected as national parks, reserves and refuges, and many more sites are under consideration for inclusion.

For now, things are in a rudimentary state. Most parks have no trails, camp grounds, guides or guards. But a start has been made, and the establishment of the parks and reserves is holding off loggers and farmers who might otherwise be cutting down the trees and chasing off the animals. And in the not-too-distant future, Honduras is sure to join Belize, Costa Rica and Guatemala as a destination for visitors interested in getting to know tropical life forms beyond the kinds that are attacked with insecticide.

Current information about conditions in National Parks may be available from the following sources:

- **Ministerio de Recursos Naturales** (Department of Natural Resources), Blvd. Miraflores, Tegucigalpa, tel. 328723.
- **Asociación Hondureña de Ecología** (Honduran Ecology Association), Colonia La Reforma C-2423, tel. 383383. The Ecology Association, in an unusual arrangement, manages La Tigra National Park for the government. It publishes guides to the mammals and ecosystems of the country.
- **COHDEFOR** (Forestry Development Corporation), Carretera al Norte, tel. 228810.

CHECKING OUT THE CORALS

NATIONAL PARKS

Unless specific facilities are mentioned, parks are not yet ready for visits on your own.

- **Montecristo-Trifinio** – *near Ocotepeque. No trails, continues into Guatemala and El Salvador. 54 square kilometers.*
- **Cerro Azul** – *10 km northeast of Florida (Copán Department). Along Guatemalan border, includes caves, cloud forest and recovering forest. The lake atop Cerro Azul mountain, known as Laguna de los Pinares, is frequented by migrating birds. 150 square kilometers.*
- **Celaque** – *5 km west of Gracias. Includes Mount Celaque, highest peak and cloud forest in country, and colonial fort and hot springs. Campsites available. 270 square kilometers.*
- **Santa Bárbara** – *in Santa Bárbara. Includes caves, and Marancho, second highest mountain in Honduras. 130 square kilometers.*
- **Cusuco** – *20 km west of San Pedro Sula. Includes cloud forest with quetzal habitat, trails. 10 square kilometers.*
- **Cerro Azul Meambar** – *30 km northwest of Comayagua. Forest and watershed reserve above the eastern side of Lake Yojoa, with falls and rapids.*
- **Pico Pijol** – *east of El Progreso. Cloud forest. 114 square kilometers.*
- **Pico Bonito** – *south of La Ceiba. Includes high tropical forest on Bonito Peak. Trails. 68 square kilometers.*
- **Montaña de Yoro** – *south of Yoro. Adjacent to Torupane Indian reserve. 155 square kilometers.*
- **Capiro-Calentura** – *in Trujillo.*
- **Sierra de Agalta** – *Olancho. Includes dwarf forest. Trails and camping. 255 square kilometers.*
- **Montaña de Comayagua** – *13 km east of Comayagua. Includes archaeological site and regenerating forest. 62 square kilometers.*
- **La Tigra** – *11 km northeast of Tegucigalpa. First national park (established 1980), protecting Tegucigalpa's watershed. Trails, dormitories. 75 square kilometers.*
- **Punta Sal** – *6 km west of Tela. Includes beaches and reefs, trails. 419 square kilometers.*
- **El Armado** – *in Olancho. Includes Montaña del Armado. 1 square kilometer.*
- **La Muralla** – *8 km north of La Unión, Olancho. Cloud forest, trails. 16 square kilometers.*
- **Cuero y Salado** – *20 km west of La Ceiba. Coastal area with river estuaries and navigable canals, includes manatee habitat. Access by boat. 85 square kilometers*
- **Laguna Guaimoreto** – *East of Trujillo. Includes Lake Guaimoreto. 50 square kilometers.*

RAFT AND KAYAK THE JUNGLE RIVERS

Honduras has white water! It's rapid, it's exhilarating, it's ecological, it's adventurous, it's off-beat, it's inexpensive, but best of all, it's warm.

There are major rivers throughout Honduras, but rafting operators mainly use those on the north coast, where water levels are most reliable during the rainy season from October to May.

The **Cangrejal River**, inland from La Ceiba, rated at Class II to Class

III, has some significant rapids, as well as many sedate stretches, where you can take a break from paddling to view the banana fields, riverside forest trailing vines into the water, and colorful tropical birds fluttering into and out of the foliage.

The **Cuero River**, running through **Cuero y Salado National Park**, west of La Ceiba, is a stereotypical lazy jungle river, lined by dense forest and abandoned coconut plantations, perfect for visitors who want to enjoy birding and wildlife observation.

The **Chamelecón River**, running to the east of San Pedro Sula, is generally more sedate than the Cangrejal, with exciting stretches.

Rafting organizers provide all necessary equipment: raft (or kayak, where appropriate), helmet, life jacket, and paddles. Participants should wear bathing suit and t-shirt or lightweight jogging outfit as protection against the sun, and tennis shoes or surf shoes. Take along a change of clothing for when you're done!

Despite the excitement, there is little danger in rafting the rivers of Honduras. Passengers wear life jackets, and in the case of an occasional capsize, you're soon washed away from any rocks into deeper, safer water.

One-day trips out of La Ceiba or San Pedro Sula, generally costing about $75 per person, are offered by:

• **Caribbean Travel** (Ríos Honduras), Hermanos Kawas building, Avenida San Isidro, La Ceiba, tel. 431361, manual fax 431360. Guides are from the Rocky Mountain Outdoor Center in Colorado.

• **Cambio C.A.**, P. O. Box 2666, San Pedro Sula, tel. 527274, fax 520523.

6. ECO-TOURISM

ADVENTURE IN THE RAIN FOREST

Talk of rain forests, talk of eco-tourism, talk of adventure travel. Whatever you call it, Honduras is the last frontier of travel in Central America, where an adventuring soul can still be one of the few outsiders to drift along a lazy river bordered by centenary trees, listen to the roar of howler monkeys trooping through the jungle canopy, spot a limpkin wading in the shallows, wonder at petroglyphs carved by mysterious ancient civilizations.

Though the pressures of logging companies and land-hungry peasants are inexorable, and more forest has been destroyed in the last few decades than in all the centuries since the Spaniards arrived in the New World, there are more jungles left in Honduras than elsewhere in the region. The forests are protected, at least nominally, in such areas as the **Río Plátano Biosphere Reserve**.

Low-impact tourism by adventurous visitors represents one of the few viable ways to make those lands valuable in a capitalistic world, without destroying their ancient treasures of medicinal plants, animal life, water-storing lowlands, and mangroves where fish breed.

The pioneer travel operator in low-impact tourism in Honduras, and one worthy of your consideration (this is not a paid ad!) is **Cambio C.A.**, which limits the size and frequency of its trips in order not to destroy what you are going out to see.

Here's what they have to say:

"Our travelers journey in dugout canoes through unspoiled, little-travelled tropical rain forest. They see the Caribbean unmarred by high-rise hotels and souvenir touts. Our travelers eat, travel, and live much as the indigenous people of the region do, and our unhurried pace allows us to get to know the local inhabitants as fellow humans and not as carnival attractions or museum pieces. . .

Our programs are designed to inform the traveler about the environmental, cultural, social, and political settings of the land through which we journey. . . . Our leaders carry basic medical supplies, two-way radios, and the many small comforts that make the difference between an adventure and an ordeal."

Among offerings from Cambio are canoe trips in **Mosquitia**, quetzal and manatee watching, hiking in cloud forest, and rafting on the **Chamelecón River** near San Pedro Sula and the **Cangrejal River** near La Ceiba. One week-long adventure trip includes camping, trekking with pack mules, and floating down the **Cuyamel** and **Patuca** rivers through the remote northeast, with opportunity to observe endangered wildlife and visit remote Indian villages. Guides speak English, German and Spanish.

Cambio C.A.'s services are available through most of the U.S. agencies that specialize in Honduras, or they can be contacted directly: **Cambio C.A.**, P. O. Box 2666, San Pedro Sula, tel. 527274, fax 520523.

9. FOOD & DRINK

As a tourist, you'll probably run across "international food," American cuisine adapted to local tastes and cooking abilities; and food served in the local *style*, without showing off too many local specialties. Your grilled steak (*bistec a la parrilla*), pork chop (*chuleta*) or chicken (*pollo*) might be accompanied by fried plantains (*plátanos fritos*), beans (*frijoles*) and/or rice (*arroz*). Garlic and onion are part of any sauce, and vegetables may include the less-than-familiar *chayote*, or vegetable pear, or *yuca* in place of potatoes. Sometimes you'll get *tortillas*, flat cakes of corn, used in place of bread.

At home, Hondurans enjoy *tapado* (vegetable-meat soup), *mondongo* (tripe soup), *enchiladas* and *tamales* (meat and sauce in tortillas or corn dough), and black beans. You can partake, too, if you get friendly with the locals, or if you take a meal or two at the bare tables and benches in a local market, where food shops cook up filling, cheap repasts for people of modest means.

On the streets, you can snack on fruits to your heart's content. Peeled oranges and bananas are sold for a few cents each, with or without salt and nutmeg, according to your taste. You'll also find *mermelada de papaya* (papaya marmalade) and other local fruit preserves at every breakfast table.

Along the highways, you'll see food stands everywhere. Field corn, cooked in the husk over open fires, is especially popular. It's not the sweet corn you might know — it's chewy, and usually quite pale — but it's fresh and delicious.

In the Bay Islands, and among the Black Caribs, or Garífuna, of the northern coast, there are some variations. Seafood of all kinds is eaten more than elsewhere, and coconut invades many a menu item: mixed with rice, or, more usually, in coconut bread.

Soft drinks are sold everywhere in Honduras, probably more than are healthy for the population. On the other hand, carbonated beverages are always safe to drink, while the local water supply may be suspect. Coke, Fanta, Stripe and Canada Dry ginger ale and soda water are major brands, sold for from 25¢ to 60¢, depending on whether you're consuming at a street stand or in a hotel restaurant. The price is for the contents only. The bottle costs as much as what's in it, or more. If you intend to walk away as you drink, ask for your soda in a plastic bag (*en una bolsa*) with a straw (*con pajilla*).

There *are* local wines in Honduras, made from fruits and imported grape concentrate, but having said this, I'll say no more — they're not worth further mention. And you can find imported California, French and Chilean wines, though by the time they reach your table, with hefty import duties, taxes and markups added on, they'll generally cost at least double what they would in the United States, and sometimes much, much more.

If you're a drinker, moderate or otherwise, this leaves you to choose between hard liquor and beer. Imported liquors, like wines, are pricey. Local rum (*ron*) is generally quite good, while gin (*ginebra*) and vodka are just so-so, though their defects can be well hidden in a mixed drink.

If you're so inclined, I can recommend that you try the beer. Salva Vida, Imperial, Nacional and Port Royal are all light beers, and to me, they all taste the same, which is good enough. Port Royal comes in a fancy bottle, suitable for taking home as a souvenir.

10. TEGUCIGALPA

INTRODUCTION

Tegucigalpa as a settlement dates back to 1578, when silver was discovered, on September 29, St. Michael's Day. The town that grew up around the mine was called Real de Minas de San Miguel, in the saint's honor, with "de Tegucigalpa" — "of the Silver Hill" in the *Nahuatl* language — appended to distinguish this San Miguel from many others. In time, Tegucigalpa was the part of the name that stuck.

Throughout the colonial period, Comayagua was the capital, but Tegucigalpa continued to grow in importance, and, after independence, the seat of government alternated between the two major settlements. In 1880, the administration of the country was installed once and for all in Tegucigalpa. Officially, the capital bears the suffix "D.C." for "*Distrito Central*," the central administrative district that also takes in adjacent Comayagüela. The city is known as "*Teguz*," pronounced "Tegoose."

Tegucigalpa Today

With more than 800,000 people, metropolitan Tegucigalpa is the most populated city of the country, but it is lacking in some of the attributes of a capital. Tegucigalpa has no railroad. The Pan American Highway bypasses the city, and an all-weather road to the north coast was completed only in the middle of this century.

In the last century, most economic development in Honduras has taken place along the north coast, leaving Tegucigalpa with somewhat of a backwater status. The central area, never laid low by earthquakes or volcanic eruptions, has a certain amount of charm imparted by colonial and nineteenth-century architecture. Some of the surrounding hillside neighborhoods are reached by narrow, winding streets, too narrow for vehicles, and by public stairways. The climate, at an altitude of 935 meters (3067 feet), is rarely too warm.

Still, modern times are catching up. Tegucigalpa has grown at a turbulent pace in the last decades, as people have migrated from the countryside to towns, and from towns to the capital. Slowly, cobblestoned streets are being covered over with asphalt. Anonymous concrete-and-glass structures are replacing venerable homes with walls several feet thick. Red-tile roofs and Italianate and colonial decorative elements are disappearing. Tegucigalpa and adjacent Comayagüela are poor cities. But Honduras has had the dubious advantage of being relatively uniformly poor, and the seething social tensions of neighboring lands are less apparent here. You can stroll around Tegucigalpa during the day and feel safe and unbothered. Only occasionally does a beggar or street vendor dare to approach a stranger. Tourism is a fledgling industry, with all of the advantages and disadvantages this implies.

ORIENTATION

It is easy to get disoriented in Tegucigalpa. The city does not have straight streets like those of San Pedro Sula, except at the very center. It's more like the pattern of a souk in the Middle East. The topography of the valley is far from flat, and you have small hills everywhere. The city is divided into units called barrios and colonias (neighborhoods and suburbs), each of which is more or less homogeneous in its social class.

Downtown is Tegucigalpa proper, or Barrio El Centro, and across the Choluteca River, connected by four bridges, Comayagüela, the poorer and flatter part of town, with few significant buildings or governmental operations. Everything of any importance occurs in Tegucigalpa, which runs northward up the slopes of Mount Picacho, and wraps around the eastern side of Comayagüela.

Streets wind this way and that through and between the different barrios and colonias, straightening out for a while, then snaking along and up a hill again. The same street will have different names, both traditional and numbered, and one or the other version will be posted.

The first step in finding any location, if you're not familiar with the city, is to ask for its barrio or colonia (neighborhood or district) and find that area on a map. Barrios are generally older or more centrally located than colonias. Once you're in the general area, ask for the street that you're seeking. Sometimes, an address will be given as a street name with a house number. Sometimes, you'll get the name of the street, and the nearby cross streets. For example, the Hotel Istmania is at 5 Avenida, 7/8 Calles (between 7 and 8 Calles, or streets). These are the lucky cases. As often as not, though, an address will be given simply as a location relative to a well-known landmark: media cuadra del Hotel Honduras Maya (half a block from the Hotel Honduras Maya). Ask for the hotel, and you're halfway there. Now, start looking!

Trying to find places in Tegucigalpa is bound to get you out and meeting people, but after a while, you'll probably want to rely on a taxi driver to help you out. Fortunately, taxis are inexpensive.

Beyond the city, within easy range by day trips, are such villages as San Antonio de Oriente, Valle de Angeles and Lepaterique which, despite their proximity to the capital, remain quintessentially rural places, with no industry to speak of beyond local handicraft specialties.

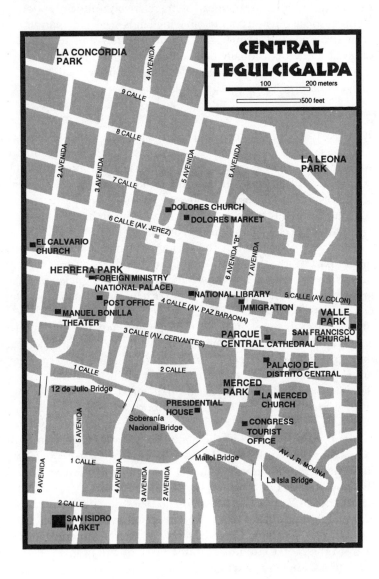

ARRIVALS AND DEPARTURES

Arriving By Air

Sahsa is the airline of Honduras, and, with its many domestic and international connections, is the company you're most likely to be dealing with. Sahsa's downtown office is on the Peatonal (4 Calle) at 6 Avenida. Numbers for reservations are 333333 and 335866. At Toncontín Airport, the number is 331134.

Sahsa flies to Guatemala, San Salvador, Managua, San José, Miami, Houston, New Orleans, Belize, Panama, and San Andrés island. Domestic routes are to San Pedro Sula ($45), La Ceiba, and Roatán, in the Bay Islands ($76).

International airlines serving Tegucigalpa, or with sales offices, are:
- **Alitalia**, tel. 3729322; and Lufthansa in the Midence Soto building downtown, tel. 376900.
- **American Airlines**, Palmira building, tel. 321347. To Miami, New York.
- **Continental Airlines**, Toncontín Airport, tel. 337676. To Houston.
- **Iberia**, Palmira building, tel. 315253.
- **KLM**, Ciicsa Bldg., Col. Palmira, tel. 326410.
- **Lacsa**, Los Jarros Bldg., Blvd. Morazán, tel. 311525.
- **Taca International**, La Interamericana building, Blvd. Morazán, tel. 312472. To Guatemala, San Salvador.

Airport

Toncontín Airport is just five kilometers south of downtown Tegucigalpa. The runway is in good repair, and that's the good news. The other news is that it isn't much of an airport. When you arrive, there are no visible airline counters, and the information desks are likely to be unattended.

If you need anything, go to the departure area (if it is open).

Entry formalities, like everything else at the airport, are minimal.

Getting to Town from the Airport

Once you go outside the terminal, you'll find a hubbub of **taxi drivers** and money changers — disconcerting, perhaps, as your introduction to Honduras, but not dangerous in any way. There's a fixed tariff of about $5 to go from the airport by "yellow cab" to any location in the capital. Or, you can walk to the main road a couple of hundred meters from the terminal and pick up a regular city taxi for about half that price. **City buses** to town also pass regularly. It's inexpensive enough to reach the airport from town by taxi, but the Loarque or Río Grande bus will also take you. One central stop is on 6 Calle (Av. Jérez) in front of Super Donuts.

Airport hours are 6 a.m. to 8 p.m. Nothing lands at night.

There's an **airport bank**, but you might as well change your money with the fellows out front. The **post office counter** is open from 8 a.m. to 3 p.m., and is one of the fastest ways to send anything home. **Hondutel**, the national telephone monopoly, has an airport outpost. There are also AT&T USA Direct phones, which you can pick up to reach an operator in the States. **Budget** has a car-rental counter, and there are other companies not far away.

Departing By Air
Isleña Airlines, tel. 331130 at the airport, flies to the Bay Islands and to La Ceiba as well. One local air taxi service is **Aeroservicios**, tel. 331287, fax 341633.

Departing By Bus
There's no central bus terminal in Tegucigalpa, but many buses for suburban and distant destinations leave from private stations in Comayagüela.

Among the bus operators:
• **To Comayagua and San Pedro Sula:** Empresa El Rey, 6 Avenida, 9 Calle, Comayagüela, tel. 333010. This station looks like a bombed-out garage. Buses leave every 90 minutes from before dawn to 10:30 p.m. Fare is less than $4 to San Pedro, less than $2 to Comayagua. Buses are comfortable and uncrowded. Also Hedman-Alas (better than other companies), 11 Avenida, 13/14 Calles, Comayagüela, tel. 377143, and Transportes Sáenz, 12 Calle, 7/8 Avenidas, Comayagüela, tel. 376521, hourly departures from 8 a.m. to 6 p.m. The ride to San Pedro Sula takes about four hours.
• **To Juticalpa and Olancho department:** Empresa Aurora, 6 Calle, 6 Avenida, Comayagüela, every hour; and Rutas Olanchanas, 8 Calle, 6/7 Avenidas.
• **To Danlí:** Discua Litena, near Jacaleapa market, (tel. 327939) five kilometers from downtown in southeast Tegucigalpa. Danlí and Paraíso: Emtraoriente, 6 Calle, 6/7 Avenida, Comayagüela, tel. 378965, 6 departures daily from 6:30 a.m. to 4:30 p.m.

Other Honduran and Foreign Destinations By Bus
Bus service for other destinations is given with descriptions of various other towns. From downtown Tegucigalpa, the Villa Adela bus will pass near many of the Comayagüela bus stations.

To reach **Guatemala** by bus, you can to travel via San Pedro Sula and Santa Rosa de Copán. Otherwise, cross through El Salvador. For **El Salvador**, take a bus for El Amatillo from the Belén market. For **Nicaragua**, take a bus from the Mi Esperanza station, 6 Avenida, 24/25 Calles, Comayagüela (tel. 382863), as far as Guasaule, on the border. Through bus service between Central American capitals is much more limited than it once was.

GETTING AROUND TOWN

Auto Rental

If you are going to rent a car, think first about hiring a taxi (see "Taxis," below). Not only is it cheaper, but roads are bad around Tegucigalpa, with many potholes, and traffic is crazy (though it doesn't move too fast, at least), and traffic signs are only an afterthought.

Generally, you will be substantially responsible for damage to a rented vehicle, even if you buy local insurance, which provides only limited coverage. Verify if your automobile insurance from home or your credit card will provide any additional coverage (such coverage is gradually being eliminated).

Among car-rental companies are:

- **Budget**, at the Hotel Honduras Maya and at the airport, tel. 335171 and 335161, fax 335170.
- **Avis**, Hotel Honduras Maya, tel. 320088, and airport, tel. 339548.
- **Hertz**, Centro Comercial Villa Real, tel. 390772.
- **National Car Rental**, Hotel Honduras Maya and airport, tel. 332653, fax 339769.

These companies have toll-free numbers in the United States and Canada, useful for making reservations and getting the latest rates. Sometimes, by reserving in advance, you can get a lower rate than you might obtain locally.

Some local car-rental companies are:

- **Amigo**, Boulevard Morazán, tel. 315135, fax 374445.
- **Maya Rent A Car**, Blvd. Morazán at Av. República de Chile, tel. 326133.
- **Molinari**, Hotel Honduras Maya, tel. 328691; airport, tel. 331307.
- **Toyota Rent A Car**, Colonia El Prado, Comayagüela, tel. 334004.

DRIVING IN TEGUCIGALPA

Driving can be a problem in Tegucigalpa, especially at rush hours – about 7 a.m. to 9 a.m. and 3 p.m. to 7 p.m. It's not that there are a lot of cars. There just aren't enough streets, and those that exist are narrow and potholed. There are only a few routes to and through downtown, and they are often gridlocked. This explains why bus terminals are on the periphery of Tegucigalpa or in Comayagüela.

Right turns are allowed on red lights, but proceed with caution. Road signs hardly exist, and if you have a choice of driving or not driving, I think you will have a better time not driving.

By Bus

Buses exist in Tegucigalpa, and it's even possible to get a sheet from the tourist office listing the number of each route, and the neighborhood where it starts and where it ends. This, however, will be useless for most visitors, as it gives no idea of the route the bus takes as it winds from one hillside neighborhood down and up to another through Tegucigalpa's tortured geography.

Local buses can be crowded, and the lineups stretch and curve like so many strands of spaghetti. Many of the points of any interest to visitors are in the small downtown area, and those that aren't can be reached inexpensively by taxi for under $3 (see Taxis, below). If you're staying at a hotel away from the center, such as the Alameda, ask the staff for guidance as to which bus will take you into the city and back out, if you don't want to take a taxi.

Fares on buses are low, the equivalent of about 10¢ U.S. Bus drivers and fellow passengers are very helpful.

By Taxi

Taxis are everywhere in Tegucigalpa. They're inexpensive, at about a dollar per person for a run around downtown, $2 for a ride to any place on the outskirts of town, $5 to the airport in the "**Yellow Cab**" taxis or $3 in a regular taxis. I highly recommend taxis as an alternative to the crowded and confusing service provided by public buses. They're also easier on your nerves than renting a car for local excursions, and usually cheaper, at about $6 per hour for time actually used.

Since taxis are not metered, it is essential to agree on the fare with the driver before you get in.

Try to find a taxi that looks as if it has been well maintained. Some are frighteningly dilapidated. The better-kept fleet of Yellow Cabs is based at the **Honduras Maya Hotel**, and charges about double the going rate for trips.

Don't be surprised if a taxi stops to pick up another passenger on the way to your destination. It's part of local practice.

Tourist Office

The tourist office in Tegucigalpa is amusing. It is located in the **Europa building** east of downtown in Colonia San Carlos (Calle República de México, Avenida Ramón E. Cruz). Look for the Lloyds Bank branch on the first floor — the tourist office is two floors up. They have no hotel information, other than a list, but they sell attractive posters as well as maps. As for buses, they will tell you where to catch them, but they have only a sketchy idea as to schedules. If you don't expect much, you won't be disappointed.

To reach the tourist office, take any eastbound Lomas bus from the main square, and get off at Hospital San Felipe. Walk one block west, then left one block on Av. Ramón E. Cruz.

My experience is that you will do better to ask for information when you first arrive at the airport, or by inquiring at your hotel desk, or any travel agency. There is currently no downtown information office.

SEEING THE SIGHTS
Downtown

Central Tegucigalpa, still somewhat colonial-flavored, is small enough that you can get a sense of the city during a walk of just a few hours. There are some fine old examples of colonial and nineteenth century architecture, city squares in which to linger, and pedestrian streets for shopping and observing the flow of city life.

A good place to start your excursion is the main square, or **Parque Central**, also known, more formally, as **Plaza Morazán**. On the east side of the square is the twin-towered **Cathedral of Tegucigalpa** (or Cathedral of San Miguel), the construction of which was started in the middle of the eighteenth century. The facade of the cathedral is noted for its inset, or engaged, columns with horizontal grooves — "accordion-fold" or "cushioned" or "pleated" columns — and pillars in the form of mermaids. While

A VIEW FROM THE HILLSIDE

the Cathedral is similar in many respects to others of the period in Central America, the pleated columns are a peculiarly Honduran characteristic that occurs here, and on some of the churches in Comayagua. Inside, the Cathedral is decorated with an elaborate pulpit, altarpieces, decorative and functional pieces plated in gold and silver, and paintings of saints, some of which pre-date the building. Part of the collection constitutes a museum of colonial religious art, open weekday afternoons from 2:30 p.m. to 6 pm., and on Sundays from 10:30 a.m. to 12:30 p.m.

South of the Cathedral, across 3 Calle, is the **Palacio del Distrito Central**, which houses the municipal government of Tegucigalpa and Comayagüela. On this site stood the old *cabildo*, or town hall, where the Declaration of Independence of Central America was ratified on September 28, 1821.

4 Calle (or Avenida Paz Baraona by its old name), along the north side of the Central Park, is a *peatonal*, or pedestrian mall. To the west, it constitutes the main commercial area of Tegucigalpa, lined by all kinds of shops and eateries, as well as the principal banks of the country, and several hotels.

At 5 Avenida, another branch of the mall runs northward, to the twin-towered **Iglesia Los Dolores (Dolores Church)**, containing, as does the Cathedral (which it predates by about twenty years, to 1732, though it wasn't completed until 1815), gold-plated altars. The pilasters on the facade are decorated with rosettes, and windows are finished with busts of angels on top and depictions of fruits underneath — altogether, along with its unique ceramic decoration and balustrade, a more elaborate treatment than on other temples in the city. It is said that the construction of the church was financed by former slaves who made a fortune in mining.

Back on the main pedestrian mall, going west, on the north side between Avenidas 3 and 4, is the **Ministry of Foreign Affairs (Ministerio de Relaciones Exteriores)**, also known as the **National Palace**. Once the San Sebastián convent, the building was taken over by the government in 1934. Note the national seal over the front door, which was never formally adopted by the government. Across the mall is the central **Post Office,** on the site of the first orphanage in Tegucigalpa.

Farther west, across 3 Avenida and then south down a side street, is **Teatro Manuel Bonilla (Manuel Bonilla Theater)**. Every Central American capital has one grand, significant performance area, and this is Tegucigalpa's, completed in 1912. The facade is neoclassical, while inside, there is an ornate double horseshoe tier of seating above the main floor, a copy of a contemporary theater in Paris.

Continuing to the west, then one block north along 2 Avenida, you'll come to **El Calvario Church**, dating from 1746.

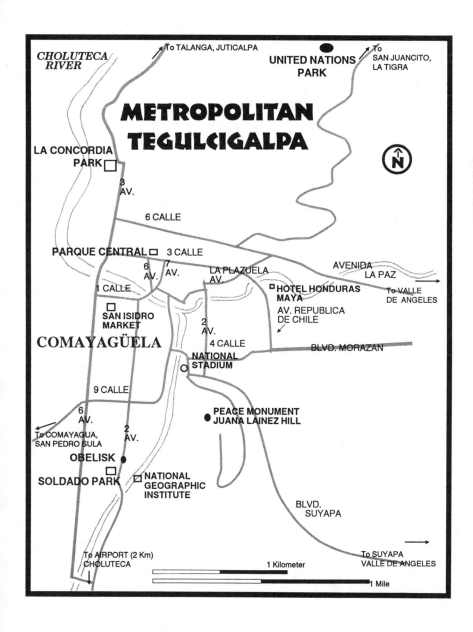

Farther afield, on the edge of downtown, four blocks north along 2 Avenida, is **Parque La Concordia** (**Concordia Park**), a block-sized square that contains small-scale replicas of Altar Q and Stela C of Copán, as well as a model of a temple at Chichén Itzén in Mexico. This is meant to be a small botanical garden as well, with assorted non-Maya statuary, pools, and plantings. Couples frequent the Bridge of Sighs and hold hands alongside the Lake of Love.

Back toward the center of downtown, along 5 Calle, at 6 Avenida, you'll encounter the **National Library and Archives**.

Walking back to the Central Park, then south along 7 Avenida (Calle Bolívar), you'll come to a small square called **Parque Merced**, after the **Iglesia La Merced** (**Merced Church**) on its east side. This church dates from the seventeenth century, and includes some colonial paintings and an elaborate altar. Also on the park is the greenish building that once housed the National University, now removed to a suburban site on Boulevard Suyapa. The University was founded in 1847 as the Academia Literaria by José Trinidad Reyes, and for some years was located in Comayagüela. Farther south is the **Palacio Legislativo**, or **Congreso Nacional** (**Legislative Palace**, or **National Congress**), a campus sort of building that dates from 1955, and is quite peculiar among the older and more elaborate governmental edifices in the city.

Walking down toward the river, you'll see the **Puente Mallol** (**Mallol Bridge**), the oldest bridge in the city. Construction was started in 1818. Back up along 6 Avenida, you'll reach the well-guarded, fortress-like former **Casa Presidencial** (**Presidential Palace**), at the corner of 1 Calle, completed in 1919. The massive, light-pink, wedding-cake Moorish-Italian architecture, with a dome at one end, ogive arches, and keyhole openings, overwhelmingly defensive, says much about the turnovers of government through the years. Air conditioners, rarely used, jut out incongruously. There's an interior courtyard, but for now, it's not open to casual visitors. It was near this site that the first silver discoveries were made in Honduras.

The executive offices have been moved to the Civic Center in suburban Miraflores, the old palace is being renovated and meticulously restored to its former grandeur, for a future incarnation as the **Museo de la República** (**Museum of the Republic**).

Back at the Parque Central, go east along 4 Calle to 10 Avenida to reach the **Church of San Francisco**. This is the oldest of the churches that remain in Tegucigalpa, started in 1592 (by Franciscans, of course), and greatly altered starting in 1740, when Mudéjar elements characteristic of southern Spain were added to the original simple structure. Inside are gold-plated altarpieces and colonial paintings. Next door is the building that formerly housed the San Francisco monastery.

Comayagüela

In Comayagüela, southwest of downtown Tegucigalpa, you'll find no high-rise buildings, only numerous bus stations, a few cheap hotels, and assorted other nondescript concrete commercial and residential structures, along with several sights that are not as historically interesting as those in Tegucigalpa proper, but every bit as rewarding for visitors who are interested in the way the broad class of Hondurans lives.

Comayagüela is a working-class area. Small businesses of every sort flourish, and if you need a piece of galvanized steel cut and hammered to a certain shape, or shoes made to measure, or a sack of feed, chances are you can find just the right merchant or craftsman somewhere in Comayagüela.

The heart of commercial Comayagüela is the **Mercado San Isidro** (**San Isidro Market**), the largest in the city. Here you can find everything, and you can bargain for anything. Yet it's not a frenzied place at all, in fact, it's very calm, and not dangerous (though, as in any market, you should keep valuables out of sight, and money in a hidden pocket). If you don't find what you're looking for at the San Isidro Market, try the **Artesanías** (**Handicraft**) **Market**, held on weekends adjacent to **Parque El Soldado** (**Soldier Park**) at 4 Avenida and 15 Calle, toward the south end of Comayagüela. Aside from the goods, the park itself is pleasant, with caged birds, and luxuriant vegetation. Soldado Park commemorates those who died in the 1969 war with El Salvador. Just north is the **Obelisco** (**Obelisk**), which was erected to commemorate 100 years of independence. Adjacent is a heavily guarded military installation, surrounded by tank traps.

Also in Comayagüela, on 6 Calle, between 2 and 3 Avenidas, is the **Escuela Nacional de Bellas Artes** (**National School of Fine Arts**), some walls of which are painted with frescoes illustrating Mayan themes.

Southeast of Downtown

East of Comayagüela, and south of downtown Tegucigalpa, the hill called Juana Laínez juts up alongside the road from the airport. At the top is the **Monumento de la Paz** (**Peace Monument**). A walk or taxi ride up to the top will give you a panorama of Tegucigalpa and the surrounding hills. The monument itself is a double-vision image of a flying saucer and complementary rings, set on concrete pillars. I'm not sure of the imagery, but it certainly isn't warlike. At the foot of the hill is the **National Stadium**. A large fruit and flower market operates here on Friday and up to noon on Saturday.

North of Downtown

North of downtown is the peak called **El Picacho** (1310 meters), one of several mountains surrounding the city. Picacho is included in **Parque**

Naciones Unidas (United Nations Park). First of all, before you go to Picacho, ask at your hotel about current conditions – a fire recently did severe damage to the vegetation on the hill, and regrowth is under way. Also, take a sweater.

There are several ways to get here. From downtown, you can walk due north, following 9 Avenida. Once you cross 6 Calle, the streets – many of them cobbled – become more winding and narrow. You pass through the neighborhood called La Leona, where some of the large, old houses have been restored to their past glory. The streets give way to paths, and with some help from passersby, and an eye toward the summit, you should be able to make it to the top. Or, you can go up in a taxi for about $5 round trip, including a wait of a half-hour.

The main reward of a visit to Picacho is the view to the whole valley spread out before you. You get a good orientation to the city. And by looking around, you'll understand why it was that your plane made a couple of sharp turns before touching down at Toncontín Airport, which is on a small plateau, one of the few flat pieces of land in this valley.

You'll also find a small zoo, in decrepit state with the animals badly cared for, and some reproductions of Mayan ruins, including pyramids. In the absence of regular maintenance, the park has become something of a ruin itself. There is long grass everywhere, and evident vandalism. There are also outdoor grills, in case you want to cook your lunch. The area is crowded on Sundays.

Also north of downtown, the **Instituto Hondureño de Antropología e Historia (Honduran Institute of Anthropology and History)** has a museum housed in a mansion, Villa Roy, built in 1936 by President Julio Lozano, and given to the state by his widow in 1981. It's really all quite limited. Part of the building is conserved as a monument to itself, and to the ex-president and his first lady. Other exhibits illustrate the lives of the Jicaques, Lencas, Chortís, Miskitos and Sumos, native peoples whose ancestors occupied the land before the Spanish arrived. And there are exhibits of fossils and colonial life. In any case, it's a quiet place with nice gardens, and good views of the city. Closed Monday and Tuesday, open from 8 a.m. to 3:30 p.m. other days, small admission charge. Take a taxi, or ask for directions from your hotel if you're walking. It's on Calle Morelo, off 3 Avenida, seven blocks north of the post office downtown. You can stop here on the way to United Nations Park.

WHERE TO STAY

Where should you stay? As far as the neighborhood goes, for most visitors, the choice is easy. Almost all hotels, in every price range, are in a one-kilometer square of central Tegucigalpa and adjacent Comayagüela. The exceptions are a few of the pricier establishments, which are located along the major roads leading out of the city.

As elsewhere in this book, the rates mentioned below for hotels include a seven-percent room tax, and reflect the current free-market exchange rate. If you change your money at a bank, or use a credit card, you'll pay slightly more.

Some of the larger hotels will offer discounts if you present your business card, or ask for the special rate. I don't guarantee that this will work for you, but this has certainly been the case recently, when occupancy rates at the better hotels have not been that high.

Better Hotels

HOTEL HONDURAS MAYA, Avenida República de Chile at 2 Calle, tel. 323191, fax 327629. 200 rooms. $107 to $120 single/$120 to $135 double, $200 to $350 in suites. $13 per extra adult, no charge for children, nominal charge for crib. Visa, Master Card, American Express. U.S. reservations, tel. 800-448-8355.

Located just east of downtown Tegucigalpa, the Honduras Maya is one of the city's landmarks, a high-rise in local terms, at 12 stories, with a trademark sculptured vertical frieze on its main tower meant to reflect the Mayan tradition of Honduras. It's the top hotel in town (though not super-luxurious and getting somewhat worn at the edges), where diplomats stay on the first days of their assignments. Rooms have the expected air conditioning, and televisions offering U.S. programs via satellite. Beds are comfortable, though furnishings are on the bland side.

Service is more than adequate, the pool is huge and heated, and views are scenic. An on-site health spa includes a sauna and steam bath. There are several restaurants, including a 24-hour coffee shop, brand-new convention and meeting facilities, extensive protected parking, and plenty of shops and services (auto rental, barber shop, travel agencies, etc.) both on the extensive hotel grounds and in the surrounding neighborhood. There is no charge for local phone calls, a plus if you're in town on business. Also complimentary (at least recently) is the buffet breakfast. Uniquely among Tegucigalpa hotels, the Honduras Maya has a casino, where the gaming includes blackjack, roulette, and slot machines.

HOTEL PLAZA SAN MARTÍN, Colonia Palmira on Plaza San Martín, P. O. Box 864, tel. 372928, fax 311366. 110 rooms. $90 single/ $110 double/$115 triple, $130 in suites. American Express, Diners Club, Visa, Master Card.

Tegucigalpa's newest major hotel, just east of downtown, is a blocky Mayan fortress of a building, with bare, slightly sloping facades terraced to the roof comb (in this case, a machine enclosure). Rooms are plainly furnished but quite comfortable, each with a balcony, refrigerator, sitting area, television, phone, and central air conditioning. Facilities include coffee shop, restaurant, bar, exercise room and indoor parking, but no pool.

HOTEL ALAMEDA, Blvd. Suyapa (P.O. Box 940), tel. 326920, 326902, fax 326932. 75 rooms. $75 single/$90 double/$105 triple plus tax. U.S. reservations: tel. 305-226-7500. American Express, Visa, Master Card.

This is one of the few hotels on the outskirts of the capital. It's about three kilometers from the airport in the hilly Alameda district southeast of downtown, and though it's not near any attractions, I can recommend it if you're interested in a quiet location. The hotel is built in a colonial-influenced style, with a white exterior, balconies, and red-tile roof. All rooms are carpeted, with color television, and the enclosed grounds include two swimming pools, one for children, and one quite large. There are also a sauna and steam bath, travel agency, car rental, barber and beauty shops, and conference rooms.

The colonial atmosphere is carried to the restaurant, with its high, panelled ceiling and heavy chairs. The menu is Tegucigalpa-standard for hotels: sea bass, shrimp, lobster and beef entrees for $7 and up, and all quite good. If you stay here, I recommend a poolside room, or one on the second floor for the most attractive views.

HOTEL TEGUCIGALPA SHERATON, Blvd. Juan Pablo II. Located in southeastern Tegucigalpa, this incomplete project could well evolve into something other than a hotel. Nevertheless, the not-yet-existent Sheraton is often used as a reference point in giving directions and addresses.

HOTEL PLAZA, 4 Avenida at 4 Calle (P.O. Box 175), tel. 372111, fax 372119. 83 rooms. $60 single/$75 double/$85 triple. American Express, Visa, Master Card.

Centrally located on the pedestrian mall of downtown Tegucigalpa, opposite the post office, the Plaza offers good-sized air-conditioned rooms, all with queen-sized beds, and televisions with U.S. programming. Some of the standard rooms have sofa beds as well. Possible negative points for some visitors will be the lack of a swimming pool, and of shops inside the hotel, though most required services are available nearby. There are two restaurants here, including an all-night coffee shop, the Papagallo. Protected parking.

HOTEL LA RONDA, 6 Calle (Avenida Jérez) at 11 Avenida, Barrio La Ronda (P.O. Box 849), tel. 378151, fax 371454. 46 rooms. $50 to $70 single/$55 to 80 double. U.S. reservations: tel. 800-742-4276. American Express, Visa, Master Card.

A nice hotel, though hardly luxurious, conveniently located downtown. Certain rooms have no view at all, but most are quite large and comfortable, with carpets, telephone, color television and air conditioning. Small apartments are available, with kitchenette and dinette. Adjacent parking, restaurant and bar.

SUITES LA AURORA, Avenida Luis Bográn 1519, Colonia Tepeyac, tel. 329891, fax 320188. 46 units. $36 single/$42 double with fan, $60/$65 with air conditioning.

These are furnished apartments in a relatively quiet neighborhood, and though room service and other hotel amenities are missing, the units are fully equipped with kitchen, air-conditioning and television. Also on site are a convenience store, pool, sauna, steam room, restaurant, bar and protected parking.

Moderate Hotels

HOTEL ISTMANIA, 5 Avenida, 7/8 Calles, No. 1438 (P.O. Box 1972), tel. 371914, 371638, 371639, fax 371446. 34 rooms. $30 single or double. Visa, Master Card.

Centrally located near Dolores church, and a few blocks from the Cathedral and Central Park, the Istmania is a modest, clean, businessmen's hotel, housed in a narrow modern building. All rooms are carpeted, air conditioned, and have telephones. Suites have kitchens, dining areas, and a combination of bedrooms and living rooms with sofa beds. A restaurant and bar are the only public facilities. This is the kind of place that receives visiting soccer teams – safe, clean, a good value, especially for families or others sharing accommodations, but nothing special. Parking is available next door.

HOTEL EL PRADO, 3 Avenida, 8 Calle, tel. 370121, fax 372221. 68 rooms. $75 single/$85 double/$100 triple plus tax. American Express, Visa, Master Card.

A modern building located near the back of the Cathedral. Rooms are air conditioned and have televisions. Coffee shop and piano bar, protected parking. Courtesy morning coffee and afternoon iced tea. Somewhat comparable to the Istmania, but larger.

GRAN HOTEL KRYSTAL, 6 Avenida/6 Calle (P. O. Box 283), tel. 378804, fax 378976. 59 rooms. $19 single/$30 double. American Express, Visa, Master Card.

A good-sized businessperson's hotel, located in the center of *everything* in Tegucigalpa, and a good value for the price. All of the modest rooms are carpeted, with air conditioning, phones, private bath, and cable television. Secure, with protected parking, and a passageway of shops. The large coffee shop has an extensive menu of American-style steaks, sandwiches, chicken and pasta and even a native-style combination plate, with no surprises and nothing priced over $5. The Krystal also has meeting and celebration facilities, and if you stay here, you might run into a wedding or some other function attended by more typical Hondurans than you're likely to meet during your passage through the country as a tourist.

Budget Hotels

HOTEL IBERIA, Peatonal Dolores, tel. 229267. $7 single/$9 double shared bath, $10 single/$12 double private bath. On the pedestrian mall near the Dolores Church. Well maintained, clean, friendly, and safe. Rooms on the second floor are better. There's a pleasant living room. I don't think that you can do better for the price. The market across from the hotel is colorful.

HOTEL IMPERIAL, 5 Avenida 7/8 Calles No. 703, Callejón Los Dolores, tel. 221973. $4 single/$6 double. Budget lodging in a good location.

NUEVO HOTEL BOSTON, 6 Calle no. 321, Barrio Abajo, tel. 379411. $8 to $9 single/$10 to $11 double. Well-located near Dolores church, and very good for the price. Take a room that doesn't face the street (which costs less). Management is English-speaking and friendly.

HOTEL MARICHAL, 5 Calle at 5 Avenida, No. 1115, tel. 370069. $8 single/$14 double. A large hotel with many basic, clean rooms, varying in size and quality. Near the Plaza Dolores.

HOTEL EXCELSIOR, Avenida Cervantes (half-block from Hotel Honduras Maya), tel. 372638. $10 single/$14 double. This is in a pretty decent neighborhood for a budget hotel, and it's frequented by volunteers of the Peace Corps, the office of which is nearby. Meals are available.

HOTEL GRANADA, Avenida Gutemburg 1326, tel. 374004. 46 rooms. $9 single/$12 double. At the eastern end of downtown, also a good buy, with a relatively quiet location. Additional rooms are available in a newer annex, a couple of blocks away (tel. 220597).

HOTEL PUNTA DEL ESTE, Avenida La Paz (eastern continuation of 6 Calle), near Avenida Juan Lindo, tel. 381094. 20 rooms. $10 double. Another case of budget lodging in a mid-scale location. Located one block east of the Mas X Menos supermarket.

CA FÉ ALLEGRO, República de Chile No. 3608, tel. 328122. $7 per person. Not formally a hotel, but the folks who run the Ca Fé rent beds (*not rooms*) to visitors, four to a room.

HOTEL MCARTHUR, 8 Calle, 4/5 Avenidas, tel. 375906, fax 380294. 24 rooms. $40 single/$55 double. This is an acceptable hotel, located a block up from the Dolores church, and updated from past years. Rooms have air conditioning and cable television, and there is a coffee shop on site.

HOTEL RITZ, 5 Avenida, 4 Calle (P.O. Box 743), Comayagüela, tel. 222769. 23 rooms. $10 to $12 double. This hotel is not luxurious, but a good value if you need to be near the bus stations in Comayagüela. Most rooms are modest, many with shared bath. Higher-priced ones have telephones, carpeting, and air conditioning. The rooftop terrace offers pleasant views of the city and surrounding piney hills.

HOTEL CENTENARIO, 6 Avenida, 9/10 Calles, Comayagüela, tel. 377729 or 371050, fax 227575. 53 rooms. $14 single/$26 double. Clean, simple, modern businessman's hotel. Check out your prospective room — some can be quite noisy. There's a basic restaurant on the top floor. The advantage of staying here is that it's near the El Rey bus company for departures to San Pedro Sula.

HOTEL COLONIAL, 6 Calle, 6/7 Avenidas, Comayagüela, tel. 375785. $8 singe/$10 doublesz. Convenient to the bus stations, all rooms with private bath, clean, good for the price.

HOTELITO WEST, 10 Calle, 6/7 Avenidas, Comayagüela, tel. 379456. $12 double. A budget hotel recommended by some readers.

There are assorted other cheap hotels in **Comayagüela**, with no advantage other than being near the bus terminals, in case you get into town late or have to leave early. In many, you'll have to share bathroom facilities.

The selection includes:

HOTEL BRISTOL, 5 Calle, 4/5 Avenidas, tel. 370988. 20 rooms. $8 single/$15 double.

HOTEL CÁDIZ, 4 Avenida, 4/5 Calles, tel. 376458. 10 rooms. $10 per person.

HOTEL TICAMAYA 1, 6 Avenida, 8/9 Calles, tel. 370084. 35 rooms. $7/$10.

HOTEL TICAMAYA 2, 7 Avenida, 4/5 Calles.

HOTEL ALCÁZAR, 5 Calle, 4/5 Avenidas, tel. 372802. 10 rooms. $5 to $6 single/$6 to $8 double.

Pensiones

Many of the cheaper places to in which to stay are in the area of the Dolores church, on Peatonal Dolores (a pedestrian street that starts in front of Dolores church and runs down to the main pedestrian street, 4 Calle). Right by the church is **HOSPEDAJE TRES DE MAYO**. Another one nearby is **HOSPEDAJE SUREÑO**, clean and basic, with airy rooms, and a rate of under $5 per night. Hospedaje Montoya, also in this area, is much less attractive. **HOTEL FORTUNA**, at the corner of Dolores and Paulino Valladares, at about $6 for a room sharing bathroom, is clean and calm, okay for the price.

And there are all sorts of other cheap places in these blocks — the **PENSIÓN SAN ANTONIO**, tel. 223801, even has rooms for less than $2 per person. If one is full, walk on and you'll find another. But just make sure that you look carefully at your prospective room before you put any money down.

Furnished Rooms

Furnished rooms at assorted price levels are available for persons on long-term stays. You'll find ads with offerings in *Honduras This Week*. Some of the establishments offering rooms are foreign-owned, include breakfast in the rate, and are located in attractive residential neighborhoods.

WHERE TO EAT

I can't say that Tegucigalpa has all the gourmet delights of a major capital. There isn't enough of an audience for fine cuisine to be very common. But if you attune yourself to what's available, you won't be disappointed — not at all.

Eating places in Tegucigalpa fall into several broad categories.

Basic eateries serving the working-class population are most common. Food is simple, and the attraction is more price than quality. For most visitors, local hole-in-the-wall diners are not worth mentioning by name. But feel free to try any that look clean, for a cheap meal of rice and beans and some stewed meat or chicken, along with local color.

It is in the *comedores* that you're most likely to encounter home-style Honduran specialties: *tajadas* (ta-HA-das), deep-fried sliced plantains; *baleadas*, beans in a flour-tortilla, close cousins of the northern Mexican burrito; *mondongo*, beef tripe stew; *nacatamal*, similar to Mexican tamales, corn dough stuffed with pork and rice and raisins and olives and sauce, and steamed in a banana leaf.

Fast food restaurants are the expanding sector of the industry in Tegucigalpa, serving standardized hamburgers and chicken and pizzas at reasonable prices, along with quick service or self-service. For visitors, these outlets offer something predictable.

Steak and Seafood Houses are what most Hondurans have in mind when they have the money and want to dine out. Seafood can be more expensive than you might expect, while steaks are a bargain. In either case, you won't be disappointed by the quality of the food.

Hotel restaurants generally serve American-style food, which they call "international cuisine" or "*cocina internacional*." Hotel coffee shops and restaurants have more extended hours than other eating places. Quality, especially for items other than standard steak and seafood, will usually be higher than at independent restaurants. One or two budget-priced items appear on most hotel menus.

There are also a few **ethnic** restaurants, mainly catering to foreign communities and employees of international agencies, and one or two genuine **French** restaurants have operated from time to time.

In general, you can count on spending from $4 to $10 for a full meal at most of the restaurants mentioned below (unless a specific price range is mentioned), not including an alcoholic beverage. A soft drink generally costs about 60 cents, a beer about $1.25, but a glass of wine or a drink with imported liquor will increase your bill considerably.

Downtown

La Terraza de Don Pepe, 5 Calle (Avenida Colón), downtown (opposite the "Pequeño Despacho"). The specialty is charcoal-grilled meats — *"carnes a la parrilla"* — which are as tasty as you'll find in Tegucigalpa. But you'll also come here for the old-time ranch atmosphere. Large, friendly, and relaxed. About $5 for most main courses.

Burger Hut, next to the church of La Merced (2 Calle, 8 Avenida) is one of many, many fast-food places. And you can also get the real thing.

Burger King has an outlet on the Peatonal mall downtown, as well as a couple of outposts in outlying areas.

Pizzeria Tito, Callejón Los Dolores (the north-south pedestrian street, by Bancahasa), is one of many pizzerias, this one Italian-owned, with an unpretentious menu that includes pastas. All items attractively served. Don't be tempted by the wine. It is not good. They also have a branch on Boulevard Morazán.

Restaurante y Pizzeria Nino, on Callejón Dolores near 5 Calle, is a small establishment owned by a Honduran-Italian family, with not only an assortment of pizzas, but hearty soups and pastas (the latter at up to $5) and saltimbocca, calamari and other specialties (up to $8).

Al Natural, near Morazán Park, just behind the cathedral on a narrow street. This is a restaurant that I recommend highly, set in an interior courtyard, quiet and peaceful despite the downtown location. The cuisine is vegetarian-style, though not strictly so, a good bet for travellers who are fearful of upsetting their tummies (or have done so already), attractively served. There's an assortment of salads for up to $3, and a daily lunch special for slightly more. The desserts, including pie and yogurt-fruit combinations, are excellent. Open until 7 p.m. most days, closed on Sunday. The restaurant is part of a family complex of shops that occupies the Argueta mansion, with a plant nursery, florist shop, gardening service, replicas of old-style furniture crafted from hardwoods, antiques, and handicrafts.

Pizza Boom, Avenida 6, Calles 6/5. A step up from your usual pizzeria, with a fireplace and fountain. About $8 for a family-size pizza. They have a branch on Morazán Blvd. at the Guadalupe church.

Pizza Hut, the real thing, off Plaza Morazán, is always packed full of people, which you can take as a real recommendation, and the speed of service leaves other eateries in Tegucigalpa in the dust. The food is attractive. Aside from regular and pan pizza in assorted varieties, including vegetarian, there are sandwiches, lasagna, spaghetti, and salad. The most expensive item, the giant super-supreme combination pizza, is just over $10. They have other branches around town.

Mediterráneo. Adjacent to Pizza Boom near Plaza Dolores. Inexpensive Honduran home cooking with a Greek touch, provided by the owner.

Ca Fé El Paraíso, located behind the defense ministry building at 4 Calle and 5 Avenida (by the Shell station, three blocks behind the Cathedral), is where ideas are hatched and debated over coffee in a variety of guises, and sandwiches, croissants and cakes, at a dollar or so per item. In keeping with the atmosphere, books and paintings are on display and sale as well.

Boulevard Morazán

For *fast food*, head to Boulevard Morazán, the strip that runs east from downtown Tegucigalpa. Follow 3 Calle onto Avenida República de Chile, past the Hotel Honduras Maya, then turn left (east) onto Morazán. There must be about 30 outlets on this street, modern and clean-looking, with names familiar and almost familiar.

Burger Hut, in Los Castaños shopping center, is a branch of the downtown emporium, and there is a **Pizza Hut** as well. Another Burger Hut outlet is in the Galerías building next the Sueños dance hall on Morazán.

Salsa, on Blvd. Morazán, serves light meals of Tex-Mex food: tacos, burritos and quesadillas, with soft drinks and pie for dessert . . . and rhythm. **Taco Loco** has similar items.

For *Chinese* food, you can head to the same area for a choice of eateries. Example: The **China Town Palace** has the usual extended Cantonese menu, with some Szechuan items, including shark-fin soup, shrimp with bamboo shoots, hot spicy chicken, and assorted combinations. About $7, more for shellfish or one of the house specialties. **On Lok** is also said to be good, with the expected Cantonese egg drop soup and noodle dishes, as well as black bean shrimp and ginger crab.

Kloster, on Blvd. Morazán, next to the On Lok Chinese restaurant (two blocks east of Av. República de Chile), is a popular spot for quaffing beer. But they also have genuine German food and, unusual for Tegucigalpa, take-out service. Dial 327676 for delivery to your hotel or wherever you happen to be. About $8 for a main course.

You'll find *steak houses* along Morazán as well. One with a Mexican flavor is **El Asador**, about three blocks up from the corner of República de Chile. They have saltimbocca, seafood dishes, and prosciutto ham.

Jack's Steak House, on Morazán at Las Lomas shopping center, is a branch of the long-established restaurant of the same name in San Pedro Sula, and has submarine sandwiches and a salad bar. **La Hacienda** on Morazán is a drive-up steak and seafood house, that regularly serves crab, either in garlic or sautéed, as well as jalapeño shrimp and standard kebabs and steaks cooked over the coals. A children's menu is available. About $6 for main courses, $3 for sandwiches.

El Arriero, half a block south of the Hotel Honduras Maya on Av. República de Chile at no. 516, specializes in steaks and seafood grilled in Uruguayan fashion, as does **El Novillero**, on the same street. **Jimmy West**, Avenida República Argentina no. 322, is a steak-and-barbecue-rib house, but it also has steak submarines, corn on the cob, and other American country favorites, as well as sausage, yucca and beans from the Latin American side. Main courses from $4 to $8.

Figure at least $10 for a full meal at any steak house — a bargain for what you get.

For *Italian* food, one more formal dining spot, as opposed to numerous pizza and pasta places, is **Restaurante Roma**, Avenida República Dominicana at 3 Calle, near the Honduras Maya hotel.

A well-established *seafood* restaurant is **Hungry Fisherman**, Av. República de Chile, also near the Honduras Maya. Prices for lobster and shrimp are a bit high, but the fish, in garlic or assorted sauces, is reasonable, at under $10 for a main course.

Right in the **Hotel Honduras Maya**, you'll find the relatively formal **La Veranda** restaurant, where the cuisine is reliable, and, though high-priced for Honduras, not at all a bad value for what you get. Specialties include steak Diane, duck á l'orange and paella for $10 and up, and there are also snapper in parchment and surf 'n turf plates for less. A top-notch hotel restaurant like this one is used to serving less than full-course meals, so if you're on a budget, have no qualms about trying a chicken-and-goat-cheese salad for just $4, or a pastry and coffee for a couple of dollars, with shelter from the hustle and bustle of the streets at no charge.

Higher on the price scale, **Alondra,** on República de Chile, opposite the Honduras Maya, serves a continental menu, and caters to groups. Expect a tab of $20 or more, with a drink.

El Bistro, Sendero San Juan (off Av. República de Chile one block below the Hotel Honduras Maya), is a French-operated establishment with light European bistro fare that includes salads, quiche, and ratatouille at lunch, and chicken cordon bleu and fondue bourgignonne in the evening, served in large portions. For a good restaurant, the prices are reasonable, at about $6 for lunch, $7 for a main course at dinner. The tab will rise considerably if you order wine.

Also serving French food is **Ca Fé du Monde**, near the Hotel Plaza

San Martín and the Honduras Maya, on Avenida Juan Lindo. **Ca Fé Allegro**, República de Chile 360, serves pastas, and the personnel are helpful to visitors. About $5 for a main course.

Avenida La Paz

Avenida La Paz, the eastern continuation of 6 Calle, is, like Boulevard Morazán, a thoroughfare through some of the better-off neighborhoods of the capital, and there are some attractive restaurants out this way.

Gauchos, Av. La Paz No. 2410, by the Alpha y Omega cinemas, specializes in Uruguayan-style steaks, roasted by an open fire. About $10 for main courses.

The **Don Quijote** restaurant on Av. La Paz specializes in paella, codfish stew, and similar hearty traditional Spanish fare, along with more familiar steaks and chops. Meals are about $6 and up.

Panoramic Dining Views

For a meal with a panorama, ask for the road (or take a taxi) to Hatillo, above the city to the north, where **La Cumbre** serves German and Hondurans food and drinks. Also here, **The Tannery** has American and European meals, at $5 or so for a main course.

Comayagüela

The **China Town Palace**, mentioned above, has a branch at 2 Avenida and 4 Calle in Comayagüela. If you're staying at one of the budget hotels in this part of town, you'll find the pickings pretty slim.

Southeast

El Rodeo, Blvd. Suyapa, near Hotel Alameda. This is a steak house, nothing special, but clean. About $8 for a steak platter and a beer. They also have a branch on Blvd. Morazán.

Pizza Hut has an outlet near the Hotel Alameda on Boulevard Suyapa. Phone 312636 (or have someone phone for you) for delivery.

BARS

You're in the wrong town if you're looking for exciting nighttime entertainment, but there are several places where you can enjoy a quiet drink without hassle.

Within the **Hotel Honduras Maya**, the bars serve snacks with drinks, and if you go at around 5:30 in the evening, you'll find the offerings fairly substantial.

Nearby, the **Hungry Fisherman** and **Ca Fé Allegro**, mentioned above as eating places, will also serve you just a drink; or, continue to one of the snack-and-drink spots along Blvd. Morazán.

Downtown, the **O'Henry Bar** of the Hotel Plaza, 4 Avenida at 4 Calle, has a happy hour from 6 to 7 p.m. daily except Sunday. Music often plays, and snacks are served with the drinks.

To find a student crowd, head toward the university on Suyapa Blvd., either by bus from the San Isidro market in Comayagüela, or, preferably, by taxi. There are bars in the area, and sometimes informal sidewalk entertainment.

SHOPPING

What you will find when shopping in Tegucigalpa, and in Honduras in general, is quite limited: leatherwork, wood carving (especially in mahogany, including boxes and statuettes), furniture, hammocks, leather bags, beadwork, silver and gold jewelry, baskets, pottery, and clothing items. And, oh yes, cigars. The wood carvings are the most typical souvenirs of Honduras, and if you have some use for an oversized set of salad servers, well, this is the place to find them. But I have to tell you that you needn't spend a great effort looking for extraordinary crafts. To my eye, except for some folk-art paintings which convey the atmosphere and spirit of the countryside, you won't find them.

For the most fun shopping, you should head to the markets. **The Artesanas (Handicraft) Market** is held on weekends at Parque El Soldado in Comayagüela (see page 93). Also in Comayagüela, nearer to downtown, is the **San Isidro market**, where you'll find not only handicrafts, but hundreds of simple utilitarian items that seem to date from a past age.

Aside from the markets, almost every hotel has a souvenir shop, where, of course, you'll pay more for anything. And there are dozens of other stores, among them:

Tienda del Artesano, facing the south side of Valle Park (No. 1001). This shop is operated by ANAH (Asociación Nacional de Artesanos de Honduras), a national guild of craftsmen, and has a selection of *everything* made by artisans in Honduras. Hours are 9 a.m. to 6 p.m. during the week, to 4 p.m. on Saturdays.

Tikamaya, on 3 Calle at 10 Avenida, by Valle Park.

Candü, opposite the Hotel Honduras Maya, on Avenida República de Chile has some interesting paintings, and a stock of maps of Honduras and Tegucigalpa. There are other souvenir shops in the immediate area — this is where the money is in Tegucigalpa.

Exposición de Arte Celajes (tel. 391971), 501 Plaza San Martín, by the Hotel Plaza San Martín, has a fair selection of crafts, as well as paintings and other fine arts. The owners are English-speaking.

Mundo Maya, in the Hotel Honduras Maya, and also in Colonia Palmira.

El Mundo Maya, Calle Adolfo Zuñiga 1114 (two blocks behind the cathedral), stocks original paintings as well as more standard souvenirs, and also provides travel information.

Honduras Souvenirs, in the Lomas del Boulevard shopping center on Blvd. Morazán, also has an assortment of gift items.

Lesanddra Leather, in the Los Castaños shopping center on Blvd. Morazán, has more finely made leather items than you'll find in handicraft stores or markets.

PRACTICAL INFORMATION
Banks

I'm not sure that you will be going to banks at all, since you can usually get a better exchange rate elsewhere, as of this writing (see "Money and Banking," pages 66-67). Street money changers can be found everywhere in Tegucigalpa, but in case you don't notice them, one place to look is in front of the Hotel Plaza on the Peatonal mall downtown.

Then there are the ca*sas de cambio* (exchange houses), which, for the moment, are legal, and provide a quicker exchange service than that provided by banks, with more security than with street changers. Their numbers are growing, and you should spot one near your hotel, but if you don't see one, look for the ads in *Honduras This Week*. One is Multicambios, Galerias shopping center, Blvd. Morazán, another is Coin, in the Mas X Menos building on Avenida La Paz. Exchange houses will in some cases handle the currencies of other Central American countries, which can be difficult otherwise to exchange.

Major banks downtown are:
· **Bancahsa**, 5 Avenida, 5 Calle, tel. 371171.
· **Banco Atlántida**, 7 Avenida, 5 Calle, tel. 321742.
· **Banco Sogerin**, 6 Calle, 6 Avenida, tel. 374551.
· **Banco de Honduras** (Citibank subsidiary), Midence Soto building, main square, tel. 371155, and Boulevard Suyapa, tel. 326122.
· **Lloyds Bank**, Europa building, Calle República de México, Avenida Ramón E. Cruz, Colonia San Carlos, tel. 321864.

For **cash advances** on a Visa card, try any bank that displays the Honducard-Visa symbol. Bancahsa (see above) and Bancahorro are authorized to make advances, or call 381111 for assistance. Otherwise, for Visa or Master Card cash advances, contact Credomatic, second floor, Interamericana de Seguros building, tel. 326030, or try any bank with a Credomatic, Ficensa or Futuro sign.

Books, Newspapers, and Magazines
English-language books, some of them used, are sold at **Book Village**

in the Los Castaños shopping center, tel. 327108, out on Boulevard Morazán, second level. The selection is the best in the entire country. You can also trade used books here. A smaller selection of English-languate books is available in the **D.T.P. bookstore** (which stocks mostly Spanish-language material), Miramonte shopping center, tel. 391081.

A newspaper and book outlet on the lower shopping level of the **Hotel Honduras Maya** carries the Miami *Herald*, *USA Today*, *Time*, and *Newsweek*. There are also stands at the **Hotel Plaza San Martín**, and, less well stocked, at the Hotel Alameda and at the airport.

Honduras This Week is an excellent English-language newspaper published weekly, distributed at major hotels and sold at some news-stands. Coverage is mainly of local, regional and international political developments, and the movie schedules, and advertisements for hotels, rentals, restaurants and travel services, will interest many visitors. A subscription in the United States costs about $40 annually. Write to Apartado Postal 1312, Tegucigalpa.

Churches

Catholic and **evangelical** churches with services in Spanish are everywhere in Tegucigalpa, of course. A mass in English is celebrated on Sundays at 11 a.m. at the Instituto San Francisco, Barrio Country Club. Call 327498 for information.

For services and other spiritual attention in English, you might try:
- **Central Baptist**, Colonia Soto, 8 Avenida, 2 Calle, tel. 378615.
- **Church of Christ**, Barrio Guanacaste, one kilometer below U.S. embassy (by the basketball court), tel. 376180. Sunday service in English.
- **Latter-Day Saints** (Mormon), Avenida Juan Lindo, Colonia Palmira, tel. 323521.
- **Episcopal Church**, Colonia Florencia, tel. 320353.
- **Union Church**, Lomas del Guijarro, tel. 323386.

The **Jewish community** gathers on Friday evenings at 7 p.m. at the Hotel Alameda.

Embassies and Consulates

Call first before visiting an embassy or consulate, in order to obtain office hours, and to get directions. Among the representatives of foreign nations are:
- **Belize**, Colonia 15 de Septiembre No. 1703, Comayagüela, tel. 331423.
- **Canada** (consulate only), Los Castaños building, 6th floor, Boulevard Morazán, tel. 314545.
- **Costa Rica**, Colonia El Triángulo, tel. 321768.

- **El Salvador**, Colonia San Carlos, No. 205, tel. 321344.
- **France**, Avenida Juan Lindo, 3 Calle, Colonia Palmira, tel. 321800.
- **El Salvador**, Colonia San Carlos, tel. 321344.
- **Germany**, Paysen building, Blvd. Morazán, tel. 323161.
- **Guatemala**, Colonia Las Minitas, 4 Calle No. 2421, tel. 321580. (Consulate, Colonia Palmira, Avenida Juan Lindo, tel. 325018).
- **Israel**, Midence Soto Building, tel. 372529.
- **Italy**, Colonia Reforma, Avenida Principal No. 2602, tel. 383391.
- **Japan**, Colonia Reforma, 2 Avenida, tel. 326828.
- **Mexico**, Colonia Palmira, Calle del Brasil, tel. 326471.
- **Netherlands** (consulate), Colonia Lomas del Mayab, Calle Copán, tel. 315007
- **Nicaragua**, Colonia Tepeyac, tel. 324290.
- **Panama**, Palmira building, Colonia Palmira, tel. 315441.
- **Sweden**, Colonia Miraflores, Avenida Principal No. 2758, tel. 325935.
- **Switzerland**, Colonia Alameda, 4 Avenida, 7 Calle No. 1811, tel. 329692.
- **U.S.A.**, Avenida La Paz. Tel. 323121 to 9.
- **United Kingdom**, Palmira building (near Hotel Honduras Maya), tel. 325429.

Gambling

The two available extremes are lottery tickets, sold for about 50 cents and up by street vendors; and the Casino Royal in the Hotel Honduras Maya, with roulette, blackjack, poker, and slot machines.

Laundry

There's exactly one coin-op (or more exactly token-operated) laundry near downtown. **Mi Lavandería** (tel. 376573) is in Comayagüela on 2 Avenida (Calle Real) between 3 and 4 Calle, opposite the Repostería Calle Real (a sweet shop). They're open every day, including Sundays, and they'll also do your laundry and dry cleaning on a drop-off basis. There are other establishments scattered through Tegucigalpa that will do your laundry at a piece rate if you want to save a few dollars over your hotel's charges.

Maps

The most easily available map is the *Mapa Guía Turístico*, sold at many hotel newsstands in combination with a succinct Spanish-language country guide. Basic maps are available at the **Tourist Office** (see "Tours and Tourist Office" section above).

For anything more detailed, you'll have to go to the **Instituto Geográfico Nacional**, located a kilometer south of downtown, at 14 Calle and 3 Avenida, across the bridge from Soldier's Park (15 Calle, 2 Avenida) in Comayagüela. They have the most up-to-date tourist maps of Honduras and Tegucigalpa, available for a couple of dollars each after official processing of your request; sectional topographical maps of the country on a scale of 1:50,000; geological maps; and regional maps. Some of these will be useful if you plan on doing any extensive bicycling or hiking. And you can look at an excellent detailed topographical map of Tegucigalpa for exactly five minutes — unless you have special permission from the high command of the army. The mailing address for orders from abroad is Apartado 20706, Comayagüela, D.C.

Movies

Look for advertisements for movies in the daily papers, and in *Honduras This Week*, which lists the original English-language title. Most of the films are foreign, and are shown in the original language, with Spanish subtitles. Ads never give addresses, so ask at your hotel as to where any cinema is located. Admission costs about a dollar in most cases.

You'll find a *simpático* atmosphere in movie houses. People smoke, talk, laugh out loud, and cheerfully share the premises with some permanent residents: the bats in the rafters.

Post Office

The **central post office** is on the pedestrian mall (Calle 4, Peatonal) at 4 Avenida, opposite the Hotel Plaza. Hours are from 8 a.m. to 8 p.m. I have found the service reliable, at least for letters mailed from this location: my letters to Montreal took about six days to arrive.

Telephones

You can make international telephone calls, with persistence, from **Hondutel**, 5 Calle at 4 Avenida. The lines are long, and once you get to the front and order your call, you have no idea if you'll get through. A far better way is to call from your hotel, if it offers long distance service, even at a surcharge; or from a private phone, if you can get your hands on one.

International direct dialing is available from Tegucigalpa, but not from most phones in the country. If you're calling the States, the easiest route is to dial 123 for AT&T's **USA Direct** service. From a pay phone, drop in a coin before dialing. There are dedicated USA Direct phones at the Hondutel office.

EMERGENCY AND SERVICE NUMBERS FROM TEGUCIGALPA
- *191– Long distance in Honduras*
- *192– Telephone number information*
- *196 –Time of Day*
- *197– International long distance*
- *198– Fire*
- *199– Public security (police)*

Water

Officially, the U.S. embassy says the water is *not* safe to drink from the tap. Drink bottled beverages and soda water. In any case, water is a scarce commodity in Tegucigalpa, and if you're not staying in one of the better hotels (which have pumps and storage tanks), you could well find nothing more than a dribble when you turn on the tap.

Weather

In terms of temperature, Tegucigalpa, like much of Honduras, has just one season, a sort of moderately warm summer. Average daily high ranges from a maximum of 86 degrees Fahrenheit (30 degrees Centigrade) in April to 77 degrees F (25 degrees C) in December and January. Average low temperature runs from a maximum of 65 degrees F (18 degrees C) in June to a minimum of 57 degrees F (14 degrees C) in January and February.

Rainfall, however, can run to extremes. The dry season in Tegucigalpa lasts from November through April. Average rainfall in November is just an inch and a half (38 mm), and drops to a trace by March. On most days in the dry times, there's hardly a cloud in the sky. Rain picks up quickly in May — May and June have the heaviest annual rainfall, 7.1 and 7.0 inches (180 and 177 mm) respectively. July and August see a drop to 2.8 inches (70 mm), then rainfall increases somewhat in September and October before tapering off again.

Even in the rainy season, however, Tegucigalpa is not a hard place to take: usually, fewer than half the days in any given month have any noticeable rainfall.

During the months of low rainfall in Tegucigalpa, especially past February, everything is dry — the air, the yellowed grass, the dust that blows up constantly from unwatered and unpaved streets on the frequent gusts of wind. The breeze can make the temperature feel cooler than it really is. But a light sweater is as much as you'll need to keep warm. The higher elevations nearby will require a bit more covering.

Tours and Travel Agencies

Is there a difference in travel agencies? Not that I have noticed, unless you have a special interest in adventure travel. I expect that if you're going to take a tour or buy an airplane ticket, you'll first try the services of the travel agency in or nearest to your hotel.

If you don't get what you need nearby, here are some of the larger agencies that are accustomed to catering to the needs of foreign visitors:

- **Agencia de Viajes Marcris**, 5 Calle, 11/12 Avenidas (near Hotel La Ronda), tel. 222151. This general travel agency can arrange local and regional tours.
- **Agencia de Viajes Brenda**, Midence Soto arcade (P. O. Box 1349), tel. 375039.
- **Agencia de Viajes Concorde**, 4 Calle, 9/10 Avenidas, No. 905, tel. 378207.
- **Agencia de Viajes Jupiter**, 6 Avenida, 2/3 Calles (half block north of Presidential Palace), tel. 375644.
- **Agencia de Viajes Intercontinental**, 5 Calle, Avenida Colón, no. 404, tel. 378370.
- **Eco-Hiking Eco-Tourist Expeditions**, P.O. Box 30037 Toncontín, Comayagüela, tel. 331208. This new company offers expeditions in four-wheel-drive vehicles to remote Lenca communities, where bases are organized for treks into countryside rarely seen by outsiders.
- **La Mosquitia Ecoaventuras**, P. O. Box 3577, Tegucigalpa, tel. 370593, fax 379398. This company specializes in ten- to fourteen-day low-impact adventures in the vast forests of Mosquitia, including the Río Plátano Biosphere Reserve, with emphasis on birding, wildlife viewing, and non-intrusive contacts with native peoples. Information is available from **Geotours**, Lomas del Boulevard shopping center, Blvd. Morazán, tel. 320466, fax 311058.
- **Honduras Tours**, J.S. Bldg., Blvd. Morazán, tel. 324415, fax 310178.
- **Honduras Copán Tours**, Edificio Comercial Palmira (opposite the Hotel Honduras Maya, P. O. Box 1373), tel. 326769, 329964, fax 326795. One of the larger agencies in Tegucigalpa.
- **Explore Honduras**, P O Box 336, Med-Cast Bldg., Blvd. Morazán, tel. 311003, fax 329800, operating through most hotels. Excursions to Copán, San Pedro Sula, Lake Yojoa and Pulhapanzak falls. Explore Honduras has a superb reputation for reliability, and is the ground operator for many U.S. agencies offering Honduras travel.
- **Agencia de Viajes Cosmos**, 3 Calle, 6/7 Avenidas, tel. 370395.
- **Jet Tours**, 1 Calle, 1 Avenida, Barrio San Rafael (next to Hotel Honduras Maya), tel. 325555.
- **Maya Travel Service**, Midence Soto Building, tel. 376979.
- **Mundirama Travel Service** (American Express representative), Fiallos

Soto Bldg. 132, tel 376111, fax 228258; branch at Ciicsa Building near Hotel Honduras Maya, tel. 323909, fax 320072.
· **Viajes Mundiales**, 2 Avenida No. 205, Comayagüela, tel. 371837.

Prices vary from agency to agency, of course. But for a half-day city tour or trip near Tegucigalpa, to Valle de Angeles and Santa Lucía, you'll pay about $25 per person. A half-day trip to Comayagua or La Tigra Rain Forest costs about $40 per person. A day trip to Comayagua and Lake Yojoa costs about $60 per person.

An overnight trip to **Copán** via San Pedro Sula, including plane and bus fares, costs about $300 per person. A two-night trip to **Copán** and **San Pedro Sula**, including banana plantation tour, costs slightly more.

A one-way trip to **San Pedro Sula**, with stops at **Comayagua**, **Pulhapanzak Falls**, and **Lake Yojoa**, costs about $75.

EXCURSIONS FROM TEGUCIGALPA

Where can you go on day outings from Tegucigalpa? Day trips, either on your own by bus or in a rented car, or on a tour, generally take in:
· **Valle de Angeles**
· **San Antonio de Oriente**
· **La Tigra Rain Forest**
· **El Zamorano**
· **Ojojona**
I'll describe these places in more detail in the following pages.

If you'll be heading to the north coast, you can stop on the way at:
· **Zambrano**
· **Comayagua**
· **Lake Yojoa**
You can also go to the above spots on day outings from Tegucigalpa. They're covered in the next chapter of this book.

Along the southern highway, on the way to the Gulf of Fonseca, is:
· **Ojojona**

The major site to visit on mainland Honduras is the archeological zone of **Copán**. Because of the way the mountain ridges and roads run, most travellers reach Copán overland from San Pedro Sula, in the north of Honduras, or from Guatemala, or by air taxi from Tegucigalpa.

And of course, you can reach the **Bay Islands** from Tegucigalpa by plane, or by a combination of bus, plane, and/or boat.

VISITING NEARBY TOWNS
SUYAPA

The religious capital of Honduras for the overwhelmingly Catholic majority, **Suyapa** is a suburb of Tegucigalpa, about eight kilometers east of downtown. The attraction for pilgrims is a six-inch statue of the Virgin, imbued with miraculous powers, which, according to tradition, was discovered in a corn field in 1743, and, no matter how many times it was moved, returned to its original place. The image was credited with the cure of a captain of the grenadiers, who organized the construction of a church in its honor.

The original church that housed the image could not handle the religious traffic, so a new basilica was started, a neat structure with two bell towers, generous vertical fluting, two triangular pediments balancing the arch directly over the door — it all could have been built from blocks or by a skilled baker of birthday cakes.

The faithful arrive at all times of the year, but especially for the **Feast of the Virgin** on February 2, and during the following weeks.

Suyapa rates as an attraction for those with an interest in the religious ways of Honduras, or for those with some extra time. If you go, catch the number 31 bus from the San Isidro market in Comayagüela, or take a taxi for about $3.

SANTA LUCIA AND VALLE DE ANGELES

The trip to these two towns will take a half-day in a car, by taxi, or on a tour, or a full day by bus if you go to both places. The bus leaves from near San Felipe Hospital, about two kilometers east of downtown on Avenida La Paz, a continuation of 6 Calle, at 7 Avenida. (Take a Lomas bus from Plaza Morazán to Hospital San Felipe; walk one block east, one block south on Av. República Dominicana, then one block east on Calle Bustamente y Rivero, an unpaved street. Departures are about every hour.)

A tour costs about $10 per person, a taxi about $20. The road is paved all the way, and in excellent condition.

Santa Lucía

Santa Lucía is 17 kilometers from Tegucigalpa, on a 2.5-kilometer spur from the main road, a small, picturesque village, its main street paved with cobblestones. Santa Lucía was once an important mining center, early in the colonial period, but as the mines were worked out, it became a backwater.

There's a colonial church, with old paintings and a statue of a black Christ that is said to have been a gift of King Philip II, sculptured in Spain more than 400 years ago. A shop sells handicrafts, and there are pleasing views of tile-roof houses and hills and patches of corn all around. There are no restaurants or hotels aimed at visitors. In the area of Santa Lucía flowers are grown for sale in Tegucigalpa.

Valle de Angeles and Vicinity

Eleven kilometers onward, **Valle de Angeles** is a larger colonial-style town of whitewashed, lime-plastered adobe houses with red tile roofs, massive wooden lintels, and porches with roofs supported by rough wooden posts. Valle de Angeles is cooler than Tegucigalpa (bring a sweater), quiet, clean and friendly, not too different from the hill villages above the Spanish coast that prosper from the visits of tourists.

There are restaurants on the main street and central plaza, and assorted boutiques selling the leather, wood and ceramic articles for which the town is known. You might be able to visit the school where some of these crafts are taught. **Lessandra Leather** is one of several shops with luggage and purses made for the tourist trade. **La Casa del Chocolate** is a tea room where you can buy home-made cookies for consumption with hot chocolate.

More formal is **POSADA DEL ANGEL**, a comfortable inn where you can take a break from walking around the village. Rooms are available for under $15 double. Phone 362233 to reserve.

The **Restaurante Turístico Valle de Angeles**, tel. 762148, set in the pines on a hill above town, serves Honduran home-style cooking — grilled meats, fried plantains, beans, enchiladas, mountains of tortillas — which is difficult to find outside of private homes, at a tab of up to $6. Open from 10 a.m. to 6 p.m., closed Monday.

And there are other establishments offering inexpensive country cooking, as well as a branch of the **Don Quijote** Spanish restaurant.

About two kilometers before you get to Valle de Angeles is **El Obrero** park, a piney area outfitted for day use with charcoal grills and a pool. It's well maintained, and if you negotiate with the guard, and perhaps provide a tip, you can also camp out. There's a small entry fee. Also near the park entrance is an American Adventist hospital.

San Juancito, north of Valle de Angeles, was once an important gold and silver mining center, and is now a quaint backwater of faded wooden houses once brightly painted, many roofed in shingles made of recycled tin fashioned from scrap metal — all quite a contrast to the whitewashed adobe houses with red baked-clay tiles of other mountain villages. San Juancito declined in importance soon after Honduran independence, but its fortunes revived when an American company took over the **El Rosario** mine and others nearby, just over a hundred years ago, and operated them into the fifties. The remains of the El Rosario mine, about two kilometers from the village, are littered with old mining equipment.

LA TIGRA NATIONAL PARK

Above San Juancito, **La Tigra** is a cloud-forest peak where the wonderland of vegetation that once covered much of the high part of Honduras still survives in parts and is regenerating in others. Covering 238 square kilometers, La Tigra National Park protects a watershed that supplies almost half of Tegucigalpa's water. Seventy-five square kilometers are an absolute reserve, the remainder a buffer zone.

Elevations in the protected area are as high as 2290 meters. As many as half of the plant species present in La Tigra are considered rare in other parts of Honduras.

La Tigra's botanical bounty is due to its location near the continental divide, and the prevailing winds that bring rain through much of the year. Broad-leafed plants, vines, mosses, bromeliads and orchids and ferns live not just on the ground, but on the trunks and branches of trees, taking up water from the air and from the ground, sending out huge leaves to take advantage of what light filters through the canopy, and roots to absorb nutrients from decaying plant matter. In parts of the park below 1800 meters, there are also pines more typical of lowland Honduras.

Birds make their nests in the trees and are attracted to the flowers that are always in bloom; the quetzal, iridescent red-and-green with an arc of tail feathers several feet long, is regularly seen, along with the goldfinch and green toucan. Animals that inhabit the park include tapirs, jaguars, ocelots, monkeys and mountain lions, many of them only at the highest and least accessible elevations.

The integrity of all this bounty is threatened by the encroachment of farming. "Park" does not indicate a pristine and inviolable area of nature in Honduras; more than 10,000 persons live within La Tigra's boundaries, cultivating corn, beans and coffee, some of it within the central zone. Much of the park consists of recovering forest — the original forest was largely leveled to supply the fuel and construction needs of the New York and Honduras Rosario Mining Company. The company even tunneled through La Tigra mountain to reach untouched forests on the western slope. Rusting mining equipment is still scattered through the park.

A network of trails is planned for La Tigra. For now, facilities for visitors are quite limited. If you go to hike, wear sturdy shoes, and take along some food. Only the most basic accommodations are available at San Juancito, or you can return to Valle de Angeles or Tegucigalpa.

A bus to San Juancito and La Tigra leaves the San Pablo market in Tegucigalpa daily at 10 a.m. Take the Colonia 21 bus from the main square to reach the market. From San Juancito, it takes about an hour at a slow pace on an ascending trail to reach the administrative office of the park, in a former mining camp, where basic lodging is available. Without reservations (by telegram to Parque Nacional, Campamento Rosario, San

Juancito), it's best to come during the week with a sleeping bag. Arrangements can also be made to sleep in private houses.

A second route to La Tigra is north from Tegucigalpa by the El Picacho road through El Hatillo to Jutiapa, where there is another visitors' center.

Bring along a sweater — it's windy and relatively cool at La Tigra. Hiking shoes are useful, though any comfortable old shoes will do. Make sure you stay on the trails. Not all are well-marked, so if you lose your way, re-trace your steps until you find trail markings again.

Management of the park has been in the hands of a private foundation, Amigos de La Tigra, since 1992.

SAN ANTONIO DE ORIENTE AND EL ZAMORANO

San Antonio de Oriente is yet another old mining town, founded around 1660, and often depicted by José Antonio Velázquez, once the town barber and mayor, and a primitive artist of world renown. Velázquez painted in great detail the town's white, twin-towered church, and sometimes included San Antonio's personalities and animal denizens.

A few kilometers past the turnoff for San Antonio de Oriente, on the highway toward Danlí, is **El Zamorano**, where the **Pan American Agricultural School** is located. The extensive installations and experimental plantings are worth a visit if you're interested in farming, or in seeing spectacular landscaping with effusive displays of tropical flowers. The main buildings are constructed in colonial style of locally quarried stone, with beams of cedar and pine. The farm covers about 5000 hectares.

The Pan American Agricultural School was opened in 1942 under the directorship of Wilson Popenoe, sponsored by the much-maligned but sometimes beneficent United Fruit Company. Teachers have included famed naturalist and essayist Archie Carr. The school attracts student farmers from all over Latin America. Arrangements can be made to stay on the premises. The school operates a store in Zamorano, where its cheeses, preserves and fresh vegetables are sold.

Uyuca Biological Reserve, on the grounds of the school, covers a couple of square miles or watershed for nearby communities.

El Zamorano is 40 kilometers from Tegucigalpa, five kilometers down a side road, at a pleasant altitude of 700 meters. The dramatic drive out takes you through a pass at 1550 meters, with surrounding, higher mountains.

OJOJONA

Ojojona is yet another picturesque hill town with cobbled streets, white houses with red-tiled roofs, and colonial churches — three of them, in fact, with paintings that date from before independence. Ojojona is also known for its pottery, especially water jugs made in the shape of roosters. Other local craft specialties are woodcrafting and leatherwork. A small museum contains the work of Pablo Zelaya Sierra, one of the most noted painters of Honduras.

Ojojona sits on a small plateau among mountains. The name of the town means "greenish water" in Nahuatl, the language of the Mexican Indians who accompanied the Spanish conquerors. The original town, now called **Pueblo Viejo**, stood three kilometers from the present site.

Ojojona is located 30 kilometers from Tegucigalpa, on a spur (at kilometer 24) from the main highway for the coast. Buses for Ojojona leave from 4 Calle, 8/9 Avenidas, Comayagüela, about every hour. There is an inexpensive pension in town.

Santa Ana, a nearby village, has a couple of colonial churches. **Lepaterique**, (**Tiger Mountain**) to the west, is also picturesque. The **Montaña Yerba Buena Biological Reserve**, just north of the town, has swimming pools.

11. TO THE NORTH

INTRODUCTION

North from Tegucigalpa is the heartland of Honduras, the connecting rift valleys between the Caribbean and the Pacific that first attracted Spanish settlers, where Honduran culture was forged as invaders and natives met and contested and finally merged, where even today the population of Honduras is concentrated. But this was a well-developed area even before the Conquest. A culture known as the **Yarumela** flourished near Comayagua more than 1500 years before Christ. Marble pieces decorated with human faces have been found from a culture called the **Ulúa**, which existed after the fall of Mayan civilization.

For all its importance to the country, it is a measure of the underdevelopment of Honduras that even much of this route was, until relatively recently, off the beaten track. Only a dirt track, interrupted by a ferry over **Lake Yojoa**, connected the two major cities of Honduras for most of the last hundred years, and only in the last twenty years has it been possible to drive this route on a paved highway. Elsewhere in Central America, the lack of roads was compensated by railroads, but in Honduras, there was nothing.

For the visitor, there is much majestic countryside to be seen during a journey along the major highway, along with **Comayagua**, the old capital where colonial churches still stand; small and little-visited towns where old ways and a slow pace of life still hold sway; and Lake Yojoa, as pleasant a stopping point and vacation area as will be found on the mainland. At the end of the route is **San Pedro Sula**, the metropolis of the north, and of modern Honduras, and beyond are the coastal cities, beaches, and the special world of the **Bay Islands**.

From Tegucigalpa

The northern highway climbs and winds for about ten kilometers out of the capital, affording pleasant views of Tegucigalpa, with its valleys and hills, and of the surrounding peaks. At kilometer 18, the road begins a descent, down to and into a long valley.

Balneario San Francisco is a swimming and picnicking area located one kilometer off the northern highway, at kilometer 20. It's nothing special, but if you're meandering through, you can make the detour. There are several warm-springs pools (only one of which is currently in use), picnic areas, a basic restaurant, and soccer fields. Accommodations are available at a small hotel.

By kilometer 23, you're climbing again, into the mountains in which the town of Zambrano is located. This is cold country, for the tropics.

At kilometer 42, half a kilometer after Zambrano, is **Aurora Park**, a picnicking and camping area in pine forests. There's a small lake, with rowboats for rent, and a little zoo. Simple food is available. There are modest fees to pay for day entry and overnight stays. Beyond, the road descends in a serpentine fashion for 15 kilometers, down into the Comayagua Valley at kilometer 60. Along the way you see many adobe houses, and poor country people selling vegetables. At the lower altitudes are coffee plantations.

At kilometer 75, you pass the **Enrique Soto Cano** military base and airport at Palmerola, with its permanently detached Joint Task Force Bravo, part of the U.S. Southern Command. The entire road has been rebuilt recently, and it is in perfect condition. Comayagua is at kilometer 87.

COMAYAGUA

Beginnings

For more than 300 years, **Comayagua** was the capital of colonial and independent Honduras. But "capital" is a grand term for what was, in fact, just the major settlement and administrative center of a backwater colony of little importance in the imperial scheme, or in the world in general. Tax collectors for the empire and the republic were based here, legislatures of important personages met and made laws, and a stream of presidents succeeded each other. The first priests built primitive churches, and modified them into more permanent structures as the capital and society became more stable, if not exactly wealthy.

It was in 1537 that Santa María de Comayagua was founded by Alonzo de Cáceres, as a strategic base for the Spanish conquerors, midway between the two oceans along the major trading routes of the Indian nations of Honduras. The traditional part of the name, Comayagua, which has endured, probably derived from the Nahuatl *comal*, the clay pan for cooking tortillas, though it could have been a corruption of the Lenca words for "well-watered plain."

The first settlement was short-lived, but the town was re-founded in 1539, after the Indians of the region were conquered and resettled under their new masters. Thereafter, Spanish encampments and headquarters shifted with Indian revolts and campaigns of pacification. For a time, Gracias, in the mountains to the West, was the seat of colonial administration. In 1543 the settlement became Villa de Valladolid de Concepción de Comayagua, when it was named as the seat of the Audiencia de los Confines, the colonial government of the isthmus.

In accordance with standard instructions laid down by King Ferdinand V in 1513, and applied in all Spanish settlements in the New World, a *plaza mayor*, or main square, was laid out, surrounded by the most important structures: the church, the governor's house, the cabildo (town hall), and the Casa Real; with a grid of streets extending outward. The first cathedral of Honduras was inaugurated in 1585. As the town grew, the main square was relocated, and new, larger administrative buildings replaced the rudimentary structures of the early days. The hospital of San Juan de Dios was established in 1590, and was the seat of the inquisition. It was flattened in the earthquake of 1785. A university, the first in Central America, was founded in 1632. A new cathedral was completed in 1715.

But the colonial period was the heyday of Comayagua. After independence, congresses met alternately in Comayagua and Tegucigalpa. The city was burned by the invading army of Guatemala in 1827, and, as Honduras settled into an existence as a satellite of other Central American countries, Comayagua never re-assumed its preeminence.

In 1880, Comayagua received its final deflation. President Marco Aurelio Soto, whose Indian wife was snubbed by the Comayagua's high society, snubbed Comayagua in turn, and moved the government permanently to Tegucigalpa. People moved away too, and Comayagua became just a stopping point on the overland mule trail to the Caribbean coast. And its churches and few governmental buildings, no longer much attended or used, remained fairly unaltered, so that today, parts of the town constitute a museum of nineteenth-century Honduras.

ARRIVALS AND DEPARTURES
By Bus
Comayagua is about an hour's drive from Tegucigalpa, or 90 minutes by bus. All San Pedro Sula buses (from Tegucigalpa) stop along the highway, a kilometer from the town center. To catch a bus to Tegucigalpa or San Pedro Sula, walk or take a taxi to the Texaco station along the highway. One yellow bus shelter is located on each side.

As well, buses operate to Villa San Antonio hourly from 9 a.m. to 3 p.m.; to San Sebastián at noon and 1 p.m. from near the market. Buses to La Paz leave from the Texaco station about every fifteen minutes. There are slower buses to Tegucigalpa from the center of town.

From Tegucigalpa, catch buses for Comayagua and San Pedro Sula at Empresa El Rey, 6 Avenida and 9 Calle, Comayagüela (departures every hour or more frequently, from before dawn to 10:30 p.m.). Fare is less than $3. Buses are comfortable and uncrowded.

Hedman-Alas, 11 Avenida, 13/14 Calles, tel. 377143, and **Transportes Sáenz**, 12 Calle, 7/8 Avenidas, Comayagüela, tel. 376521, also offer hourly departures from 8 a.m. to 6 p.m.

ORIENTATION

Comayagua has a **population** of about 30,000. The **altitude** of about 300 meters makes it warmer than Tegucigalpa, but not a sweltering tropical town by any means.

To reach the **market**, follow the street that passes in front of the Cathedral, toward the south, past the colonial museum. Local **fiesta** days are February 2 through 11 in honor of the Virgin of Lourdes, December 8 (Immaculate Conception), and December 12 (Virgin of Guadalupe, especially celebrated by Indians of the surrounding area).

SEEING THE SIGHTS - COLONIAL COMAYAGUA

What remains of colonial architecture in Comayagua dates mainly from the eighteenth century. The rustic churches and palaces of the early Spanish administrative center were repaired, expanded, rebuilt and relocated as the town and colony matured. A new flurry of building followed earthquake damage in the middle of the eighteenth century. But

COMAYAGUA

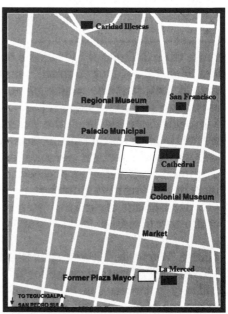

independence brought conflicts between government and church, and endemic civil turmoil. Construction fell off, and the architectural fashions of the late colonial period lived on.

The florid rococo style in Spain, known as *Churrigueresque*, had its own peculiar expression in the Americas in the eighteenth century, taking into account local conditions. Heavy, thick-walled, ground-hugging structures were built, on the theory that they would vibrate less and so suffer more limited damage in earthquakes. Decorative detail — flutings, plaster decorations of flowers, saints placed in niches, metal and wood grilles — relieved the heaviness of the buildings. Columns set into walls are especially characteristic of Comayagua and Honduran colonial architecture.

Many of the buildings of Comayagua fell into disrepair, as the population declined following the definitive relocation of the capital. Some eventually were replaced by nondescript structures. But, with time, many of the principal buildings of the old capital have now been restored. These, and the cobbled streets and red tile roofs that predominate, lend to Comayagua the air of a city from the past.

In the next few pages you'll find the principal colonial buildings and museums of Comayagua.

Church of La Merced

The **Church of La Merced** was started in 1550 under Bishop Cristóbal de Pedraza. Tradition has it that the church was built on the site of the first mass in Comayagua. It was consecrated as the first Cathedral of Comayagua in 1561 and remained the principal church for fifty years. The square on which it stands was, at the time, the main plaza of the city, the location of the market and of all notable public events.

Originally a rudimentary structure of mud on a framework of sticks, with a thatched roof, La Merced was reconstructed around 1590, of stone and adobe. In 1644, it received an altarpiece as a gift from Philip IV of Spain. To judge by the building seen today, the present structure largely dates from the early 1700s. One of the two bell towers was demolished after it was damaged in earthquakes in 1774.

La Merced is a relatively simple structure, recalling mission churches in the southwestern United States, with a fluted border outlining the curving edge of the façade, and a single niche above the door, containing a sculpture of the Virgin of Mercy. Above it, a circular window illuminates the choir. The cupola of the surviving short bell tower is pierced by a lantern-like projection. Inside, the church is largely bare, but for the carved altar.

Cathedral of Comayagua

Three blocks north of the Merced Church, and one block west, is the **Cathedral of Comayagua**, or **Iglesia de la Inmaculada Concepción (Church of the Immaculate Conception)**.

The growth of Comayagua by the end of the sixteenth century had led to the enlargement of the urban plan, and relocation of the *plaza mayor*, or main square. All the important buildings of the town had to be moved as well. The new cathedral, constructed under Bishop Gaspar de Andrade, had three naves, adobe walls, and a tile roof. It was not well built, however — a 1699 report describes the Cathedral as being in a terrible state, needing total reconstruction. By 1708, still another Cathedral was completed on the site. This one was, and remains, the most impressive ecclesiastical structure of the old capital.

The multi-tiered façade of the Cathedral is especially rich in decoration and detail. Two niches to either side of the door contain figures of St. Augustine and St. Jerome. St. Gregory and St. Ambrose are placed in niches on the level above, while on the third level is the figure of the Immaculate Conception, flanked by St. Joseph and St. John the Baptist. Above them rises Christ, with His hands extended. Palms and grapes are depicted in low relief throughout, and characteristically Honduran engaged columns climb the entire height. Unfortunately, all of this is white on a white background, and stands out only when the sun strikes in such a way as to create an interplay of light and shadow.

Alongside the Cathedral is the bell tower, jutting forward and supported by buttresses, with arched openings in four tiers, and crowned with a cupola covered by two-toned ceramics. The smooth walls contrast the detail of the Cathedral fa_ade. The tower clock, crafted by Moors in Seville 800 years ago, reposed in the Alhambra of Granada, before it was donated to the original Cathedral of Comayagua by Philip II. It is quite possibly the oldest working clock anywhere.

Inside (enter by the side door if the main door on the square is closed), the Cathedral is a formal, three-nave structure with a floor plan in the form of a Latin cross.

Pillars allow natural light to flood the main nave. Formal pews, numerous altarpieces, mosaic floor and paintings are a sharp contrast to the bare, country-church aspect of the other colonial monuments of Comayagua. The Cathedral holds some of the treasures of colonial art in Honduras. The pulpit and three retables are richly carved—one retable, in a side chapel, dedicated to the Holy Sacrament, has a wrought silver front. Solid silver accessories were gifts from Philip IV. The many paintings include the Martyrdom of St. Barth by Murillo, and there are notable statues of saints.

Other Cathedrals and Museums

The **Colonial Museum**, opposite the Cathedral at the southeast corner of the main square, houses a display of religious objects. It's open daily from 10 a.m.

The **Regional Museum of Archeology** is located in the building that was the house of government when Comayagua was capital of the republic. One-story, attractive, it reflects simpler times when the administration of an entire country, such as it was, could be carried out from what today would barely contain a municipal bureaucracy. It's located off the street that runs in front of the Cathedral, one block to the north. Hours are Wednesday to Friday 8 a.m. to noon and 1 to 4 p.m., weekends 9 a.m. to noon and 1 to 4 p.m. The museum may sometimes be visited on other days.

La Caxa Real (or "Caja," in modern Spanish), begun in 1739 and finished 1741, was the depository for royal taxes. The building suffered in earthquakes, and now only the front wall remains. If nothing else, its naked state, bare of the plaster and decoration of restored edifices, illustrates colonial construction techniques. Massive stone blocks, bricks, and rubble from older buildings were piled and mortared to form walls up to a meter in thickness.

Of the old **City Hall** of Comayagua, rebuilt in colonial style in 1880, on the north side of the main square, only the façade remains.

The **Column of the Constitution** dates from 1820, the eve of Central American independence. The name of the monument refers to nothing local, but to the 1812 Spanish constitution, which was an inspiration for liberal thinkers in the Spanish colonies. Locally, it's called **La Picota** ("the gibbet"), since the gallows and stocks of the town were adjacent.

Another important church, that of **El Señor Cruxificado de los Reyes** (Crucified Lord of the Kings), once stood just a block to the north of the main square. Destroyed by earthquake in 1809, there were plans to rebuild it on a site where it would compete less with the Cathedral for worshippers; but as administration and the position of the church declined after independence, the plans lay unfulfilled.

The **Church of San Francisco** was constructed starting in 1574. The Franciscans were the second religious order in Comayagua, after the Mercedarians, and erecting this church was their first task, and a continuing one. The building was renovated numerous times — in fact, this is the second site of the church. Damaged in a mid-eighteenth century earthquake, its roof crashed down in 1806. In another earthquake, in 1809, the bell tower collapsed. The current bell tower is three stories high, of the original four stories. The side fa_ade features a Renaissance-style pediment over the door, inset with a niche containing an image of St. Anthony. Another niche contains an image of St. Francis. The monastery next door contains a bell cast in Alcalá in 1464, possibly the oldest church bell in the Americas.

In the northern part of Comayagua, the **Church of Caridad Illescas** is one of the lesser churches of the town, as it was meant to be. This was a neighborhood parish, serving Indians and mixed-bloods who were required to come here for indoctrination. Construction was started in the early nineteenth century, and not completed for another hundred years.

Basically in baroque style, the Church of Caridad Illescas has a pediment over its main door, and, characteristic of Comayagua churches, a round window toward the top of the façade. The decoration along the top is more flamboyant than that of the earlier Merced church, but the general aspect is simple. As is the case elsewhere in Comayagua, the bell tower once stood higher. Inside, there are several colonial retables and sculptures.

The **Church of San Sebastián**, six blocks south of the Merced church, was founded in 1558, also by the Mercedarians. Poorly built, it was reconstructed, probably in the mid-eighteenth century. The building was taken over as a headquarters by the invading anti-clerical army of Guatemala in 1827. The bell towers were rebuilt only in 1957.

Inside, a stone on the floor is carved as a monument to José Trinidad Cabañas, president, national hero, and native of Comayagua. There are samples of colonial furniture, retables, and paintings, but basically, the church is bare, as it, like the church of Caridad Illescas, was meant to serve Indians and blacks.

WHERE TO STAY

Be advised that given the proximity of the **Soto Cano air base**, some of these hotels do an hourly trade.

HOTEL IMPERIAL, Barrio El Torondón, tel. 720215. 24 rooms. $8 single/$12 double. A two-story hotel with a few colonial details on the façade. Simple rooms. Well protected, though the street here is not well lit.

HOTEL EMPERADOR, on El Boulevard, the access road to town from the main highway. Tel. 720332. 19 rooms. $12 per person. Simple, adequate rooms.

HOTEL NORYMAX, tel. 721210. $18 double. On the same street as the Emperador. Clean and pleasant, charming balconies. Nice, modest rooms, and quiet. Small handicraft store. Washing machine available. Restaurant for breakfast. A good buy.

HOTEL LUXEMBURGO, Boulevard Comayagua. Bare rooms, but the beds are clean. About $10 double.

HOTEL QUAN, Barrio Abajo, tel. 720070, 720190. 20 rooms. $6 single/$10 double with private bath and fan; $20 double with t.v. and air conditioning. Visa. U.S. contact: Avenues to the World, 1091 Industrial Blvd., San Carlos, CA 94070, tel. 415-592-2090, fax 415-591-8986. A more than adequate hotel for the price, especially in the air-conditioned rooms. From the end of the Boulevard, go half a block north.

Other small and inexpensive hotels are near the main square and around the market.

WHERE TO EAT

Pájaro Rojo. Located one block north of Hotel Emperador on the entry road. The "Red Bird" is a more formal restaurant than others in Comayagua, with meals of paella, grilled steaks, seafood and chicken served on an attractive patio. Main courses range up to $6, sandwiches and snacks are lower-priced. There are dancing and live music on some evenings. The same owners operate the **Pájaro Azul** ("Blue Bird"), an eatery with breakfast and lighter fare right along the highway.

The **China** restaurant a couple of blocks west of the square is what it sounds like; and there is another Chinese eatery on the square itself.

SPORTS AND RECREATION

Climbing and **hiking** have some enthusiasts in this area. If you're interested, ask for the Alianza Francesa (Alliance Française), which has a mountaineering club.

PRACTICAL INFORMATION

There are several **banks** in Comayagua, including **Bancahsa**, Calle del Comercio; **Banco Atlántida**, Calle del Comercio; and **Banco de Occidente**, Calle de Comercio.

Amigo Renta A Car has an agency in Comayagua, tel. 720371, and **Cramer Tours** has a branch in town.

Near Comayagua

La Paz, 21 kilometers to the southeast of Comayagua, is the capital of the department of the same name, which stretches southward to the border of El Salvador. Poor roads connect La Paz with regional towns. La Paz probably originated around 1750, as an outpost of Comayagua, serving the few Spanish haciendas in the area.

Ajuterique along the road from Comayagua to La Paz, is an older town that dates from 1650, and has a colonial church. The name probably means "turtle hill."

Both La Paz and Ajuterique are easily reached on shuttle buses that run several times an hour from the highway bus stop outside Comayagua. There are also buses from the center of Comayagua, and fixed-route taxes from the highway junction. Buses operate also from 8 Avenida, 11/12 Calles, Comayagüela (Transportes Flores, tel. 373032).

These towns make for worthwhile short excursions if you're interested in detouring from the usual tourist path. To continue to more remote towns to the southwest, such as **Marcala** (see page 226), you'll have to pack your luggage along, as buses run less frequently and the trip is longer.

El Rosario, about 20 kilometers north of Comayagua on a branch of the old road northward, was a great silver-mining center for several centuries. Another road northward heads to coffee-growing country on the way to La Libertad. A branch to the northeast crosses pine forest to reach the colonial villages of **Esquias** and **Minas De Oro** ("Gold Mine," named for obvious reasons), each with a colonial church.

By sturdy vehicle or by infrequent bus, you can continue through to the highway that runs inland from San Pedro Sula to Trujillo. In the northern part of the zone live some Jicaque Indians, who migrated from the coast and took up stable farming only in the last century.

TENAMPUA

Ten kilometers southeast of Comayagua via a track that departs from the paved highway, **Tenampua** is the fortress where Honduras' Lenca nation held out under their chieftain Lempira against the Spaniards. Easily accessible to the curious for centuries, and unprotected, nothing much of interest remains, but for some deteriorated walls.

Archeologists both professional and amateur excavating over the years have found mounds with four layers of superimposed construction, as well as a ball court. The site is naturally protected by steep slopes, but great walls, as high and as wide as five meters, roughly built of uncut stone fitted as closely as possible, and terraced on the side of the defenders, block the easiest routes of access.

North of Comayagua

The main highway continues through the warm, fertile **Comayagua Valley**. From kilometer 94, there is a steep climb, to a pass at kilometer 105, on the continental divide. On one side, waters flow toward the Caribbean; on the other, toward the Pacific. The descent is to the **Siguatepeque plateau**, which is forested with pines, the Honduran national emblem.

Siguatepeque, "Hill of Women," is four kilometers off the highway, from a junction at kilometer 114. There is a good American Adventist hospital here, and, at 1140 meters, the climate is relatively cool. From the highway junction, another road cuts to the southwest, to the towns of Intibucá and La Esperanza (see pages 225-226). Buses operate to Siguatepeque from 8 Avenida, 11/12 Calles, Comayagüela (Transportes Maribel, tel. 373032).

At kilometer 115 is the forestry engineering school. There are more climbs to the village of **El Socorro**.

Near kilometer 131, you can see from the road a large kiln, where people burn lime for use in mortar, an activity that has gone on since the time of the ancient Maya. Modern cement still has not replaced old methods. You also see small-scale sugarcane mills — *trapiches* — emitting great plumes of smoke. The view in this region is spectacular, out to multiple peaks, and pastured hills and mountains. Unexpectedly, in the midst of a tropical country, it looks as if you were in Switzerland.

At kilometer 137, a kilometer before **Taulabé**, after an abrupt descent, you can visit the caves called Tarule, or Taulabé. There are stalactites and stalagmites, and, if you look straight up, bats. A boy will guide you through at no charge, though you should leave a few lempiras as a tip. The cave is 400 meters long.

The road is very good this way, but watch out for unexpected potholes. There are many small shops and eateries, where you can stop for a drink, and a plain, home-cooked meal.

Northwest of Taulabé, via a branch road, is **Santa Barbara** (population about 16,000), a regional center that dates from the late colonial period. There are several inexpensive hotels. Palm hats woven here are sold all over Honduras and in neighboring countries.

LAKE YOJOA

At kilometer 149, you get your first spectacular view of **Lake Yojoa** (yo-HO-ah), surrounded by mountains. One of the beauty spots of mainland Honduras, Yojoa has clear waters, and, for a mountain lake of its size and depth (175 square kilometers, up to 40 meters deep), its waters are surprisingly warm. The altitude along the shore is about 600 meters.

Yojoa is best-known, perhaps, for its bass. These are not indigenous — they were stocked, years ago — but they have taken well, and the lake is now a sport fishing center. Anybody can swim, of course, and the few hotels usually have boats and water-skiing equipment available for rent.

ARRIVALS AND DEPARTURES
By Bus

Buses on the Tegucigalpa-San Pedro Sula route will let you off at either the Motel Los Remos or at the turnoff for the Motel Agua Azul, near kilometer 164. From the latter point, buses run along the north shore of the lake about every half-hour.

ORIENTATION

Lake Yojoa lies beside the main north-south highway, which follows its eastern shore. From the road, you'll see marshes, and trees growing out

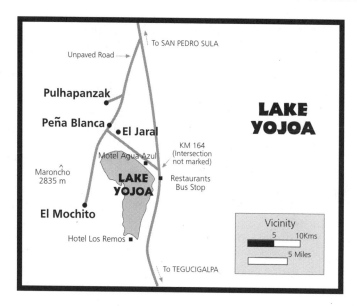

of the water, draped in Spanish moss. It is a true paradise for birds. From kilometer 165 (about 80 kilometers from San Pedro Sula), a branch road traces the northern shore, and it is mainly along this route, and right at the junction with the main highway, that you will find the few lodging and eating places and boating facilities that serve visitors. From the western shore of the lake, a secondary road reaches San Pedro Sula by way of the falls of Pulhapanzak. Hills and mountains overlook the lake, the highest being Mount Marancho, to the west.

Weather and Climate

The Lake Yojoa region gets copious amounts of rain, from clouds trapped by **Mount Marancho**, or Santa Bárbara (2744 meters). September, October and November are the rainiest months around Yojoa, though most of the rain falls at night. February through June are dryer.

During these months, farmers burn the land to ready it for the next crop season. Sometimes, you cannot see the mountains for all the smoke.

Around Lake Yojoa

The lake itself is largely fed by underground streams. It acts as a natural humidifier — everything around is green, and you can feel the moistness. If you spend any time in the area, inspect your camera lens for fungus.

Two islands poke out of the lake. The larger is near the south end.

The flat lands around the lake, well-watered and well-drained, afforded good access by roads, are intensively farmed. Sugar cane, coffee and pineapple are the main crops. Coffee especially is grown — the abundant water means that the coffee bush and the trees that shade it can both prosper.

Shade allows for a slow ripening of the coffee bean, and a maximum development of flavor. Gradually, the fruit of the coffee (the *cereza*, or "cherry") turns from green to red, at which point it is ready for picking. The outer skin is removed by simple machines, then the coffee is dried in the sun, which causes the "parchment" layer to flake off. Further drying is accomplished with hot air blowers fueled by oil. The beans then are classified by size and quality. Different sizes and types go to different markets. Italians get small beans sorted by hand. Mechanically sorted coffee ends up in the States (though experts say that the shape has no effect on the taste).

You can visit the coffee dryer at **Peña Blanca** village (see "West of Lake Yojoa" section below), and the coffee plantation at the Adventist school on the road to El Mochito from Peña Blanca. Or ask any farmer in the area for permission to look around. People are very friendly.

The expansion of agriculture in the rich lands around Lake Yojoa has some notably unfriendly effects. The forests on the slopes of Mount Marancho and nearby are legendary for their wildlife. But as trees are cut, some of the jaguars, pumas, ocelots, deer and bears are, in fact, becoming nothing more than legends. There is also concern that agricultural runoff and mining are poisoning the lake's waters.

WHERE TO STAY

There isn't much in the way of accommodation around the lake, and the hotels are scattered.

HOTEL AGUA AZUL (telephone 527125 in San Pedro Sula) is located along the north shore of Lake Yojoa, about 3.5 kilometers from the junction at kilometer 165. There are 21 units. You'll pay $16 double in regular rooms, and up to $25 for a "chalet" (cottage) with six beds. Rooms are simple, with old furnishings, but comfortable, and the water from the taps is hot. Maybe I should call this a well-kept fishing camp. The hotel makes arrangements for bass fishing and boating and water skiing. And the bird watching in the area is excellent. The gardens and landscaping are a fantasy world, and everything is quiet, but for the forest noises, and the nocturnal burps of giant frogs. And there's a pool, if you don't want to jump into the lake.

If you're just passing through for the day, the Agua Azul's shaded lake-view terrace is a good place to try black bass, available here as a filet (you can get it bones and all from any number of roadside stands). They also have a full menu of steaks, chicken and sandwiches, with nothing over $6.

LOS REMOS (tel. 570955 in San Pedro Sula) is a cluster of motel units and cottages at the south end of the lake, where the road from Tegucigalpa reaches the shore. It's not a luxury place by any means: the rooms are bare, there's a smell of damp in the air, and the pool is not well maintained. But everything is clean, and the balcony of the restaurant offers good views. There are 19 sleeping rooms in total. The rate is about $15 per person. The owners will make arrangements for fishing and boating. There's a launching ramp, in case you're towing your boat.

The **BRISAS DEL LAGO**, 10 kilometers from the highway turnoff, has about 72 rooms going for $60 double, along with several suites at a higher rate. Some rooms are air-conditioned and have television and lakeview balcony. There are also a play area, dance hall, tennis courts, bar and pool. Boats can be rented for fishing or for cruising, and there are canoes and pedal boats. For reservations, call 527030 in San Pedro Sula, 222874 in Tegucigalpa, or fax 533341.

WHERE TO EAT

You can eat reasonably at the above hotels. Try the lake fish, of course. There are also numerous eateries where the bus stops along the highway, but I'd be careful about them.

The West Side of Lake Yojoa

The road from kilometer 164 to Peña Blanca, on the west side of Yojoa, is one of the nicest in Honduras (in my opinion), with good views to the lake and the surrounding peaks. You will see sugar cane and pineapple plantations. The village of **El Jaral** is off the road, and was once of considerable importance. It was there that the ferry across Lake Yojoa docked, in the days before the highway between Tegucigalpa and San Pedro Sula was completed.

Farther on is **Peña Blanca**, where the paved road ends. The view is attractive from the main street. The village derives its name from the white peak, or outcrop (*Peña blanca*), that can be seen by looking to the west. Buses run between Peña Blanca and the main highway about every half-hour. The **HOTEL MARANTA** in Peña Blanca charges less than $10 double for clean, basic rooms. There's a snack bar at the store next to the hotel, charging less than $4 for a home-cooked meal.

El Mochito, to the southwest of the lake, is a mining center for lead, copper and silver, exploited in colonial times.

PULHAPANZAK

About 11 kilometers to the north of Peña Blanca, via a rough road, the **Pulhapanzak Falls** drop down to a natural pool, a great place for swimming. The site is a park, and there's a small admission charge. Groups from San Pedro Sula crowd the facilities on weekends.

To reach the falls by public transport, take the **bus** from Peña Blanca that runs to San Pedro Sula. One passes about every hour. Ask the driver to let you off at Pulhapanzak village. Or, if you're starting from San Pedro Sula, take the bus for El Mochito. It's a slow ride with many stops. The falls are a kilometer from the village. There are some Mayan ruins, but to inexperienced eyes they look like hillocks covered with vegetation. Farmers around the lake have discovered numerous Mayan artifacts, though there has been little intensive exploration of the local ruins.

MOUNT MARANCHO
AND SANTA BÁRBARA NATIONAL PARK

It is possible to hike to the top of **Marancho** (also known as **Santa Bárbara** mountain), but this is a task for expert adventurers. According to Michael Bell of the U.S. Peace Corps in Honduras, hikers should:
• be experienced
• have a topographical map, obtainable from the Instituto Geográfico Nacional in Tegucigalpa, and a good compass
• carry plenty of water
• have overnight camping equipment; and • carry a machete to clear trails when necessary. The ascent, for people in good condition, takes 15 hours — that's a two-day excursion.

Rainfall is high at the top of the mountain, and vegetation is largely as it was created by nature, due to the difficulty of access. You will walk where no human has gone before, and see vegetation and animal life that looks as if it came from a prehistoric world: giant vines dangling from trees and twisting through vegetation, and huge transparent butterflies. At some places, the ground-level layer of living and rotting vegetation is a meter thick. This is all a very special experience.

Santa Bárbara National Park, covering 130 square kilometers, includes the Yojoa basin, as well as Mount Marancho with its cloud forest, and several caves. The core area covers 5500 hectares. A buffer zone comprises 7500 hectares in which agricultural activities and wood-cutting are controlled. Mount Marancho and its underground sink holes, caves and hollows feed Lake Yojoa and numerous streams, forming one of the major watersheds of Honduras.

North from Yojoa

From the Yojoa junction (kilometer 164), the main highway rises for several kilometers. You see pineapple plantations, newly established in this area. From kilometer 169, the road begins to descend toward the hot lowlands, winding gently all the way. Many stands sell bananas, oranges and pineapples, all fresh of course, and in the case of pineapples, cut to order.

At kilometer 184 is **Flores**, a wide spot in the road at the junction for **Santa Rita**, 15 kilometers away, on the Comayagua River.

Upriver from Santa Rita is **El Cajon dam**, a huge (for Honduras) hydroelectric project. Placed into operation in 1985, the dam is the tallest in Central America (over 700 feet), and one of the highest in the world, forming a lake covering almost 100 square kilometers snaking and branching through Central Honduras in the valleys of the Comayagua, Sulaco and Humuya rivers. The electricity produced is more than can be used in Honduras, and much is sold to neighboring countries. The dam can only be visited with official permission from the state electric company.

From Flores, you descend another three kilometers, then follow a mostly straight road through the lowlands to San Pedro Sula, crossing the **Chamelecón River**, a brown, muddy, unnavigable river of rapids.

SAN PEDRO SULA

One of the oldest cities in Honduras, **San Pedro Sula** is also the newest, the center of industry and trade in the fastest-growing part of the country, with a population of over 300,000. San Pedro Sula is just 246 kilometers from Tegucigalpa, and a continent away.

Tegucigalpa has venerable governmental buildings and institutions of learning. San Pedro Sula has factories.

Tegucigalpa is where the Mestizo culture of Honduras was formed. San Pedro Sula, if not polyglot, is multicultural, with evident African and Levantine strains.

Tegucigalpa, in the mountains, has hills and winding streets. San Pedro Sula, in the lowlands, is flat. Tegucigalpa has buses. San Pedro Sula has buses *and* a railroad.

Tegucigalpa developed as the isolated capital of a backwater. San Pedro Sula knows no limits. In the Honduran context, it is Chicago.

Beginnings

This old-new city's roots go back to June 27, 1536, when it was founded as Villa de San Pedro de Puerto Caballos by Pedro de Alvarado, one of the maximum leaders of the Spanish onslaught. The traditional name for the valley, Sula, (from the Aztec for "birds") was added in short order.

San Pedro was for a time a military headquarters, but the center of Spanish power soon moved to the highlands. The outpost near the coast was destroyed by pirates in 1660, and intermittently attacked by Indians and Sambos (mixed-bloods of part-African descent) allied with English pirates. Much later, in 1892, the town was almost abandoned in the wake of a yellow fever epidemic.

But that was the low point. A railroad reached San Pedro Sula from the coast in the 1870s, part of a transcontinental system that was never completed. Bananas were planted widely by American companies, low-lying lands were drained, port facilities were constructed nearby, malaria and tropical diseases were conquered or controlled by chemicals and medicines, and San Pedro Sula began to attract new residents not only from the highlands, but from outside the country. West Indians came to work on the banana plantations, and Lebanese arrived to smooth the flow of trade. Factories were established to produce cloth and processed foods and construction materials for the local market.

All this development occurred in relative isolation from Tegucigalpa: a paved road to the capital opened only in 1971.

Modern San Pedro Sula

Today, San Pedro Sula is a clean, modern, growing town. Yet it is still of a manageable, or human, aspect. Prosperity is obvious, and everything looks efficient. There are no beggars, or few of them. And strangely, there is no visible military presence, which can make you feel uncomfortable if you've become used to seeing soldiers around, as you will in some other parts of Honduras.

Downtown San Pedro Sula is small and mostly uncongested, reflecting the rapid growth of the city after the period of motorization. There are pockets of wealthy suburbs, and little evidence of grinding poverty.

There is also very little in the way of points of interest or attractions, except for some annual feasts and celebrations. But San Pedro Sula is *the* starting point for excursions to many other places. You can fly right in from abroad, stay in good accommodations, and continue by road to the ruins of Copán and to points along the coast, on day or overnight trips.

ARRIVALS AND DEPARTURES
By Air
- **Sahsa,** 4 Avenida, 3 Calle SW, tel. 526051. Daily service from Miami, Belize, Tegucigalpa (three flights daily), Guatemala, La Ceiba (four flights daily, $45 one way), New Orleans, Roatán (two flights daily, $53 one way).
- **Aero Costa Rica,** to Orlando, Florida.
- **Continental,** Gran Hotel Sula, tel. 574141; 574740 at airport.
- **Copa,** 10 Avenida, 1/2 Calles SW, tel. 520883 (562518 at airport). To Mexico City, Panama, San José, Costa Rica.
- **Isleña Airlines,** tel. 562218. To La Ceiba (three flights daily).
- **Lacsa,** 8 Avenida, 1/2 Calles SW, tel. 526888., to Costa Rica, Guatemala, Miami, New Orleans, Cancun, Mexico City, New York.
- **Taca,** 9/10 Avenidas, 1/2 Calles NW, tel. 532646. To San Salvador,

Guatemala, Miami.
- **Aero Servicios**, Gran Hotel Sula, 10 Avenida, 9 Calle NW, No. 9, Los Andes, tel. 534401.
- **American Airlines**, Firenze Bldg., Barrio Los Andes, tel. 580518; 682356 at airport. To Miami, New York
- **Aviateca**, 2 Calle, 1/2 Avenidas NW, tel. 532580. To Guatemala

The Airport
   Ramón Villeda Morales Airport is located about 12 kilometers east of San Pedro Sula, off the road to La Lima. A taxi will take you out for about $6. Buses for La Lima will leave you more than a kilometer from the terminal. The terminal is in the process of being rebuilt. (It needs it!)
   The airport has a large duty-free shop, well stocked with perfumes, cigarettes and liquors. Both lempiras and dollars are accepted, and you can buy goods *when you enter* Honduras at this airport, as well as when you're leaving, which saves possible breakage.

By Bus
   At least three bus companies provide hourly or near-hourly service between Tegucigalpa and San Pedro Sula. The ride takes about four hours, and the fare is less than $3.
   San Pedro Sula to Tegucigalpa: Empresa Hedman Alas 3 Calle, 7/8 Avenidas NW, tel. 531361, hourly, with newer buses than those of other companies; Transportes Sáenz, 9/10 Avenidas, 9/10 Calles SW, tel. 531829; and Empresa de Transportes El Rey, Avenida 7, Calles 5/6, tel. 534264, every 90 minutes.
   Tegucigalpa to San Pedro Sula: Empresa El Rey, 6 Avenida, 9 Calle, Comayagüela, every hour or more frequently from before dawn to 10:30 p.m. Buses are comfortable and uncrowded. Also Hedman-Alas, 11 Avenida, 13/14 Calles, Comayagüela, and Transportes Sáenz, 12 Calle, 7/8 Avenidas, Comayagüela, hourly departures from 8 a.m. to 6 p.m.
   To Puerto Cortés: Empresa Impala, 2 Avenida, 4/5 Calles NW; and Empresa Citul, 7 Calle, 5/6 Avenidas SW, tel. 530070. Buses operate about every 20 minutes until 6 p.m.
   La Lima, Tela, and La Ceiba: From the Tupsa station, 2 Avenida, 5/6 Calles SW, every five minutes to La Lima (the banana capital) and Progreso. Change buses in Progreso for Tela; or take a La Ceiba bus to the Tela junction, and a taxi into town (less than a dollar for the taxi ride). Buses leave every hour for La Ceiba.
   Copán Ruins: Empresa de Transportes Torito, 6 Calle, 6/7 Avenidas SW, tel. 534930, has buses going to Santa Rosa de Copán. To reach the ruins of Copán, take this bus as far as La Entrada (two hours), where you can pick up another bus for Copán Ruinas, 64 kilometers and almost two

hours and a travel-sickness pill onward. A couple of direct buses are operated daily by Etumi, 6 Calle, 6/7 Avenidas SW, at 10 a.m. and 1 p.m. **Santa Rosa de Copán**: Every hour or more frequently by Empresa Torito, 6 Calle, 6/7 Avenidas, SW and Transportes Copanecos, 6 Calle, 4/5 Avenidas SW.

To Guatemala: There are several choices. Continue by bus from Copán Ruinas; take a bus to Santa Rosa de Copán, then continue by bus to the border past Nueva Ocotepeque; or Transportes Impala, 2 Avenida, 4/5 Calles SW with several through buses a day to Nueva Ocotepeque and the border.

Departing By Train

A slow, cheap train leaves in the morning for Puerto Cortés and Tela (with a change of train en route) from the station near 1 Avenida and 1 Calle. For information, call 531879 or 532997. If you're a train buff, hurry up and climb aboard before the service is discontinued.

ORIENTATION/GETTING AROUND TOWN

The central area of San Pedro Sula is divided by 1 Calle (running east-west) and 1 Avenida (running north-south) into four quadrants, or zones: *Noreste* (*NE*, or Northeast), *Noroeste* (*NO*, or Northwest), *Sudoeste* (*SO*, or Southwest) and *Sudeste* (*SE*, or Southeast). Streets are numbered, and addresses in the central area always give the quadrant, using the Spanish abbreviation. (For convenience, I will use the English NW and SW for Northwest and Southwest).

Calles run east-west, *avenidas* run north-south. 4 Avenida downtown is a pedestrian mall (*peatonal*). Avenida Circunvalación is the ring road around the central area. There are also various *colonias*, or suburbs.

Auto Rental

Among car-rental companies in San Pedro Sula are:
- **Avis**, 1 Calle, 8/9 Avenidas NW, tel. 530955, fax 578877.
- **Auto Usados**, 3 Avenida, 19 Calle NW, tel. 534038.
- **Molinari**, Gran Hotel Sula, tel. 532639, fax 522704.
- **Budget**, tel. 526749, 522295, fax 533411. At Gran Hotel Sula and airport.
- **Maya Rent a Car**, 3 Avenida, 7/8 Calle NW, tel 522670, and at the Hotel Copantl and the airport.
- **Blitz**, 1 Calle, 3/4 Avenidas NW, tel. 522405.
- **Toyota Rent a Car**, 4 Avenida, 2/3 Calles NW, tel. 572644.

AIDS WARNING

San Pedro Sula is said to have an AIDS infection rate of as high as four percent – comparable to that in Haiti and Thailand. According to journalist Larry Luxner, the prevalence of prostitution, a high incidence of cervical cancer (which leaves women vulnerable to infection), and the proximity of Puerto Cortés with its transient population of sailors, are all factors in this alarming statistic.

Whatever the causes, San Pedro Sula is not the place in which to take risks.

Tourist Office

The local tourist office is on the third floor of the building at 4 Calle, 3/4 Avenidas NW. They're not very helpful, but if you're starting your Honduras trip here, you can pick up some free maps and accurate information on buses, and weed through the piles of fact sheets that are lying on various counters.

SEEING THE SIGHTS

If I told you there were sights to see in San Pedro Sula, in the usual touristic sense, I would be pulling your leg. Despite San Pedro's long history, all of the city is modern, and there are no notable parks or museums or public institutions. Even the **Cathedral**, with its neo-colonial appearance, is a post-war structure.

You can, however, stroll the streets and get a sense of the commercial life of the town, or shop for handicrafts; though the city is hot for much of the year, especially from April to October, without the cooling sea breezes of the coast. If you're not here for business, you will use San Pedro as a base for visits to Copán, banana country, and the coast to the north. See below ("Trips from San Pedro Sula") for more details.

For an in-town excursion, you can go up to the **Mirador Caprí** (viewpoint) west of the city. This is just a parking area and a Coke stand on a hill, about four kilometers from downtown. Take a taxi ($5 or less) or your own car. There are no buses. On a clear day you can see for miles, to the mountains that look over Lake Yojoa to the south.

WHERE TO STAY

GRAN HOTEL SULA, 1 Calle, 3/4 Avenidas NW (P. O. Box 435), tel. 529999, fax 576215, 527000. 118 rooms. $85 single/$96 double/$107 triple, $128 in suites. U.S. reservations: tel. 800-223-6764. No charge for children under 12.

This is a nine-story building right on the main square of San Pedro Sula. The staff is competent and friendly. The rooms (and the hotel in general) are very clean, the mattresses are excellent, and all are provided with coffee makers. All rooms in the main tower have balconies (I recommend those with a view to the pool, a courtyard work of tiled art, complete with cascades and tributaries), and suites have kitchenettes and sleep sofas. There are also some poolside units. Other amenities include a restaurant, 24-hour coffee shop, casino, and assorted boutiques, entry to health club, and twice-daily maid service (extraordinary!).

The Gran Hotel Sula is a trip back in time to the late fifties, when staying downtown did *not* mean staying in a dangerous, decaying area. The hotel has been well maintained, but fortunately, it has not been updated (except for such necessities as air conditioning and color televisions with satellite programming), so that it maintains the sort of charm associated with a meticulously restored ocean liner or railway car, or a South Beach Miami hostelry.

Take the Skandia coffee shop. You can take spin on revolving stools at the lunch counter and order a banana split, club sandwich, and apple pie, and drink of atmosphere that says, this is a *diner!*

Of course, if you're not a kid, you can sit at one of the tables. Egg plates, club sandwiches and burgers in the Skandia run $3 and under. For more formal dining, the Granada restaurant overlooks the pool from the mezzanine, and serves filet mignon, shrimp casserole and daily specials for $7 and under, a lunch buffet for about $6. The cuisine is excellent.

Discounts — significant ones — are available to Hondurans and resident foreigners.

HOTEL COPANTL SULA, Colonia Las Mesetas (P. O. Box 1060), tel. 530900 or 537656, fax 573890. 205 rooms. $90 to $95 single or double. U.S. reservations, tel. 800-328-8897, fax 512-341-7942.

This is the *other* large hotel in San Pedro, located on extensive grounds on the southern outskirts of the city, on the way in from Tegucigalpa, more a grand hotel than any other in town. It's nice, clean, quiet, and modern, with a soaring, dark, multi-story lobby, bar, disco, and country-club facilities that include an Olympic-size pool with diving blocks, pool snack bar, four tennis courts, handball courts, sauna and whirpool, exercise equipment, and massage service for a fraction of U.S. prices.

Of the several restaurants, the Pergola, on the seventh floor, is a grill room with reasonably priced fare — steaks, chicken and shrimp brochettes for $7 and less. The ground-floor coffee shop is informal, features quick service, and is frequented by locals as well as hotel guests — a good sign.

Rooms are less attractive than the public areas, on the small side, with a hard feel and less-than-top-notch taste in furnishings, but they're air-conditioned and carpeted, and have color televisions. Shops and services include car rental and travel agencies, and if you need it, there's a casino with card games, slot machines and roulette. All in all, you could stay here for an off-beat Latin vacation and feel that nothing is lacking, or happily use the hotel as a base for touring Honduras.

A free shuttle bus runs every half hour to downtown during daylight hours on weekdays and till noon on Saturday, otherwise you'll have to take taxis or have a rental car if you're going anywhere in town. When the hotel is not full, you might try asking for the corporate rate, the military rate, the resident's rate, or some other discount.

HOTEL BOLÍVAR, 2 Calle, 2 Avenida NW No. 8 (P.O. Box 956), tel. 533224, 531811, fax 534823. 70 rooms. $28-$30 single/$32-$38 double. American Express, Visa, Master Card.

This is a good, middle-range hotel, a modern building with an excellent central location and attractive grounds, though it could be better maintained. Orientation to interior courtyard and pool makes it relatively quiet in most rooms, despite traffic outside. There is air conditioning on the top (third) floor and in poolside rooms. Main courses in the restaurant run $6 or less, with an emphasis on seafood. Protected parking. The hotel is well publicized and often booked up, so reservations are advisable.

JAVIER'S HOUSE, Calle 9, Avenida 23-24 SW (house 239D), tel. 576322. $45 double with breakfast. U.S. contact: tel. 1-800-553-2513.

Something new, a bed-and-breakfast, operated by Javier Pinel, a Honduran travel agent who lived many years in the States.

HOTEL INTERNATIONAL PALACE, 3 Calle, 8 Avenida SW, tel. 577922, fax 522838. 24 rooms. $40 single/$45 double.

Plain, fairly new, modern and clean, the International Palace has air-conditioned rooms with televisions, phones, beds with foam mattresses, and tiled bathrooms. Rooms facing the street have balconies and cost a few dollars more than inside rooms, which face light wells.

HOTEL AMBASSADOR, 5 Avenida, 7 Calle SW, tel. 576824, fax 575860. 39 rooms. $27 single/$32 double.

A low-rise, motel-style building in a shopping center the southwest part of San Pedro. Rooms are air-conditioned, some have balconies, there is a coffee shop, and protected parking is provided.

HOTEL-SUITES LOS ANDES, Av. Circunvalación 84/17 Avenida NW, tel. 534425, 532526 fax 571945. 40 units. $55 single/$70 double/ $80 triple.

A low-rise complex of furnished apartments on San Pedro's ring road, each with television, air conditioning, kitchenette with dishwasher. Though most hotel services are lacking, there are a convenience store, coffee shop, restaurant and bar, and whirlpool.

HOTEL PALMIRA. Two locations under one management: **Palmira**

1, 6 Calle, 6/7 Avenidas SW, tel. 576522, 26 rooms; and **Palmira 2**, 7 Avenida, 4/5 Calles, SW, tel. 522363, 19 rooms. $19 single/$34 double with fan, slightly more with air conditioning. In either location, your money buys you a modern, plain room, short on decor and soothing surroundings, but clean and secure.

Businessman Hotels

Somewhat similar to the Palmiras in facilities and atmosphere, or lack of same – Central American businessmen's hotels – are:

HOTEL TERRAZA, 6 Avenida, 4/5 Calles SW, tel. 533108. 42 rooms. 10 and up single/$18 and up double. Restaurant, bar, air-conditioned rooms.

HOTEL COLOMBIA, 3 Calle, 5/6 Avenidas SW, tel. 533118 or 575345 . 25 rooms. $17 single/$35 double.

HOTEL LA SIESTA, 7 Calle, 2 Ave SE, tel. 522650 or 529290. 44 rooms. $10 per person. A plain hotel with plain rooms. Some have balconies, facing a busy street.

GRAN HOTEL SAN PEDRO, 3 Calle, 1/2 Avenida SW, tel. 531513. 75 rooms. $15 single with fan to $26 double with air conditioning. Near the central plaza, about a ten-minute walk. Not grand, as the name implies, but a good budget hotel, and often full. There's a coffee shop and protected parking.

HOTEL BRISAS DEL OCCIDENTE, 5 Avenida, 6/7 Calles SW, tel. 552309. A basic sort of place where you get what you pay for – about $3 per person with shared bath. It's clean, anyway, and near the Citul bus station for Puerto Cortés.

WHERE TO EAT

There are few restaurants worthy of mention in San Pedro Sula. I have found good eating in some of the better hotels, especially the two noted below:

Gran Hotel Sula, 1 Calle, 3/4 Avenidas, NW. On the first floor, you'll find the 24-hour Skandia diner, with good, simple meals for just a couple of dollars. On the second floor, the more formal Granada restaurant offers a buffet at noon for about $6, and full dinner at night, and, sometimes, entertainment. The cuisine is genuinely continental, and excellent, aside from which it is a very good value. Even Peace Corps volunteers, who stay in two- and three-dollar hotels, come out to dine at the Gran Hotel Sula.

Comparable food, with a higher tab, will be found at the **Hotel Copantl Sula**, on the southern outskirts.

Fast Food

Pizza Hut is at 1 Calle (Boulevard Morazán) and 16 Avenida, NW. Just what you'd expect, with filtered water. A couple of blocks closer to the square on 1 Calle is Toto's Pizza, at 11 Avenida. **Burger King** has a shop on the ring road, Av. Circunvalación, two blocks south of 1 Calle.
La Estancia, 2 Calle, 9/10 Avenidas NW, is a good beef restaurant, serving steaks radiant-roasted by an open fire, in Uruguayan *fogata* style.

Chinese

Chinese restaurants with standard Cantonese fare include the **Copa de Oro**, 2 Avenida, 2/3 Calles SW No. 4; **Lucky**, 3 Calle, 3/4 Avenidas, just south of the main square; the **Central Palace**, 4 Calle, 6/7 Avenidas No. 43, SW; **China Town**, 5 Calle, 7 Avenida SW; and **Taiwan**, 5 Avenida, 2/3 Calles, NW.

Other Fare

Some of the restaurants that cater to middle-class residents are located on the outskirts, especially along Avenida Circunvalación, the ring road, and you'll probably take the detour to try them if you have a car.
Pat's Steak House, out of the way at 5 Calle, 17 Avenida SW (on the ring road, in the vicinity of the Hotel Copantl Sula) is your best choice if you're looking for a thick cut of beef or a surf 'n turf combo. $10 and up for a meal. Owned by an American, it's often full. Phone 530939 to reserve before going out. **Las Tejas**, nearby along the curve in the ring road at 9 Calle, 16/17 Avenida, also serves grilled meats, to a hacienda theme. José y Pepe's, on Circunvalación at 6 Calle SW, has steaks, seafood, and Mexican specialties. They have a more pleasant branch above town in Colonia Palmira, at Avenida República de Panamá 2027.
Charlie's Chicken is a huge roast chicken emporium at 4 Avenida and 15 Calle NE, near the ring road. The fare won't hurt your stomach, and it's a good place to take kids if you've had too many burgers with them. **Don Udo's** is a coffee shop-bar on Circunvalación at 5 Calle NW, with a long menu, said to be a good place for breakfast as well as heftier meals.
Without much searching, you'll also find fried chicken palaces and hamburger eateries; though there are fewer eating places in San Pedro Sula than in Tegucigalpa.

SHOPPING

The **Mercado de Artesanías Populares**, 6 Calle, 8/9 Avenidas NW, sponsored by the tourist office, has a variety of sculptures in wood, straw items, pottery, hammocks, silkscreen prints, and primitive paintings. Another large store is **Dicias Novedades**, 4 Avenida mall, 2/3 Calles SW, a half-block from city hall.

The **Central Market** is at 6 Calle and 2 Avenida SW, a few blocks south of the main square. The wares are foods and spices, but if you go without great expectations, you might find straw hats or utilitarian items to your liking. The **Guamilito Market** is at 6 Calle and 8 Avenida NW, with more handicrafts than at the Central Market.

Look on the side streets around the Gran Hotel Sula for handicraft shops, and at the small booth in the Central Park. Items offered include wood carvings, paintings, and leather items. And don't pass up the pi_atas and many other items intended for local use that make for interesting knick-knacks once you get them home.

Alongside the highway to Puerto Cortés are stands with fabulous wicker creations: baskets in the form of animals, pendant chairs, benches, sofas, love seats, and much more. You'd need a shipping container to get the big stuff home, but don't let that keep you from stopping and shopping for the small items.

PRACTICAL INFORMATION
Banks

For street money exchange, go to the Central Park (Parque Barahona), or the pedestrian mall nearby. Don't take the first offer — rates vary by quite a bit even within the park. From appearances, nobody's worried very much about security. Dexterous traders flip inch-thick wads of 100-lempira notes in your face with one hand as you pass, and display a calculator in the other.

If you need a real bank, among those in San Pedro Sula are:

Banco Atlántida, 1 Calle, 3 Avenida NW, tel. 531215; **Banco Central de Honduras**, 5 Avenida, 3 Calle SW, tel. 533804; **Banco de Honduras** (Citibank), 3 Avenida, 1 Calle NW, tel. 523151; **Banco Continental**, 3 Avenida, 2/3 Calles SW, tel. 522744; **Banco Mercantil**, 1 Calle, 2/3 Avenidas NW, tel. 534444; Lloyds Bank, 4 Calle, 4 Avenida SW, tel. 531379.

For cash advances on a Visa card, contact Bancahsa, 5 Avenida SW No. 46, or any bank with a Honducard-Visa sign, or call 580323. For a cash advance on Visa or Master Card, contact Credomatic, Ficensa building, tel. 532404, or any bank with a Credomatic sign.

Churches
- **Latter Day Saints**, Bancatlan building, 3 Avenida, 1_Calle NW, tel. 528152.
- **Episcopal**, El Buen Pastor, 23 Avenida, 21 Calle, Colonia Trejo, tel. 522140.
- **Mennonite**, 2 Calle 1507 NE, tel. 527821.
- **Second Baptist Church**, 4 Avenida, 10/11 Calles SW, tel. 534039.

Consulates
- **Belgium**, 4 Calle, 4 Avenida No. 28, tel. 527989.
- **El Salvador**, Edificio Rivera y Cía, 5th floor, tel. 534604.
- **Germany**, Berkling Industrial, Puerto Cortés road, tel. 531244.
- **Guatemala**, 8 Calle, 5/6 Avenidas No. 38, tel. 533560.
- **Italy**, 5 Avenida, 1/2 Calles NW, Constancia building, tel. 523672.
- **United Kingdom**, Teminales Cortés, tel. 532600.

Fiesta
   The big local celebration is on June 29, in honor of Saints Peter and Paul. The festivities run for an entire week — at least.

Film
   One store well stocked with a variety of film is El Indio, 7 Avenida, 2/3 Calles SW.

Gambling
   San Pedro Sula's casinos are in the Hotel Copantl and the Gran Hotel Sula.

Movies
   What the heck, they're cheap. Newspapers don't give the addresses of the cinemas. **The Tropicana** is at 7 Av, 2 Calle SW; **The Aquarius** at 11 Avenida, 2 Calle NW; the **Presidente** on 1 Calle west of the park; Los Andes on the ring road.

Post Office
   3 Avenida, 9 Calle SW, No. 75.

Telephones
   Hondutel, for long-distance calls, is at 4 Avenida, 4 Calle SW.
   Emergency numbers in San Pedro Sula are the same as in Tegucigalpa:
   - **191** – Long distance in Honduras
   - **192** – Telephone number information
   - **196** – Time of Day
   - **197** – International long distance
   - **198** – Fire
   - **199** – Public security (police)

Tours and Travel Agencies
   The usual destinations for day trips from San Pedro Sula are the ruins of Copán, Lake Yojoa, the fortress of Omoa on the Caribbean, banana plantations, Tela, and the Lancetilla botanical garden; but there are other

possibilities, including Comayagua and even Tegucigalpa.
Among the travel agencies in San Pedro Sula are:
- **Maya Tropic** in Gran Hotel and Copantl Sula, P.O. Box 480, tel. 522405, 525401. Arranges bass-fishing trips to Lake Yojoa, tours to the Bay Islands, and day trips and longer excursions to the ruins of Copán, banana plantations, and along the coast. Maya Tropic is the company that arranges many of the side trips to the mainland offered in conjunction with Bay Islands dive trips.
- **Eco Tours**, Calle 9, Avenida 23-24 SW (house 239D), tel. 576322. U.S. contact: tel. 1-800-553-2513. Operated by Javier Pinel, recently of Americas Tours and Travel in Seattle. Mr. Pinel keeps a boat at Lake Yojoa, and arranges custom trips, as well as operating a week-long "Honduran Highlights" tour.
- **Cambio C.A.**, P. O. Box 2, Trujillo, Colón, tel. 527335 in San Pedro Sula, arranges rafting trips on the Chamelecón River and hikes in Cusuco National Park (see below), at $90 per person per outing and up.
- **Explore Honduras**, Paseo del Sol Building, 2 Avenida, 1 Calle NW, tel. 526242, fax 526239. Considered a reliable operator of trips in northern and western Honduras.
- **Transmundo Tours**, 6 Avenida 2/3 Calles SW No.15, tel. 534752.
- **Cramer Tours**, on the Peatonal (4 Avenida SW No. 2, near the Central Park, tel. 577082, fax 576867) and at the Hotel Copantl Sula. Tours to banana plantation, Copán, the Lancetilla garden.
- **Alas tours**, 3 Calle, 4/5 Avenidas SW, tel. 530345.
- **Brenda Tours**, 2 Calle SW No. 25-D, tel. 530360, 531770, fax 528129. Mainly they offer excursions to the Bay Islands.
- **Mundirama Travel Service**, Edificio Martínez Valenzuela (American Express representative), 2 Calle SW, 2/3 Avenidas, tel. 530490.
- **Agencia de Viajes Mundiales**, 8 Avenida, 1/2 Calles SW, Roma Building, tel. 532309.
- **Cosmos**, 10 Avenida, 3/4 Calles, NW, tel. 527270.

Approximate prices of trips from San Pedro Sula are:
- **Banana plantation** tour, $30
- **Lake Yojoa** and **Pulhapanzak Falls** (see pages 128-132), $65

- **Cusuco National Park** overnight, including camping, $160
- **Copán ruins** and **Pulhapanzak Falls** (see pages 213-222 and 131-132), $75 and up for a day trip, $130 and up overnight
- **Telamar beach resort/Lancetilla Botanical Garden** (see pages 156-159), $65
- **Omoa**, $65
- **Tegucigalpa** and **Valle de Angeles**, $105 ($140 overnight)
- **Trujillo**, $140 overnight.

If you speak some Spanish and can negotiate with a taxi driver, you can arrange some of these trips for a group of four for considerably less.

West of San Pedro Sula

Cusuco National Park, 20 kilometers west of San Pedro Sula in a straight line, takes in a section of just 10 square kilometers of cloud forest on **Tilineo Peak**, divided into a central absolute reserve and a surrounding buffer zone of recovering forest, where agriculture is subject to controls to protect the central area.

Quetzals are said to be readily sighted in April and May. Other wildlife includes toucans, and monkeys. Conifers grow at the higher levels.

Nature trails are in the works, and a visitors center has been set up in the village of Buenos Aires. Access is via a roundabout route, south from San Pedro, then west and north.

Information on trails and current conditions in the park is available from **Cohdefor** (Honduran Forestry Corporation), 10 Avenida, 5 Calle NW, San Pedro Sula, tel. 534959. Tours are operated to the park by Cambio C.A.

North of San Pedro Sula

Lake Ticamaya, about one by two kilometers, is a relatively shallow body of water that attracts herons and other water-loving birds. It lies southeast of **Choloma**, off the highway north from San Pedro Sula.

East of San Pedro Sula

The road from San Pedro Sula to the east, toward El Progreso and the coast, is straight and flat — but watch out for banana peels! Past the airport, nine kilometers out, is an industrial zone. Then you enter banana country.

LA LIMA

Two kilometers past the airport is the turn for **La Lima**, capital of bananas. You are surrounded by bananas for as far as you can see. In La Lima, turn right, and you will cross a bridge over the brown Chamelecón River. Alongside is another, pedestrian bridge. Above, **Chiquita** on the water tank watches over.

Past the bridge, on the left side, are the banana company operations, which you can visit if you arrive between 7 a.m. and 10 a.m., or from 12:30 p.m. to 2:30 p.m. It is all impressive. I have eaten bananas all my life, yet until I went to La Lima, I was in the dark about the basics of cultivating this fruit and transporting it to markets worldwide.

Well, the guides will show you everything. Bunches of bananas are covered with plastic to protect the fruit from insects. Plants at different stages of maturity are color-coded. Branches laden with bananas are supported with a special tool while they are hacked off the plant with a couple of expert strokes of a machete. The whole mature plant is then cut down, but for a single shoot that will grow up to replace it. The stem of bananas, meanwhile, is transported to the processing plant, where fruits are washed, separated into bunches, sorted, and washed again. Chemical treatment retards ripening, then the fruit is packed and weighed. Blemished fruits go their separate way, to be processed into baby food. As industrial tours go, this one is off-beat, and well worth taking.

Beyond La Lima, just two kilometers before Progreso, there is a smaller banana processing plant on the left side of the road. With a small tip, you can arrange to visit it, and it takes less time than to see the one at La Lima.

Buses operating on the route to Tela will take you to La Lima for less than 50 cents. While you're out this way, you can also view the classic two-level arrangement of banana towns: standardized housing for the field laborers, which, though it is better than what most people would otherwise inhabit, is still visually dreary and sterile; and pools, golf courses and attractively designed and landscaped residential bungalows for the upper ranks of employees.

EL PROGRESO

Just before **El Progreso**, you cross the **Río Ulúa**, no more attractive than the Chamelecón. El Progreso is a transit town, as much for bananas as for people, on the shortcut from Tegucigalpa to Tela. The bus stop for Tela is two blocks from the main square.

The **GRAN HOTEL LAS VEGAS**, 11 Calle, 2 Avenida Norte, is the only three-story hotel in town, with air conditioning and restaurant. Rates are less than $10 per person.

DEPARTMENT OF YORO

Most travelers will head north from El Progreso to Tela, La Ceiba (takeoff point for the Bay Islands) and, possibly, Trujillo. These places are covered in the next chapter. To the east, however, is an area little visited and lightly populated, the **department of Yoro**, covering the long valley sheltered from the coast by a ridge of mountains. Some of the residents are the remaining Jicaque Indians who were displaced from the coast by migrations of Black Caribs, and, under the influence of missionaries, adopted settled corn agriculture, much like the Indians of western Honduras.

The **town of Yoro**, capital of the area, dates from 1578. The name derives from the Nahuatl for "center." Many place names in Honduras are in the language of the Mexican Indians who accompanied the Spanish conquerors.

An odd phenomenon is said to re-occur every year between June 14 and 25 in **El Pantano**, just over a kilometer to the southeast of the center of Yoro, when a fierce combination of downpour, thunder, lightning and winds leaves in its wake a scattering of stranded fish. This "**rain of fish**" has given rise to many theories as to its causes. One is that fish from the Atlantic, at the end of their life span, sense and follow an extreme low-pressure system up the Aguán valley to Yoro, and jump ashore when the storm is at its worst.

Montaña de Yoro National Park, covering 155 square kilometers of rain forest south of Yoro, is adjacent to Torupane reserve of the Jicaque Indians.

Ayapa Volcano, south of Yoro, holds caves with pools inhabited by blind fish.

Olanchito, 243 kilometers from San Pedro Sula, is the center of one of the fastest-growing agricultural areas of Honduras, along the Aguán River. The town was founded in 1530, moved to a new location, and never flourished until recent times. Accommodations for visitors are available at the **HOTEL VALLE AGUÁN**. There are frequent buses to La Ceiba.

Tocoa, to the east, is a bustling commercial center with good, plain accommodations at the **HOTEL SANABRIA**, tel. 443400.

12. THE NORTH COAST

INTRODUCTION

The northwestern lowlands of Honduras — a strip about 50 kilometers wide, backed by mountain ridges for almost 200 kilometers — are the banana republic of Honduras. I don't mean this in any demeaning, stereotyping way. It's just that banana cultivation and commerce in bananas have made this area what it is today.

Farther east, toward the border of Nicaragua, where the land is poorly drained and considered mostly uncultivable, things are much as they were 100, 200, even 300 years ago. Hardly a road penetrates the marshes and forests, transport is mainly by boat, and Indian bands live in scattered groups.

Just 130 years ago, the northwestern coast was also a lightly inhabited area, where remnant towns dating from colonial days held on precariously, amid drenching rains, enervating heat, swarms of insects, yellow fever, thick undergrowth, and assorted other maladies and negatives.

Beginnings

Christopher Columbus was probably the first European to sail along the northern coast of Honduras, during his fourth voyage to the Americas, in 1502. Puerto Caballos, Omoa, and Trujillo were established as towns in succeeding decades, and if the government and mining and agriculture all functioned inland, it was at least necessary to maintain a presence along the coast in order to protect the lifeline of Honduras and neighboring colonies: the Spanish sea lanes.

But even these fortified positions declined in importance after independence. English ships, once forbidden, became the major carriers of trade. And the fractious United Provinces of Central America were no serious opposition to the English navy, or to merchants under its protection who set up outposts along the shore. Honduran military concerns were elsewhere: in the repetitive wars within Central America, and in rebellions within Honduras itself. The coast was ignored.

The Banana Industry

And then bananas happened.

Wild bananas, offshoot of a plant that originated off the coast of Africa, grew in the Honduran lowlands, and a commercial, edible kind came to be cultivated in small quantities, after bananas were first exported from Costa Rica in the 1870s. But the banana business stayed in Costa Rica, from where all the refrigerated shipping was controlled by the **United Fruit Company**.

Around the turn of the century, merchants based in New Orleans began to look at Honduras as an alternative to the United Fruit monopoly. The **Standard Fruit Company** was organized in 1899 to plant and ship Honduran bananas. The fabled Sam Zemurray, an immigrant to New Orleans, founded the **Cuyamel Fruit Company**. United Fruit itself moved in soon after, and eventually bought out Zemurray (who was to come out of retirement later to manage the enlarged company to greater and greater market penetration).

The banana companies cleared land and drained swamps. Port facilities were expanded to receive banana ships, and rail lines were extended to carry the fruit to port from all over the lowlands. With virtually nothing to rely on in the way of governmental services, the banana companies established their own medical and social benefits, and paid wages above local standards to insure a steady supply of labor. Immigrants were attracted to work on the banana plantations, not only from central Honduras, but from the West Indies as well. Lebanese and Syrians became fixtures in commerce. Research centers were established to study new crops, and plant pathogens.

Honduras soon became the largest exporter of bananas in the world, and remained the leader well into the 1940s. Decaying colonial outposts revived, and what was a remote corner of the nation became its most dynamic area. Today, all of the large towns of Honduras after Tegucigalpa are on or near the north coast, along with all of the railroads, and most of the better highways.

Uneven Progress

The progress of the north was not, of course, uniformly smooth. In the 1930s, Panama disease attacked the plantations, and some were abandoned, or planted in Abacá (manila hemp). It was only with rotation of planting areas, the replanting of new strains over a period of time, and the application of large amounts of pesticide that the industry was saved.

Meanwhile, the banana companies, and especially United Fruit, came under attack for meddling in local politics, for restricting their investments to the coastal area, and for not building a railroad to the interior, as once promised. Things came to a head in 1954, when banana workers refused to work on Sundays without double pay. Other salaried workers joined in. So novel was the strike that it became a Central American issue, with the government of Guatemala taking the side of the workers. The dispute was settled with wage boosts and such "radical" benefits as paid vacations. Collective bargaining was legalized, and Honduras had its first effective labor unions.

Over time, Honduras' share of the world banana market declined, as the banana companies expanded to other countries. Eventually, seeking to lessen its exposure, United Fruit diversified into cattle-raising, pineapples and palm-oil production, and began to buy its bananas from independent farmers. But bananas and the banana companies remain the engine that drives the economy of the north coast, and of all of Honduras.

Banana Tours, Indigenous Peoples, and Beaches
All this, of course, is background for the visitor to the north coast, though there *are* aspects of the banana trade and associated ventures that are well worth looking at even for casual visitors. The tour of banana company operations at La Lima, mentioned in the previous chapter, is one example; the Lancetilla Botanical Garden, near Tela, is another.

There are also attractions for the visitor interested in peoples. The **Garífunas**, or Black Caribs, near Trujillo and Tela, and the **Miskito** and **Sumo** and **Paya Indians** along the eastern stretches of coast, are little known, and little understood, outside their territories.

The main attraction of the north coast, however, is **beaches**. There are miles and miles and miles and miles of sandy strip, bordered by palms, as idyllic as any. The most accessible parts, near the ports, have some hotels, and even a few rather good resorts. And if it's isolation that you're after, you do not have to travel very far from any coastal town to find a stretch, away from major roads, where hardly anybody has gone before you.

PUERTO CORTÉS
Puerto Cortés is the major port of Honduras, and one of the largest in Central America, with modern container facilities, stretching for five kilometers along a bay near the mouth of the Chamelecón River. Located 57 kilometers from San Pedro Sula and 303 kilometers from Tegucigalpa, it's a hot and humid place, with more than 100 inches of rainfall every year, though some sea breezes relieve the heaviness of the climate.

Puerto Cortés dates from the first days of the Spanish conquest. An expedition led by Gil González Dávila, in danger of sinking during a storm, jettisoned 17 horses in great secrecy, to avoid revealing to Indians the mortality of the strange animals. Once ashore, the Spaniards called the place Puerto Caballos ("Port of Horses"), and so was it known until 1869. Puerto Caballos was the major port of colonial Honduras, and for Guatemala as well. In came wine and oil from Spain, and out to the metropolis went indigo, silver, cacao and cochineal. When pirate depredations disrupted trade — the city was sacked in 1591 and 1596 — the principal depot for trade was moved up the coast to Omoa, where a major fortification was erected.

The modern city of Puerto Cortés dates from 1869, when it was founded on swampland across the bay from the old Spanish port, as the terminus of a new interoceanic railway. The railway never got very far, but Puerto Cortés prospered anyway, as a banana port, and later as a center for oil refining. Oddly, it was also the base of the Louisiana lottery from 1893 to 1895, after a run-in with the U.S. Post Office.

ARRIVALS AND DEPARTURES

By Bus

Lodging and eating places are limited; consider taking a local bus for the day to Puerto Cortés from San Pedro Sula. Departures are about every 20 minutes until 6 p.m., from 2 Avenida, 4/5 Calles NW (Empresa Impala) and 7 Calle 5/6 Avenidas SW (Empresa Citul). In Puerto Cortés, the Impala station is at 3 Avenida, 3 Calle, tel. 550606. Local buses will take you along the coast to Omoa and Pinalejo (see below).

By Train

A narrow-gauge banana-era train leaves for San Pedro Sula in the morning, and there is daily service to Tela with a change of train. Hurry up and buy your ticket! The railroad has been in a decrepit state since the banana companies switched to trucks and shipping containers, and could disintegrate without prior notice.

By Sea

Puerto Cortés is a port, you are within your rights to insist that it is possible to continue to somewhere by sea. Indeed you can, but patience is required. Large canoes sometimes leave for the Carib towns of Lívingston in Guatemala and Punta Gorda in Belize. This can be a soaking voyage even in mild seas. If you find such a trip, make sure you get your passport stamped before you leave, at the Oficina Regional de Migración on the main square (tel. 550582). The officials there might be aware of any pending departures.

If you're heading up the coast, you'll usually spend less time if you go the long way around, by Copán, to Esquipulas in Guatemala, and then to Puerto Barrios.

ORIENTATION/GETTING AROUND TOWN

For the visitor, Puerto Cortés is almost a dead end. Despite its proximity to Guatemala, there's no way out from here by scheduled transport. Of interest, though, are the old Spanish fort at Omoa, just up the coast, and the beaches nearby. Local buses will take you to the Garífuna villages of **Travesía** and **Baja Mar** just east of Puerto Cortés, or you can walk. There are few facilities.

For use of a beach with services (restaurant, boats, horseback riding), try the **Hotel Playa** or the **Costa Azul**.

Maya Rent A Car has an agency at 3 Avenida, 2/3 Calles, tel. 550064, fax 550218.

WHERE TO STAY

HOTEL MR. GGEER, 2 Avenida, 9 Calle, tel. 550444, fax 550750. 30 rooms. $25 single/$35 double. No, I didn't misspell the name, nor will I explain it. This is a modern hotel, the best in the port, with restaurant and bar, air conditioning, and carpeted rooms with television. A buffet lunch is available most days.

Around Puerto Cortés, you'll find pleasant beaches along the road to the west. And not far from downtown, in the opposite direction from the port, there's one acceptable hotel, the **COSTA AZUL**, tel. 552260, fax 552262, at the El Faro beach area, $45 single/$50 double.

HOTEL PLAYA, Barrio Cienaguita, tel. 551105 or 550453, fax 552287. 25 rooms. $45 single/$50 double.This hotel is on the outskirts of Puerto Cortés, four kilometers toward Omoa, then half a kilometer down a side road. Rooms in motel-style low-lying wings, practically on the water, have hardwood panelling, t.v., air-conditioning, phone, and a double and single bed; and there are larger apartments. Landscaping and public areas are somewhat harsh in aspect.

WHERE TO EAT

Two restaurants in Puerto Cortés have no unexpected surprises for your tummy. **El Torito** ("The Little Bull") specializes in red meat, and **Playa Azul** ("Blue Beach") serves sea creatures.

PRACTICAL INFORMATION

Banks include Bancahsa, Banco Atlántida(2 Avenida, 3/4 Calles), Banco de Occidente (4 Calle, 2/3 Avenidas) and Lloyds Bank (2 Avenida, 3 Calle).

OMOA

Omoa dates from late in the colonial period, when the captain-general of Guatemala ordered the founding of a new port, in 1752. The purpose was not only to protect insecure Spanish sea lanes and control smuggling, but to halt the advance of the British, who already had outposts in Belize, the Bay Islands, and at Black River (Río Tinto) in Mosquitia.

Situated east of the mouth of the **Motagua River**, at a deep harbor, Omoa was well situated to serve not only the commerce of indigo from Guatemala, but of silver from Honduras as well, and it remained the major port on the coast for many years.

A major port required a major defense, and in 1759, work was started on the construction of the **Castillo de San Fernando (Castle of San Fernando)**, named for the saint of King Ferdinand VI of Spain, who ordered its construction. The task was monumental. With no suitable building materials nearby, stone was brought from Santo Tomás de Castilla on the Bay of Amatique in Guatemala. As Indian laborers died off, they were replaced by black slaves. Omoa became known as the graveyard of Honduras. By 1775, the castle was considered complete.

It was also ready to be attacked.

In 1779, Spain was again at war with England, this time as an ally of the newly independent United States. On October 16, Omoa was assaulted from land and sea by a mixed English force of regular troops, Baymen from Roatán, and Sambo, Miskito and Carib allies. After four days the fortress fell, and with it, several hundred prisoners, along with two ships full of cargo. In November, Spanish forces mounted a counter-siege, and managed to oust the invaders, frustrating a British plan to control the coast and drive on through Nicaragua.

Omoa stood unchallenged thereafter, functioning as a gateway for trade, though the British managed to dig in at less defended points on the coast. Eventually, Omoa lost its importance as a port, and the fortress was used for a time to house political prisoners. Until well into this century, it served as the nation's foremost penitentiary. Despite its age, the fortress of San Fernando, solidly built, remains in excellent condition. Triangular in shape, it is roughly 200 feet on a side, with walls 12 feet thick and 18 feet high.

Offshore, ships are known to have foundered with Spanish treasure, and at least one wreck with a trove of gold coins was found, in 1972.

ARRIVALS AND DEPARTURES
By Bus
Local bus service is available on **Transportes Omoa** from the center of Puerto Cortés to Omoa and the beaches nearby. There are other companies operating directly to the center of Omoa only.

VISITING THE FORT

The **Fortress of Omoa**, 70 kilometers from San Pedro Sula, is open to visitors weekdays from 8 a.m. to 4 p.m., Saturday and Sunday from 9 a.m. to 5 p.m. A nominal admission charge is collected at the visitors center alongside, an old building with displays that include maps, illustrations regarding Honduran history, cannon, cannonballs, and an anchor. If you insist on taking a camera into the fortress, *they* will insist in turn on collecting a fee of about $5.

The fortress is *massive*, and yet, oddly, it has today the air of a blinded giant, surrounded as it is by pasture and banana fields. A utilitarian work, it is bare of decorative detail, topped by ramparts, with a lower outer wall with corner turrets.

Arched chambers line the interior courtyard, some of them replastered and restored. Certain of the chambers were used as lodgings by Spanish officials, others as kitchens, a chapel, a prison, a gunpowder store. One contains hundreds of cannonballs.

Visitors can walk on the ramparts, where rusting cannon lie, and look out over the fields toward the now-somewhat-distant sea.

Note: Be aware that most of the Fortress of Omoa is unrestored, and conditions are not up to those at tourist sites in countries that have more experience in handling visitors. Restrooms are filthy. Beggars and car-watchers grope tourists. There are no refreshment facilities. However, Omoa is a potential gem, and things can only get better.

Adjoining the fortress is **Centeno Lagoon**. Variations in water level, or perhaps seismic movements, cause its waters to turn sulfurous during the dry season, poisoning many fish.

WHERE TO STAY AND WHERE TO EAT

HOTEL ACANTILADOS DE OMOA (Caribbean Cliff Marine Club), P. O. Box 23, Chivana, Omoa, tel. 551461 (526182 in San Pedro Sula), fax 551403. 18 units. Visa, Master Card.

New and attractive stone-and-stucco cabanas facing the sea on a grassy hillock dotted with pines and bushes. Each unit has a porch and hammocks. There is no pool, nor television, but this is the best hotel in the area, with air-conditioned rooms, private beach, bar, and restaurant. Rates range from about $40 for a unit with a queen and single bed, to $60 for a room with two double beds and refrigerator, to just over $100 for a cottage with two bedrooms and space to sleep eight or more persons. Discounts are available midweek.

The hotel, about four kilometers east of Omoa, is part of a recreational complex, and available on site are a convenience store, marina, disco, fishing and other rental boats, and a couple of watering holes and a second restaurant.

Under development is **Centro Ecoturístico La Bambita**, a 325-hectare tropical forest area for hiking, horseback riding, birding and wildlife observation.

If you're just in the area for a day to visit the fortress at Omoa, the **restaurant** here is probably your best bet for a meal. They have large breakfasts for up to $4 (for steak and beans), but the specialty is seafood, at $7 and under for shrimp or fish in assorted preparations. Sunset views are provided at no charge.

Right in Omoa are several inexpensive pensions, the **TULIA**, the **PUERTO GRANDE** and the **CENTRAL**, none of which can be considered "tourist-class," but they'll do if you're on a budget, at $10 or less for a single or double room.

Aside from Acantilados, mentioned above, the safest places to eat near Omoa are the stands on the beach, which offer fried fresh fish and Carib-style conch-and-coconut soup for a couple of dollars and up.

EXCURSIONS

Southwest of Omoa, at **Pinalejo**, is the former residence of President Miguel Paz Baraona, now a small museum. Daily hours are 8 a.m. to 5 p.m.

TELA

Fifty kilometers east of Puerto Cortés, and one kilometer off the main Progreso-La Ceiba highway, **Tela** is a banana port of clapboard houses that give it something of the aspect of a Far West frontier town. The beaches are attractive, and though the waters are not as crystalline as those off the Bay islands, and there are some currents, they are as nice as you'll find on the coast. In fact, there are rather ambitious plans to take advantage of the area's tourist potential with new resorts, to the dismay of many who like things just as they are.

A spur of mountains rises to 2000 feet just inland, backed by the higher peaks of the **Nombre de Dios** range that forms the southern boundary of Atlántidadepartment.

Tela was, for a time, the principal port of the United Fruit Company. But Panama disease and the relocation and rotation of banana plantings led to Tela's decline. The banana company residential compound has been converted into a resort, and the former United Fruit Company experimental station is now a unique botanical garden. But you can still see ships being loaded with bananas at the Tela pier. The western, "modern" side of town is known as **New Tela**, or Tela La Nueva.

ARRIVALS AND DEPARTURES
By Bus

From San Pedro Sula, take a bus from the Tupsa station, 2 Avenida,

5/6 Calles SW, for Progreso, and change there for a bus into Tela; or take a La Ceiba bus to the Tela junction, and a taxi into town (less than a dollar for the taxi ride).

Buses leave from the terminal two blocks east of the main square in Tela. Service to La Ceiba is every hour or more frequently from 4:30 a.m. to 7 p.m.; to Progreso, every half hour from 5 a.m. to 6 p.m. These are local buses, and in either case, the ride takes about 90 minutes.

For San Pedro Sula, take a Progreso bus, and change there. For Tegucigalpa, pick up a bus in San Pedro Sula. There is also slow through service to the capital from La Ceiba.

By Train
Slow trains operate daily to Puerto Cortés and, with a change, to San Pedro Sula.

WHERE TO STAY
VILLAS TELAMAR, P. O. Box 47, Tela Nueva, tel. 482196, fax 482984. 120 rooms. From $57 single/$65 double for rooms, $97 to $175 for villas with up to four bedrooms and eight beds. U.S. reservations, tel. 800-742-4276. Visa, Master Card, American Express, Diners Club. Children up to 12 no charge.

Much advertised, Villas Telamar is a resort, but in an off-beat kind of way, more like a sheltered residential enclave for banana-company families, which is what, in fact, it once was. It's clean and adequate and a good deal, though not an elegant destination – you won't find the carefully tended luxuriant tropical vegetation of some Bay Islands resorts, for example, nor crass diversions from pure relaxation.

Accommodations are in clapboard cottages set above ground on stilts to catch the breeze, surrounded by picket fences. Rooms have air conditioning, and you have the option of choosing an apartment with kitchenette, or a bungalow with up to eight beds and kitchen. Rates vary by type of accommodation, and how close you are to the water.

Facilities for all members of the family include two pools, tennis courts, an honest restaurant (grilled fish and shellfish, mainly), white sand beach with orderly rows of palms, golf, play areas, and a small, offbeat zoo, with felines, crocodile, toucans, and monkeys, among others.

This is a good place to catch the air of romance of old-time tropical travel, not luxurious in the modern sense (there are no uniform rooms with wall-to-wall carpeting, for example) but civilized, with the necessary amenities and details, and class: highly polished hardwood floors, towering ceilings and equally towering potted plants, wicker and rattan and mahogany furnishings, ample staff . . . ahh . . .

In addition to tennis on-site, fishing, golf and water skiing can be arranged. Horses are kept in Telamar's stables.

SAHRA'S BOARDING HOUSE, on the beach in the old part of Tela (Tela Viejo). Simple rooms with sea views for about $3 per person.

HOTEL MAR AZUL. $15 double. Located a block from the main square opposite the Texaco station. Clean, fans in room, a good budget hotel.

NUEVO HOTEL PUERTO RICO, on the beach, has air-conditioned rooms for $25 to $35 double, with higher rates for sea view accommodations.

Other lodging places are the **MARABU INN**, near the bridge on the road to Villas Telamar in Tela La Nueva (New Tela, the suburban-appearing section west of downtown, 10 rooms, $6 per person); and the **HOTEL TELA**, downtown (Calle José Trinidad Cabañas, tel. 482150), 15 rooms, $9 per person).

HOTEL SHERWOOD, Avenida Guatemala, tel. 482416, fax 482294. 14 rooms. $18 to $30 single/$23 to $40 double. Master Card. Beachfront rooms with telephone, cable t.v., air-conditioning, bar and restaurant.

HOTEL ATLÁNTICO, Av. Nicaragua, tel. 482202. $10 per person, or $30 with air conditioning. Beachfront hotel.

HOTEL TURICENTRO LANCETILLA, Progreso road, tel. 482007. $20 double or triple. An option if you have a car, located about one kilometer before Laguna de Tela.

WHERE TO EAT

The **Marabu Inn**, near the beach on the way to Telamar, has, beyond any dispute, the best restaurant in town, open for lunch and dinner. The fare is mainly seafood, all of it fresh. There are assorted basic eateries around the main square and beach, and fast-food places in New Tela.

PRACTICAL INFORMATION

There are several **banks**, including **Bancahsa**, on Calle José Trinidad Cabañas, and **Banco Atlántida**, on the same street, at the corner of Avenida Guatemala.

Near Tela

LANCETILLA EXPERIMENTAL STATION

Just south of Tela is the **Lancetilla Experimental Station**, a wonderland of tropical effusiveness and variety. United Fruit established this center in 1926, as part of a program to diversify its plantings in Central America.

The amphitheater of hills around the Lancetilla site protects it from the worst extremes of tropical weather, while the elevated situation provides natural drainage for the copious amounts of water that drop from the sky and flow from the surrounding mountains. By the time the property was turned over to the government of Honduras in 1974, following extensive hurricane damage and rising costs, over a thousand varieties of plants had been established. Some of them were notable success stories. The African oil palm has supplanted bananas on many United Fruit plantations; and eucalyptus and teak have also shown themselves to be comfortable here.

But the longtime director of the gardens, famed botanist Wilson Popenoe, to whom they are dedicated, did not limit plantings to crops with commercial potential. Ornamental plants have also been an important feature from the beginning, and these, in turn, attract a great variety of birds.

ARRIVALS AND DEPARTURES

To reach Lancetilla, take the road from Tela out to the San Pedro Sula highway. The Lancetilla turnoff is about a kilometer out of Tela. Follow the dirt road for three and a half kilometers to the entrance. It's also a rather pleasant walk from Tela of about an hour.

LANCETILLA'S TREES AND PLANTS

Among the many, many species of trees at Lancetilla:

Mahogany, which occurs naturally in the surrounding hills, is notably non-gregarious: one mahogany tree is isolated from the next in the forest or on a plantation. Mahogany wood is used for carving, and for furniture.

Teak, also used for furniture and dishes.

Bamboo plants, examples of different types gathered from all over the world. Some are more than 50 years old, and over 50 feet tall.

Nutmeg trees, which come as male-female pairs.

Cinnamon trees in several varieties.

Strychnine trees, which you cannot even touch without serious consequences, including, possibly, death. If you go out in the morning, you can see the bodies of birds that pecked at strychnine trees and dropped dead on the spot. Only certain ants can consume this tree.

A tree native to Africa produces a fruit that can be eaten only during four days a year, when cyanide compounds are absent. The rotting fruit is deadly. (Could this be the original forbidden fruit?)

Another tree produces a delicious fruit after 35 years of growth, under the best of conditions — obviously not a candidate for commercial plantations.

I'm also told that there are coca plants in the park, which you might recognize by the parallel veins in their leaves.

The orchid collection can also be viewed, and plants are available for purchase. Check import regulations before leaving home, or else pass up this opportunity.

Everything at Lancetilla is labeled with color-coded tags: *yellow* for ornamental, *red* for fruit, *green* for timber, and *black for poisonous.*

HOURS

The garden is open from 7:30 a.m. to 3:30 p.m. weekdays, 8:30 a.m. to 4 p.m. on Saturday and Sunday, closed on Monday except for the nursery. You should arrive an hour before closing at the latest in order to see anything.

I recommend that you go in the early morning, about 6 a.m., if you're on foot, in order to beat the heat, and to see all the birds that congregate in the trees along the way, toucans and many other parrots, motmots, oropendulas, and the Central American curassow, among others. There are more than 200 species, in fact, which can be seen in the area and in the park. A checklist is available at the visitors' center.

PRACTICAL INFORMATION

There is a **restaurant** at the entrance of the park, or you can picnic in designated areas. A **map** is given to visitors, but you should look into **guide service** when you arrive. There is no fee for a tour, but a tip is appropriate. Not all guides speak English.

SAN JUAN AND TORNABÉ

Several small **Garífuna** villages lie along the coast not far from Tela. **San Juan** is four kilometers to the west, and **Tornabé** is another three kilometers beyond. Both are reached by local bus from Tela.

The Garífunas, or Black Caribs, speak a language all their own, which is said to be of Amerindian origin, though some of their vocabulary can be recognized as coming from Creole English. Their houses are of bamboo and thatch, and blasting out from them is reggae music. In fact, Garifunas walk as if they are dancing. They are interested in visitors, not least to be included in their photos.

If you're lucky, you can join the Garífuna in a meal of conch soup or some other stew-type dish based on seafood. Or, at the very least, buy coconut bread.

Buses for Tornabé leave from Tela as they fill up. The fare is minimal, or you can take a collective taxi from the main square for less than a dollar.

WHERE TO STAY IN TORNABÉ

THE LAST RESORT, P. O. Box 145, Tela, tel. 482591, is a new colony of eight bungalows on the edge of Tornabe, offering one of the few comfortable beach accommodations outside a major town. Managed by a Swiss-and-Honduran couple, the complex has a bar, restaurant, palm-shaded deck, and individual units that sleep up to five persons, equipped with fans and private bathrooms. Water craft (including a catamaran) are available for exploration of the adjacent Micos and Diamond lagoons, and of nearby Punta Sal National Park, and diving and snorkeling can be arranged. The resort also has a van available for excursions to Lancetilla Gardens and other coastal attractions, and to pick up guests in Tela.

PUNTA SAL MARINE NATIONAL PARK

Punta Sal Marine National Park, adjoining the Garífuna villages, is a protected area of beach and sea that includes reefs, wrecks, beaches, swamp, wet savanna, coastal lagoons, and cliffs – a varied combination in a small area. Wildlife in the park includes ducks, manatees, caimans, and various species of monkey. The park stretches inland over more than 400 square kilometers.

Access is on foot or by boat from Tela. There are trails in the most easily accessible sections, and a couple of isolated fishing villages offer supplies in a pinch.

Nearby Laguna de los Micos

On the way to Punta Sal is **Laguna de los Micos**, a lagoon stretching for 15 kilometers along the seaside track. Birders will appreciate the marine avian species, including herons, ducks, swallows and pelicans.

El Triunfo

East of Tela, about seven kilometers, is the village of **EL TRIUNFO DE LA CRUZ,** reached by an unpaved road, site of one of the first Spanish settlements in Honduras. A bus leaves for El Triunfo from one block east of the main square of Tela. Or you can walk out, as you can to other Garífuna villages, along the beach.

In Triunfo de la Cruz is the Caracol beach restaurant, with seafood and cold beverages.

LA CEIBA

La Ceiba, 65 kilometers east of Tela, is **Standard Fruit's** town, a banana port where ships move in, and sailors move about, with all their traditional carousing. Hondurans say that "Tegucigalpa is where we think, San Pedro is where we make money, and La Ceiba is where we have fun." This is the only city in Honduras where Carnival is celebrated in the great fashion of the Caribbean islands. La Ceiba's *carnaval*, nominally in honor of San Isidro, takes place during the third week in May, with dances, parades, beauty queens, floats, and general fooling around.

In the annals of banana exploits, La Ceiba and Standard Fruit are known for developing the giant Cavendish variety of banana to substitute for the gros Michel, which is regularly laid low by Panama disease. Out in the market, Standard is better known by its brand name, **Dole**. Dole pineapples as well as bananas now keep the port busy. For visitors, La Ceiba is the main jumping-off place for the Bay Islands.

ARRIVALS AND DEPARTURES
By Air
Service is provided from **Golosón Airport** west of town (about $2 by taxi) by:

Sahsa, Standard Fruit Company Building, Avenida La República, tel 432030. Service to Tegucigalpa (two flights daily, $55 one way), San Pedro Sula ($45 one way) and Bay Islands, and to Miami, New Orleans and Belize.
• To Roatán *(Bay Islands)*: currently at 6 a.m. and 12:30 p.m. daily; at 7 a.m. only on Sunday; fare $40 each way.

Isleña Airlines, Av. San Isidro at the main square, tel. 430179, fax 432632. To San Pedro Sula (four flights daily), Tegucigalpa (two flights daily), Bay Islands, Puerto Lempira, Palacios.
• To Roatán *(Bay Islands)*: at least five times daily, currently at 6:30 a.m. (except Sunday), 8 a.m., 10 a.m., 2 p.m. and 4:30 p.m.; fare $20 one way.
• To Guanaja *(Bay Islands)*: daily except Sunday at 6 a.m., 12:30 p.m. and 4 p.m.
• To Utila *(Bay Islands)*: daily except Sunday at 6 a.m. and 4 p.m.; fare $15 one way.

Lansa Airlines, Avenida San Isidro by Central Park, tel. 422354. To Bay Islands.
Aerolíneas Sosa, tel. 430884. Flights in coastal region, to Tegucigalpa and Bay Islands in Twin Otters.

By Bus
The bus station is off Calle 11 at Blvd. 15 de Septiembre — go south, then west from the main square. Tupsa buses direct for San Pedro Sula depart every one to two hours from 5:30 a.m. to 5:30 p.m., stopping only at El Progreso. Fare is about $3.
Buses leave about every two hours for Trujillo, from 4 a.m. to 3:45 p.m. Service to Tela is almost continuous, and there are less frequent buses to other regional towns.

By Train
The morning train will take you from San Pedro Sula to Tela. An early afternoon train will take you back.

By Boat to the Bay Islands

If you want to go to Utila, Roatán or Guanaja by boat, head for the pier and ask around for the next boat out, or inquire at the San Carlos bar. Usually, boats leave two or three times a week, and charge $5 or less for the trip. Travel time is four to five hours, depending on the craft. Boats leave when they are full — and you'll learn what "full" really means. As for the crew, you'll see characters with one tooth, and I'm told that a Captain Hook-type is sometimes espied. Some boats go to Roatán only, some stop at Utila or Guanaja. Just let me remind you here that the air fare is reasonable and the flight is short.

ORIENTATION/GETTING AROUND TOWN

La Ceiba, with a population of about 60,000, is low-lying and hot, but, despite its banana-port history, it's a surprisingly pleasant place. Streets are paved, and clean. Breezes blow through. Along the sea is a single great pier, culminating in a lighthouse, and, until repairs are made, severed neatly in two, a hurricane casualty. A canal with clean water cuts through, lined by the shady, broad-crowned *ceiba* trees (silk-cotton, or kapok) for which the city is named.

To me, La Ceiba could be Amsterdam, but for the tropical birds that gather in the morning and **Pico Bonito** (2580 meters, or 8464 feet) towering to the south in the Nombre de Dios mountain range.

Auto Rental
• **Molinari**, Gran Hotel París, tel. 420055 or 432371.
• **Maya Rent A Car**, Hotel La Quinta, tel. 430224.

Tourist Information

Visitors' information is available in the office at 1 Avenida and Avenida San Isidro, near the sea.

WHERE TO STAY

HOTEL COLONIAL, Av. 14 de Julio, 6/7 calles, tel. 431953, fax 431955. 60 rooms. $22 single/$32 double.

A newish hotel with conference facility, sauna and whirlpool (if no swimming pool), rooftop bar, restaurant, and souvenir shop. Rooms have air conditioning, telephone and color television. Safe-deposit boxes available, protected parking. And as the name suggests, decor is wrought iron and dark wood.

GRAN HOTEL PARÍS, Parque Morazán (P. O. Box 18), tel. 432371, fax 432391. 89 rooms. $40 single/$45 double.

The Gran is the oldest of the good hotels in La Ceiba, a secure, three-story office-type building overlooking Ceiba's main square. Rooms are clean and air conditioned, there is a nice, clean pool, and personnel are well trained and helpful; though this is hardly a luxury hotel, and maintenance could be better. Take a room on the pool side, which is quieter. If you miss your connecting flight to the Bay Islands, because of bad weather, delays into the night, or whatever, this is where you'll probably end up. Coffee shop, good restaurant, parking.

HOTEL PARTENON BEACH, Barrio La Isla, Calle de la Barra 12 tel. 430404, fax 430434. 45 rooms. $22 single/$28 to $34 double/$57 in suite. Master Card, Visa.

A modern, new beachfront hotel. Rooms are carpeted, with private bath, air conditioning, television. On-site are a pool, one of the better restaurants in Tela, and car-rental agency. A good value — and rooms without sea view are slightly lower priced. Reliably answers faxed reservations requests — unusual in Honduras!

HOTEL LA QUINTA, tel. 430223, fax 430226. 113 rooms. $30 to $40 single/$36 to $40 double/$50 for four persons.

Booming La Ceiba's most booming hotel is opposite the golf course, about ten minutes from the airport. Recently enlarged, La Quinta consists of motel-style rooms surrounding a pool, each air-conditioned, with carpeting, television, and phone. Some rooms have refrigerators. Construction is workaday, with industrial-style materials, and sparse decoration and detailings to suggest an estate (*quinta*). The restaurant is large, and there are conference facilities and protected parking. Two suites are also available. The beach is ten minutes away, with transportation available from the hotel.

GRAN HOTEL CEIBA, Avenida San Isidro, 5 Calle, tel. 432737. 40 rooms. $25 double. Master Card, Visa. This is a plain, modern hotel with an eighth-floor view terrace, air-conditioned rooms, bar, and coffee shop. Only the name is grand. Second-best in town, centrally located. Rooms have private bath and phones.

HOTEL IBERIA, Avenida San Isidro, 5 Calle, tel. 430401. 44 rooms. $18 single/$25 double. A simple hotel, with rooms facing an interior courtyard (more like an airshaft, bare of vegetation), and some amenities: air conditioned rooms, restaurant, parking area.

HOTEL PRÍNCIPE, 7 Calle between Avenida 14 de Julio and Avenida San Isidro, tel. 430516. 36 rooms. $9 double ($14 air conditioned) This is supposed to be the best of the budget places, according to taxi drivers, but I wouldn't want to spend more than one night here.

Less Desirable Hotels

Other hotels, less desirable, are **HOTEL ITALIA**, Avenida 14 de Julio No. 48, tel. 420150 (54 rooms, some air conditioned, $8 single/$15 double); and **HOTEL LIGERO'S**, Avenida Atlántida, 4/5 Calle, tel.

420181 (26 rooms, $6 single/$10 double).

There are numerous other small and cheap hotels downtown, and along the rail line that leads to the pier.

WHERE TO EAT

Ricardo's, Avenida 14 de Julio at 10 Calle. This could be where you'll have your best meal in Honduras. Owned by a Honduran-American couple, Ricardo's offers air-conditioned seating, or dining on a very nice terrace, decorated with plants and protected from the rain.

There is a variety of seafood, beef and pasta dishes, and a good selection of wines. Service is excellent. For what you get, it's not all that pricey, $10 per person or less.

Partenón Beach, at 12 Calle on the way to the Tela highway, offers Greek-style food. The seafood crepes are excellent.

The **Gran Hotel París** is also said to set a good table.

NIGHTLIFE

For many visitors, and for many Ceibeños as well, night and dancing and drinking are what Ceiba is about.

Among dance halls (locally called *discos*), popular spots include the **Coco View**, in Barrio Potreritos. Music is decidedly Caribbean, including reggae and the punta rock of the local Garifuna people. The dance area is air-conditioned, and patrons are required to leave their shooting irons at the door. (This is a fact, and it is not necessarily the case at other establishments.)

La Costa, along the beach, specializes in salsa and other popular Latin music, and serves light meals. The **Ocean Club**, located where Avenida 14 de Julio meets the beach, is owned by gringos, and as of recently, was not charging admission. Music is Latin and rock, and burgers and under-graduate-style filling foods (spaghetti and meatballs) are served. **El Cayuco** is a dancing shack right at the water's edge, active at almost every hour. Away from the beach, in Barrio La Isla, **Black and White** is popular for all-night dancing, and piñata-busting on Sunday afternoons.

Cover charges of a dollar or so, more on weekends, are collected at most dance halls.

The **San Carlos Bar** (with hotel rooms) is near the Hotel Iberia. Don't forget your cowboy hat and kicker boots. Park your horse in front and flop the saloon doors open.

SHOPPING

Various shops offer wood crafts and the like; one is **El Buen Amigo**. **Deco-Arte**, near Ricardo's Restaurant, has handicrafts and works of art selected with good taste, and of a quality much higher than you'll generally find in Honduras. Unusually, they have crafts from other Latin American countries as well.

Other shops are **El Regalito**, north of the Plaza, and the large **El Buen Amigo** store, which sells maps.

PRACTICAL INFORMATION
Banks
Banco Central de Honduras, Avenida la República, tel. 420622; **Bancahsa**, 9 Calle, Avenida 14 de Julio/San Isidro, tel. 430547; **Banco Atlántida**, Avenida San Isidro, tel. 431008; all these in addition to street money changers on the main square (*parque central*) in front of the Gran Hotel París.

Churches
For English-language services, check the **Episcopal church**, Avenida Morazán 48, tel. 432641.

Gambling
The **Casino Royale** is where you can lose your money.

Insects
For visitors interested in insects, the high point of La Ceiba will be a visit to the **entomology museum** (*museo de entomología*) at the **Regional University Center of the Atlantic Coast** (*CURLA*). More than a thousand specimens are on display, including many, many spectacular butterflies, and a rare homoptera known as the peanut head.

Hours are 8 a.m. to 5 p.m. during the week, and a free bus to the campus leaves every half hour from Manuel Bonilla Park, downtown.

Travel Agencies
For assistance in getting to the Bay Islands, or out of the country, try:
- **Lafitte Travel**, Hotel Iberia, tel. 420115, fax 431391.
- **Caribbean Travel**, Hermanos Kawas building, Avenida San Isidro, tel. 431361, manual fax 431360. Rents houses in Utila and arranges **rafting** trips on the Cuero and Cangrejal rivers. The cost is about $75 per person, including lunch and pickup at your hotel or at the airport. The season runs from October to May, and the guides are from the Rocky Mountain Outdoor Center in Colorado.
- **Transmundo**, Hotel París, tel. 422820.
- **Honduras Tours**, Calle 12, Avenida 14 de Julio, tel 432828.
- **Cambio C.A.**, P. O. Box 2, Trujillo, Colón, tel. 431399 in La Ceiba, specializes in **low-impact nature-oriented trips** (also known as ecotourism). They offer tours to Cuero y Salado National Park (see

below), hikes through rain forest in Pico Bonito National Park to the south of La Ceiba, and arranges rafting on the Cangrejal river. Rates range upward from $60 per person per outing.

Near La Ceiba

As elsewhere along the coast, beautiful and near-deserted beaches lie to the east and west of town.

At **Perú**, a fishing village about 10 kilometers east of La Ceiba, there are roofed shelters with barbecues and picnic tables available for day use, for a nominal fee.

Corozal, a Garífuna beach village about 15 kilometers east of La Ceiba, can be reached by hourly bus. Along the way is **Piedra Pintada** ("Painted Rock"), a greenish-yellow outcrop in an otherwise flat landscape. And there are other fishing villages with attractive and little-visited beaches in both directions from La Ceiba.

Esparta and **El Porvenir**, to the west, aside from their sands, are known for the so-called "crab invasions." In July and August, the creatures race through town in the thousands toward inland destinations.

CUERO Y SALADO NATIONAL PARK

Cuero y Salado National Park, roughly 20 kilometers west of La Ceiba, takes in 85 square kilometers of coastline, river estuaries and navigable canals lined by lush vegetation, and includes the major protected manatee habitat on the Caribbean coast of Central America. Spider, white-faced and howler monkeys, crocodiles and caimans, jaguars and many kinds of small mammals also inhabit the area. Plant species include water lilies an royal palms.

Access to Cuero y Salado is by hand-operated coconut railway cars (*"burras"*) from the village of La Unión, just off the highway – the park includes old coconut plantations, canals dug by United Fruit, and villages. Dormitories, campsites and trails are being developed. Limited sleeping and eating facilities are available at the moment.

For details of current conditions, inquire at the "**Fucsa**" (Cuero y Salado foundation) office in La Ceiba, on 1 Calle at Avenida Atlántida, near the sea, or at **COHDEFOR**, tel. 420800. Fucsa can arrange overnight stays.

Near Cuero y Salado

Catarata del Bejuco ("Vine Falls"), about 15 kilometers southeast of La Ceiba at Las Mangas, cascades 80 meters into a dense vine-laden forest.

Pico Bonito National Park, south of La Ceiba, takes in 8025-foot (2433-meter) Pico Bonito mountain. In addition to high, mountainside tropical forest, the park includes lowlands with mixed deciduous forest (mahogany and Spanish cedar are characteristic trees), as well as jaguars, tapirs, and a wide variety of birds. Access to the park is usually with a guide, and by four-wheel-drive vehicle.

TRUJILLO

Like other coastal ports, **Trujillo** languished between the colonial period and the twentieth century. The city was founded on May 18, 1825, by Francisco de las Casas at Punta de Caxinas, where Columbus had first sighted the mainland on his fourth voyage to the New World. Las Casas named the settlement for his home town in Spain.

Trujillo was the first seat of the bishop of Honduras, and for a time during the colony, was a shipment point for gold. Several forts were erected here to protect against pirates, though the town was intermittently sacked by Henry Morgan, among others, and for a time was abandoned. Late in the eighteenth century, Trujillo was a base for attacks against English trading posts in Mosquitia, to the east.

Remote Trujillo gave refuge to such outcasts as Black Caribs, deported by the British from the West Indies late in the eighteenth century. The one glorious note during the town's long decline came in 1860. The American adventurer William Walker, ousted from power in Nicaragua, supposing that English-speaking Bay Islanders chafing under Honduran rule would lend him support, gathered a new force and captured Trujillo. Britain, concerned about repayment of debts out of port revenues, induced Walker to surrender under a guarantee of safe conduct. In an act of treachery that is largely uncondemned, the British commander turned Walker over to the Hondurans. Walker was promptly shot, and buried in the Trujillo cemetery.

Trujillo saw some revival in the twentieth century as a banana terminal, and decline again as Panama disease hit the nearby plantations. More recently, its fortunes have climbed with the expansion of agriculture in the valley of the **Aguán River**, which flows to the south.

ARRIVALS AND DEPARTURES

By Bus

Buses run about every hour from the main square to La Ceiba.

By Air

Air service is provided by **Isleña Airlines** twice daily, with connections from Tegucigalpa, San Pedro Sula and La Ceiba.

ORIENTATION

Trujillo lies on the south side of a large bay, opposite the bend of the Cape of Honduras. With most of the modern fish-packing and shipping facilities going in at Puerto Castilla, on the opposite shore, Trujillo still maintains some of the romantic atmosphere of its turbulent past.

Visitors can walk through the **fortress of Santa Bárbara de Trujillo**, open daily from 8 a.m. to 5 p.m. The **San Juan Bautista church** was completed in 1809 (though its clock wasn't installed until 1899). The odd folk-Gothic church is worth a view, and the sleepy streets are ideal for strolling.

Trujillo lies about 100 kilometers east of La Ceiba by sea, or 240 kilometers by road, much of it in poor condition but currently being improved. Along the way are the **Balfate falls**. The easiest access is by air from La Ceiba.

WHERE TO STAY

VILLAS BRINKLEY, Barrio Buenos Aires, tel. 444444, fax 444045. 15 units. $52 single/$60 double.

Unexpected all the way out at Trujillo, "The Brinkley" is quite suitable to the old atmosphere of the town, a bay-view complex of cottages in Spanish-colonial architecture on the hills above town, with pool and health-club facilities. Arrangements are made for fishing, boating, horseback riding and diving. Restaurant, bar.

HOTEL CHRISTOPHER COLUMBUS. When complete, this will be the major resort hotel in Trujillo.

AGUA CALIENTE RESORT, Silin, tel. and fax 444249. 14 units. $50 double. A new "turicentro" in the Latin tradition, a pool and roadhouse with overnight accommodations, and a difference. The pools here — for kids and grownups — are fed by natural hot springs, which may or may not have medicinal properties, but which, in any case, are soothing. There are also a whirlpool, playground, mini-zoo, and massage room. The individual cabanas are set in a shallow semicircle, built with industrial-style materials. Each is air-conditioned, has cable television, and comes with two double beds. Grounds are informal, with many native trees left in place. About four kilometers from the beach, American managed. Local tours available. The pools may be visited for the day only for a charge of about $2 to $6, depending on which pools are used, or slightly more with a massage.

TRUJILLO BAY RESORT HOTEL, P. O. Box 22, tel. and fax 444732. 25 rooms. $25 single/$30 double, children no charge. Visa, Master Card. U.S. reservations tel. 615-883-4770.

A new, secure, American-operated hotel located near the airstrip and 90 meters from the beach. Rooms are air-conditioned, with television, and everything is up to U.S. standards, right down to the double-filtered water. Inexpensive and attractive coffee shop. Boats available for rent, and fishing, car rental and diving arranged.

O'GLYNN HOTEL, tel. 444592. $18 single/$25 double. Located in central Trujillo, air-conditioned rooms.
HOTEL TRUJILLO, Calle Cementerio, tel. 444202. $8 single/$14 double.
HOTEL COLONIAL, 12 rooms. $20 single/$30 double. Some rooms are air conditioned, and there is a restaurant.

WHERE TO EAT
There are no particularly recommendable restaurants in Trujillo. Basic eateries along the beach serve fish and breakfasts. One restaurant on the square is air-conditioned.

NIGHTLIFE
For a taste of Garifuna music, the **Black and Night** bar serves up drinks, punta rock and reggae well into the night.

EXCURSIONS
• **Cambio C.A.**, P. O. Box 2, Trujillo, 444044, fax 444045. Specializes in ecologically oriented excursions, including canoe trips in Mosquitia, cultural interchange with the Pech indigenous group (including a native meal and visits with villages elders), and trips to a remote beach. Prices range upward from $55 per person per outing.
• **Turtle Tours**, based at the Hotel Villa Brinkley (tel. 444444, fax 444200), offers tours to Mosquitia and the Río Plátano reserve. A five-night package from La Ceiba, including a night at the Brinkley and flight to Palacios, costs about $500. Or, you can arrange a half-day trip into the tropical forest for about $30, as well as boat tours, snorkeling from remote beaches, and visits to Garífuna villages.

PRACTICAL INFORMATION
Banks include **Banco Atlántida** and **Bancahsa**, both on the main square.

Near Trujillo
Riberas del Pedregal, on the outskirts of Trujillo, is a private, off-beat complex with a collection of pre-Columbian artifacts, some of them found in caves in nearby La Brea. There are also a couple of river-fed swimming ponds. There are several **Garífuna** (Black Carib) villages nearby, clusters of high-peaked, thatched houses. The most easily reached is **Santa Fé**, 12 kilometers west via an unpaved road along the sea.
To the east, off the road to Puerto Castilla, is **Guaimoreto Lagoon**, easily reached on foot, by car or by local bus, surrounded by mangroves, a good spot for birding.

Los Lirios Lagoon, to the south off the highway into town, also has varied bird life. On the northern, seaward side of the lagoon are stretches of nearly deserted beach.

Los Farallones are a rock formation on which waves produce thunderous and frightful sound effects.

Capira y Calentura Biological Reserve, along the road into Trujillo, covers a small forest area that includes two hills overlooking the bay, and includes some remains of ancient Indian cultures. Significant wildlife includes monkeys and macaws.

Piedra Blanca ("White Rock"), east of Trujillo, is said to be perforated by caves, still unexplored.

Important archeological discoveries have been made in the **Cuyamel Caves**, which lie in hills about ten kilometers south of Trujillo. The importance of Cuyamel comes from the virtual absence of artifacts from the pre-Columbian nomadic hunters who lived along this part of the coast of Central America. Elsewhere in Honduras, and to the north, in Guatemala, pre-Columbian civilizations left cities that are in some cases virtually intact.

The appliqué and incised decoration on objects found at Cuyamel indicate a South American origin of the people who frequented the caves. But there are also indications of contact with Mexican and Mayan peoples during pre-Classic times. There is evidence that some of the inhabitants of the region practiced head hunting, and used alcoholic beverages in their rituals.

East of Trujillo

Northeastern Honduras is virtually trackless, barely populated by Miskito Indians along the coast, and Sumos and Payas inland. Sovereignty over much of the area was in dispute between Nicaragua and Honduras, until a 1960 decision of the International Court of Justice set the boundary for once and for all at the **Coco River** (also known as the Wanks, or Segovia). It was only in 1957 that the department of Gracias a Dios was established, taking in much of the region.

Coastal lagoons and rivers are the main transport routes, though a few dirt roads run inland from **Puerto Lempira**, on the Caratasca Lagoon in the far northeast. Only the most basic, frontier type of accommodation is available in Puerto Lempira and the villages along the road to the south. Planes operate regularly to Palacios and to Puerto Lempira, and irregularly to scattered airstrips in the region. It's also sometimes possible to ship aboard a dugout canoe, or simply hike along the bar, though there are many intervening waterways.

The Coco River was a gold-exporting route in the colonial period — gold was mined near the rapids at the source of the river, near the Pacific.

But Spanish presence was usually minimal. **Brus Laguna** (Brewer's Lagoon) and **Black River** (Río Tinto, later Fort Inmaculada Concepción) were British trading posts and forts and timber depots in the nineteenth century. Black River, 25 kilometers from the coast, had a population that approached 4000.

But even after the British were expelled in 1782 there was little interest in the area by the weak central government. Under the remnants of British influence, and foreign missionaries, many of the inhabitants speak English, as well as their native languages. The Miskitos on both sides of the Coco River give allegiance to no government, and many of those from Nicaragua crossed over as refugees after disputes with the Sandinistas.

Inland from the mangroves and swamps of the coast are great stretches of sandy soil covered by Caribbean pine, and exploited in part for timber.

MOSQUITIA

Seeing Mosquitia with a Tour Group

Organized excursions to the forests and tribes of the interior are offered by **Cambio C.A.**, the low-impact travel service based in Trujillo. Among offerings are a visit to the Tawahka, a Sumo group three days' journey from the coast, who have maintained their traditions.

La Mosquitia Ecoaventuras, a younger company than Cambio C.A., also offers ten- to fourteen-day low-impact adventures in Mosquitia, with emphasis on birding, wildlife viewing, and non-intrusive contacts with native peoples. Information is available from La Mosquitia Ecoaventuras, P. O. Box 3577, Tegucigalpa, tel. 370593, fax 379398.

Seeing Mosquitia On Your Own

There are no guarantees about getting into, through, or out of Mosquitia. There are only a few dirt tracks into the region that radiate from Puerto Lempira. Most transport is by water (unscheduled, of course), and hotels and pensions are difficult to find, or non-existent in many localities.

Arriving By Air

Isleña Airlines, in La Ceiba (Av. San Isidro at the main square, tel. 430179, fax 432632) operates at least one flight daily to Puerto Lempira and Palacios along the coast of Mosquitia, fare $35 to $45. Air taxis can also take you to the landing strips in the interior (if you happen to have a contact with a missionary who will put you up).

ORIENTATION

If you arrive in Palacios or Puerto Lempira on your own, you certainly won't be the first gringo adventurer. You can find a room, and there are people who will hire out dories and dugouts for trips along the waterways. You can hike along the beaches from village to village, and rent sleeping space or pitch your tent (above high tide, please). Boats can be found to take you across estuaries, and at the village of Plátano, pilots will negotiate trips of up to several days into the Río Plátano Biosphere Reserve, though you can't expect any mercy when it comes to rates.

Stocks of food in the few stores are limited, so take your own reserve. Insect repellent, water purification equipment, jungle camping equipment, tropical boots, rain protection and plenty of time and tolerance and patience will also come in handy.

Río Plátano Biosphere Reserve covers a huge mass of land from the Caribbean inland to the fringe of Olancho department, where a rising population threatens the survival of primeval forest and the plant and animal species that inhabit the region. Agricultural and hunting activities by settlers are supposed to be controlled within the reserve, but in practice, land is cleared and animals are hunted with little restriction.

Río Plátano reserve includes **petroglyphs**, designs carved into rocks by ancient peoples. The banks of the River Plátano are especially rich in these prehistoric remnants. Other such designs are found in the caves of the Ayasta Canyon in south central Honduras, and cave paintings have been found in Nueva Armenia, south of Tegucigalpa. The Plátano petroglyphs, on riverside boulders, are generally serpentine in appearance, though at least one notable figure, at Walpunbantara, is recognizably an iguana.

A "lost" city called **Ciudad Blanca** is also said to lie within the confines of the reserve, the remains of a vast city built by a mysterious ancient culture. While no individual metropolis has been found, any of the petroglyph sites could well have been the origin of the legend of the lost city. Some consider that the archeological site known as Limonsito is, in fact, the lost White City.

Smaller reserves to the east include **Caratasca**, surrounding much of the Caratasca Lagoon, and the **Río Kruta** reserve, on the border with Nicaragua, where the rare harpy eagle is found.

13. THE BAY ISLANDS

INTRODUCTION

You will have noticed, by now, that the title of this book is **Honduras** *and* **Bay Islands**, not simply "Honduras," or "Honduras in*cluding* the Bay Islands." Aren't the Bay Islands part of the country?

Yes and no.

Legally, constitutionally, formally, administratively, economically and institutionally, the Bay Islands do, indeed, form part of the *República de Honduras*. But more than a stretch of water separates mainland from islands. Mainlanders speak Spanish, while Bay Islanders speak English (sort of). Mainlanders are farmers. Islanders are fishermen and mariners and boatbuilders. Mainlanders are mostly *mestizos*, descended from Spaniards and native Americans. Bay Islanders are largely descended from Africans and Englishmen, from slaves and buccaneers and pirates.

And for the visitor, the Bay Islands are a world removed not only from the mainland, but from everywhere else in the universe, a paradise of beach and rain-forested peaks in the sea, with few telephones, clocks, or cares, and some of the best fishing and diving in the hemisphere.

HISTORY

Before the Spanish came to the Americas, the Bay Islands were most likely populated by Paya Indians. Many old dwelling sites have been identified, and pieces of pre-Columbian ceramic are still occasionally found.

In 1502, Christopher Columbus, on his fourth voyage to the New World, landed on **Guanaja**, which he called Isla de los Pinos (Pine Island).

Discovery, as elsewhere, meant disaster for the natives. Though Columbus came in peace, Spaniards soon after carried off the inhabitants to slave in Mexico and the West Indies. Later, the islands were something of a breadbasket for the Spanish fleet, provisioning ships with fruits, vegetables and meat for the return voyage to Spain.

With their broken topography, swamps, and reefs blocking the approach from the sea, the Bay Islands attracted limited Spanish interest as sites for permanent settlement. But what repelled the Spanish is precisely what attracted buccaneers and pirates. Pirate ships could easily navigate shallow passages to harbors behind the reef, and lie safe from the larger and heavier vessels of the Spanish. And the islands were not far from Trujillo, whence gold was shipped to Spain.

Early English settlers came in peace. The Providence Company colonized Roatán in 1638 with Puritan farmers from Maryland. They called the place Rich Island, cut logwood trees for export, and grew tobacco and indigo, and cassava as a staple. Their colony, possibly located near today's Old Port Royal, lasted four years. In 1642, the Spanish threw out the Puritans, helpless and defenseless as civil war raged in England.

Spain followed a policy of keeping *everybody* out of the islands, so that no food could be grown, no shelter erected, that might be used by enemies. This policy turned many Indians into allies of the English pirates who continued to use the islands, despite the best efforts of the Spanish. A pirate camp at Port Royal was overrun by the Spanish in 1650, and all natives who could be found were exiled to the mainland. But pirates still returned to take on fresh water from island streams, hunt wild pigs, and dry turtle meat. Some say the loot from Morgan's 1671 raid on Panama is buried on Roatán.

Sometimes the borderline between pirate and merchant was hazy. Pirates cut logwood to ship home and sell, and the islands made a perfect base for trading cloth and manufactured goods to the Indians along the coast, in defiance of the Spanish monopoly.

In 1742, the British government moved to take the islands as part of a military campaign against Spain. New Port Royal on Roatán was fortified. Spanish attacks failed to dislodge the British, but diplomacy did the trick. The British evacuated in 1748.

When war between Britain and Spain broke out again in 1779, Roatán became a refuge for woodcutters displaced from the coast. Troops and refugees resisted bitterly at Fort George in 1782, but were obliged to surrender after two days. As many as 500 dwellings are said to have been burned. The fort was destroyed, and the black survivors sold into slavery.

The islands were nearly deserted once again, but not for long. In 1797, Britain marooned 5000 Black Caribs on the Bay Islands. The unfortunates, descendents of Carib Indians and shipwrecked African slaves, had rebelled against British rule on the island of Saint Vincent. Spain, still maintaining a no-go policy, obliged the Caribs to move to the mainland near Trujillo, by that time virtually abandoned due to repeated British attacks; though some managed to stay on at Punta Gorda on Roatan's north shore.

The modern culture of the Bay Islands really dates to Central American independence. After 1821, Central America maintained a garrison in the islands, but the weak, decentralized country was no longer

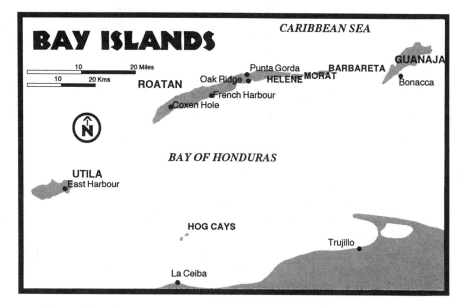

able to defend its territorial claims. White Cayman Islanders, fearful of black domination after the abolition of slavery, began to migrate to the Bay Islands, which some knew from fishing and turtling expeditions.

After 1838, a new wave of black Cayman Islanders began to arrive, as their indentured service during the transition from slavery ran out. The new settlers came into conflict with the Central American garrison, and with the aid of the British superintendent at Belize, packed the soldiers off to Trujillo.

Most of the modern towns in the Bay Islands were established during this period. The islanders built the kind of houses they were familiar with, on stilts, above the range of insects. They lived from fishing and from garden crops.

In 1849, the residents applied to be governed by the authorities in Belize. A local 12-man legislature was established, and in 1852, England formally annexed the Bay Islands. The new British expansion caused a fury, however, especially in the United States, despite the long tradition of British involvement in the islands and along the coast. In 1859, Britain gave in to U.S. pressure, and ceded the islands to Honduras.

For many years thereafter, despite the abolition of English-language schools under Honduran administration, and the settling of small numbers of mainlanders, the islanders were mostly ignored by the distant government in Tegucigalpa, and continued to live lives apart from the mainland mainstream. The Bay Islands developed an export agriculture of coconuts and plantains long before the mainland. When a hurricane destroyed many of the plantations in 1877, many turned to service on U.S. merchant ships.

The Bay Islands Today

Today, many islanders are still merchant seamen and skilled boatbuilders. And fishing, for the dinner table or for the market, remains the most important occupation. Though tourism is fast becoming the mainstay of island life, and migrants from the mainland are becoming a more and more significant part of the population.

ORIENTATION

Located about 60 kilometers offshore, the islands, running in a 125-kilometer arc, are the tips of undersea mountains that extend out from the mainland's Omoa ridge. Their peaks, rising as high as 400 meters (1300 feet), are covered with oak and pine and cedar and dense, broad-leafed undergrowth, and studded with caves and cliffs. Coral reefs, often within swimming distance of shore, virtually surround most of the islands, forming natural breakwaters, and creating ideal, calm pools for diving, fishing, swimming and sailing.

Roatán is the largest of the Bay Islands, with the major towns, though there are also settlements on **Utila** and **Guanaja**. The smaller islands are **Morat**, **Helene** (Santa Elena) and **Barbaret** (or Barbareta). With more than 60 smaller cays offshore, the Bay Islands cover about 92 square miles.

Population

About 22,000 persons inhabit the Bay Islands altogether, about 15,000 on the main island of Roatán, about 5500 on Guanaja, and 1500 on Utila. In addition to fishing and boatbuilding, some make a living harvesting and drying coconut meat, or copra, and many keep gardens of root vegetables, especially cassava. Local cuisine is heavy on fish, of course, but also on coconut, as in coco bread.

Most residents are Protestant and English-speaking and live right along the water. But there have long been a couple of small inland settlements of Spanish Hondurans, at Juticalpa and Corozal on Roatán, where the inhabitants grow corn and beans and live just like mainland farmers.

In recent years, as tourism has presented opportunities not available on the mainland of Honduras, the numbers of Spanish-speaking residents has been rising. Meanwhile, the close-knit, church-centered life of English-speakers has been hard hit by the ways brought not only by visitors from the outside, but also by satellite television, and a government and educational system, once semi-autonomous, that now operate in Spanish and are administered by mainlanders.

ARRIVALS AND DEPARTURES

By Air

Guanaja and Utila have airstrips, while the runway on Roatán can handle jets. Approximate schedules from La Ceiba, San Pedro Sula and Tegucigalpa to the islands are given elsewhere. From Tegucigalpa, the round-trip fare to the islands is about $130; from La Ceiba, about $40. Runways on the islands have no electric lighting.

If there is an evening delay in your connection, you could be "forced" to overnight on the mainland at San Pedro Sula or La Ceiba before continuing to the islands the next morning. If you have a confirmed connection, the airline picks up the tab, and you get to see more of Honduras than you might have otherwise.

Private Planes must land and clear customs first on the mainland, most conveniently at La Ceiba.

By Boat

Yachties and others of that ilk can consult the *Cruising Guide to the Honduras Bay Islands*, available from Wescott Cove Publishing Co., P O Box 130, Stamford CT 06904. Fuel is available at the larger towns. Seas are generally choppy, with steady south-southeast winds of about 15 knots.

If you don't sail down, you can find a sailing vessel for hire in the Bay Islands. Start your search by contacting **Roatán Charter**, Box 877, San Antonio, FL 33576, tel. 800-282-8932, fax 904-588-4158. One of the vessels they represent is the 46-foot sloop *Honky Tonk*, currently for hire at $900 per person and up on a weekly basis, including beach barbecues and nights spent in ports and coves throughout the Bay Islands.

Passenger boats operate to the Bay Islands several times a week from La Ceiba (see page 162), though it's generally more convenient to fly.

Bay Islanders are famed boat builders. Many craft are *dories*, elongated and similar to sailboats, and now often fitted with rudders, though traditionally they have had none; and dugout *cayucas*, canoe-like vessels made from hollowed logs.

Mainland Excursions

Since the Bay Islands are the principal tourist destination in Honduras, a whole network of inland treks, tours and ventures has developed as adjuncts to diving packages. Samples of add-ons that can be booked through hotels in the Bay Islands, or when arranging your dive package:

• Copán ruins, from $125 day trip, from $160 overnight.
• Banana plantation tour, from $40 day trip, $65 overnight.
• Trekking in Cusuco Cloud Forest, with camping, $435 for three nights.
• River adventure in Mosquitia, with camping, $810 for eight nights.

SPORTS AND RECREATION

DIVING

What can you say about the diving? First, diving is what the Bay Islands are most known for. Second, the water is warm. Temperatures range between 79 and 84 degrees Fahrenheit (26 degrees to 29 degrees C). Third, underwater visibility is good. The water is not as clear as in Bonaire, but it is crystalline nevertheless. Visibility can vary with the weather. The sea is calm within the fringing reefs, and there are practically no drift currents along the south side of the islands.

And if you like **coral reefs**, you'll find the corals around the Bay Islands spectacular, intact, and very much alive (coral can get silted up and damaged by hurricanes, among other things).

The islands are each surrounded by coral reefs, from 20 to 40 feet down. Almost all of the coral types specific to the Caribbean can be found in the reefs off the Bay Islands. One of the most unusual and characteristic types is pillar coral, which reaches several feet in length. Others are elkhorn, star, lettuce and brain coral. And there are multi-hued rope, vase, finger and barrel sponges, flittering sea fans, and schools of rainbow colored fish, indigo hamlets, parrot fish, rock hinds, chromis and others that favor the reefs, seahorses, sea urchins, anemones, polyps, and more ordinary snappers and jacks and groupers and sea turtles. In deeper waters are manta rays.

The underwater landscape features wandering clefts and caverns, sheer walls, cracks, tunnels, caves and ledges, reverse ledges, and dropoffs of 100 to 200 feet. Walls start as little as twenty feet under the surface, which affords more natural light than is usually available in wall diving.

Famous sites include **Mary's Place**, off Brick Bay, a huge crack in the ocean floor (called the Grand Canyon of wall diving, and currently off limits because of over-visitation); **Bear's Den**, a formation that in earlier times was a waterfall, until the shifting of continental plates submerged it; the **Enchanted Forest**, planted with black coral and sea fans; **West End Wall** and **CoCo View Wall** off Roatán, and **Captain's Crack**, off Guanaja.

Wrecks include the ***Prince Albert***, off CoCo View Resort on Roatán, and the ***Jado Trader***, off southern Guanaja, and there are proprietary wrecks near some of the resorts. Others, reputed to be from colonial times, are only discussed in whispers.

I'm told there are few sharks, and, for what it's worth, I haven't seen any.

Most of the resorts that offer diving make life easy. The diving equipment and compressors are on the dock, right at the diving boat. There is nothing to lug, and no loss of time. Diving sites are usually no more than 20 minutes away. Many hotels have interesting coral formations and submarine landscapes within easy range of shore dives.

DIVING HIGH POINTS

Major points to consider about diving in the Bay Islands:
- *Decompression chamber available (at Anthony's Key Resort)*
- *Wall diving a major feature*
- *Several wrecks to dive*
- *Easy diving from shore – unlimited at a number of resorts*
- *Excellent variety of coral and fish*
- *Lowest package diving prices in the Caribbean*
- *Diving available on opposite shores of Roatan – sheltered diving off the south when winds are up on the north side.*
- *Live-aboards available*
- *Minimal travel time to dive sites—minutes in many cases.*
- *Many small resorts and representative agencies willing to answer visitors' questions before money is put down*

DIVING LOW POINTS

- *Sand flies are a nuisance on shore*
- *Limited entertainment and other non-diving resort amenities*
- *Limited dive shops outside of resorts*
- *Diving is built into most rates. Non-diving companions get little or no discount*

Waters are generally clearest for diving during the periods when there is the least rain: mid-February to mid-September. The onset of hurricane season and winds can churn up the waters during the late months of the year. But the same conditions help to distribute the nutrients in the water, and encourage growth of undersea life.

You *must* be certified to dive at Bay Islands resorts. If you're not, you can arrange to take courses for PADI or SSI certification.

Airlines have the usual baggage limits of about 45 pounds or two pieces. Sahsa will take an additional bag of diving equipment for a small charge.

Diving Live-Aboards

Terrific diving is within easy reach of almost any hotel on the Bay Islands, even if you just wade out from shore. Absolutely superb diving, at sites where the sea creatures are not yet accustomed to seeing masked humans, is a little farther out. To reach a number of such sites requires dragging your gear to the dock every morning, setting out for a long ride, returning for lunch, setting out again, and returning to your hotel, followed by repeated packing up and unpacking as you move on to your next diving base.

Or, you can live aboard your dive boat, and roll off the dive platform shortly after you roll out of bed.

Live-aboards come at a price. A week-long trip, with six days of diving, runs from $1000 to $1500, based on double occupancy. And the diving can be tougher. You'll spend more time in the water, probably at greater depths than if you dive from a shore base, sometimes in uncharted seas. Medical help in an emergency is *not* at hand.

But live-aboards also come with amenities: sundecks, video libraries for evening entertainment, good-sized rooms, and often photo-processing facilities. And since the diving is usually limited only by decompression tables and safety considerations, the cost *per dive* can turn out to be even more reasonable than from a land base. As many as five daily dives are scheduled.

Here are some of the live-aboards currently operating in the Bay Islands:

The *Bay Islands Aggressor*, 110 feet, carries 18 passengers in air-conditioned cabins (two to four persons each). Showers and toilets are shared. Features include sun-and-shade deck, video entertainment, bar, equipment and underwater cameras for rent, and on-board slide processing. Certification and specialty courses are available. The rate is about $1400 per person for a weekly trip with five-and-a-half days of diving throughout the islands and the Hog Cays, *with discounts available from September to February*. Resort and certification courses are available on board. Contact **Aggressor Fleet**, P O Drawer K, Morgan City, LA 70381, tel. 800-348-2628 or 504-385-2416, fax 504-384-0817. For information within Honduras, contact **Romeo's Resort**, tel. 451127, where the boat docks.

The *Isla Mia*, 75 feet, takes 14 divers in seven air-conditioned cabins, each with private bathroom, to sites around Roatan, Morat and Barbareta. Also on board are sundecks, slide-viewing tables, video player, two compressors, and a small library.The ship avoids using anchors on reefs, and offers naturalist seminars during selected weeks. The cost of an eight-day, seven-night package with unlimited diving is $1000 at any time of year, slightly more during seminar weeks. Guests are expected to be certified, in order to avoid excessive guiding. For information, contact **Isla Mia**, 1315 Post Office St., Galveston, TX 77550, tel. 800-874-7636 or 409-765-1776, fax 409-765-1775. In Roatan, contact the **French Harbour Yacht Club**, tel. 451478, fax 451459.

The *Maid'en Desert* is a 60-foot air-conditioned sailing ketch with just three double rooms and compressor, available at a weekly rate of $900 to $1250 per person. For bookings, contact **Roatán Charter**, Box 877, San Antonio, FL 33576, tel. 800-282-8932, fax 904-588-4158.

Costs

Diving in the Bay Islands is almost always part of a package included with your hotel booking, and if you compare prices, you'll find that a week of diving will cost several hundred dollars less than in Belize. Partly, this is because Honduras is a real country, that grows its own food and provides many of the services that must be imported for visitors elsewhere in the Caribbean.

If you're not in the Bay Islands on a dedicated dive vacation, here's an a la carte price list for services and rentals at Reef House Resort, which are representative of the *high end* of what you'll pay throughout the area: $25 per single tank dive, $35 per two-tank dive, $30 per night dive, $75 for a resort scuba course, $350 for full certification. Daily tank rental $7; regulator $10; buoyancy compensator, $8; masks, fins and snorkel, $7; dive light, $5.

What to Bring

When resorts talk about inclusive dive packages, they generally mean that air tanks, weights, guides and boat transport to dive sites are provided. You should bring your own regulator with tank pressure gauge, buoyancy compensator, and depth gauge, along with fins, masks, and, optionally, booties, gloves (to protect against abrasions), underwater light and dive watch. Anything you don't bring can be rented.

And don't forget your certification card.

FISHING

This is the how most resident islanders make their livings, either directly or indirectly. Traditionally, fish have been caught and kept fresh in pens made of closely placed stakes driven into the shallow seabed offshore, then transported to markets in La Ceiba and elsewhere on the mainland. But commercial catches of lobster and shrimp for export are becoming increasingly important.

Sport fishing isn't quite as developed as in some other Caribbean locales, though not for the lack of resources. Among the species found in the shallows near shore are bonefish and permit, which are caught all year, and grouper, snook, and all sorts of snapper, including yellowtail and red. Tarpon has a more limited season, generally from February through June.

Deeper waters have mackerel (king and Spanish), bonito, blackfin tuna, and wahoo, kingfish, and, seasonally, marlin, while jewfish are caught around the Hog Cays. Commercially fished are shrimp and lobster, red snapper, and conch ("conk," or sea snail), a somewhat tough species that is consumed locally but not much exported.

Tournaments

An annual **billfishing tournament** operates out of the Fantasy Island Resort and Marina on Roatán, usually at the end of September or beginning of October. The fee for participation has recently been just $50 per angler, and the winning fish in 1992 was a 400-pound marlin. Boat rentals can be arranged with registration. For information, contact **Fantasy Island** at tel. 800-676-2826 in the U.S., or 451222 on Roatan.

Lodging and Fishing Packages

Hotels offering fishing facilities usually quote a price inclusive of boat, equipment, and guide. See hotel listings in the pages that follow.

Fishing Gear

Choice of equipment can be limited, however. For bonefishing in shallow waters, a light spinning rod is suitable, with 200 yards of four- to six- pound test line (or eight-pound line, according to some anglers), and light lures. Heavier line and tackle are suitable for casting from shore, or for trolling. Take an assortment of lures to suit different conditions, jigs (hair, nylon, white, yellow, pink), hook sizes 1-0, and tipped leader 20- to 30-pound test, 18 to 20 inches long.

PRACTICAL INFORMATION
Beasts, Bugs, Bites, and Bonks

There are no poisonous snakes or dangerous wild animals in the islands, though sandflies ("no-see-ums") are placed by some in the latter category. I should say that this is without justification. There are some sandflies, but if there is even the slightest wind, they will not be a problem. On a still day, it would be hard to stay for very long on the beach unless you have insect repellent, so come prepared with your favorite brand. Residents place their houses on stilts above the level of molestation.

Hikers and treasure hunters venturing into the hills need have no particular concerns about wildlife, such as deer, lizards, rabbits, and parrots.

Don't nap under coconut palms on the beach. Plummeting coconuts can cause serious injury or death. In a storm, do not shelter under a coconut palm. Ample fallen palms are evidence that they don't have much of a supporting root structure.

Costs

Things cost more in the Bay Islands than elsewhere in Honduras, but it's still possible to live cheaply in the towns. Everything depends on where you stay. At Anthony's Key, the price of a beer is triple the price at the best hotel in La Ceiba. But this is not how things are everywhere.

Island Talk

Open belly? It's just how you say diarrhea in the local language, which is English, sort of, with many, many modifications. Bay Islands sayings have been collected in a fascinating illustrated booklet entitled *Wee Speak*, by American resident Candace Wells Hammond, which you'll find on sale here and there. Black Caribs, or Garifunas, speak their own language, and a perfectly intelligible version of English.

Standard English is also understood and tolerated. And since the Bay Islands have been part of Honduras for the last hundred years, you'll find that some people speak Spanish as well, though residents of Hispanic origin usually have to learn some English in order to get along.

Land

Oddly, the entire area of the Bay Islands is classified as urban, which, among other things, allows foreigners to own land along the water (prohibited in rural areas). Real estate operators have moved in, in a small way, and you can buy a piece of the islands from one of them. Can time-sharing be far away?

Phones and Fax

Now that phones have reached the islands, the easiest way to reach any hotel is to dial direct. Mail is slow, telegrams are fast and expensive. Many hotels have fax machines.

Souvenirs

Avoid picking, carrying, harvesting, buying, or otherwise acquiring to take home the following: coral (black or otherwise), fish, shells, and pre-Columbian artifacts (in plentiful supply, and commonly known as *yaba-ding-dings*). It's either illegal to take these out of Honduras without a license, or illegal to bring them back to your own country, or both, and it doesn't help to conserve what you came to see and do. This leaves t-shirts and hardwood carvings.

Weather

If you like rain, come in October or November or, with less certainty, in December — 50% of the yearly total falls just in these three months. If you have just a week of vacation, and don't want it spoiled by rough seas or airplane delays, come from January to September. The best months are March to August.

Expect to see some rainfall at any time of year, as storms blow through the Caribbean. Average rainfall in October and November is about 450 mm (almost 18 inches). The lightest months are March, April and May, with under 75 mm (less than three inches) of rain. January and February

— when the islands are heavily visited — see moderate rainfall of about 200 and 125 mm (8 and 5 inches) respectively. Temperatures are generally perfect in the Bay Islands. The yearly average is about 27.5 degrees C (81 degrees F). The coolest month is January (25.8 degrees C, 78 degrees F), the warmest month is August (28.8 degrees C, 84 degrees F). With a sea breeze usually blowing, it's not hard to take.

On the average, a serious hurricane strikes every ten years.

The Islands of the Bay

For no particular reason, I propose to take the islands from west to east across the Caribbean.

UTILA

Utila is the nearest of the Bay Islands to the mainland, just 35 kilometers from La Ceiba. Measuring about 14 kilometers east to west, and almost five kilometers across, it is the island that sees the fewest visitors. Mostly this has to do with the island's geography. It is low-lying, something like an atoll, and the central portion, taking up a good two-thirds of the surface, is mangrove. A fringe of dry land surrounds this near-lake. Most of the high ground is at the east end — the absolute high spot is 200-foot Pumpkin Hill in the northeast, a walk of less than an hour from town. A canal through the mangrove bisects east-central Utila.

Utila is where most of the white Cayman Islanders settled after 1830, and to this day, most of the inhabitants are fair-skinned.

You don't find any big resorts on Utila, though you can see the foundations of a resort that was planned for a hilltop. Utila is difficult to reach, and has a small population. There are **no beaches**.

But these "disadvantages" for big-time tourism make Utila a great place to go and rest and hang out, away from the crowds, and from touristy expectations. People are friendly, and there are small stores, bars and restaurants where you can get to know them. Prices are lower than elsewhere.

There is one road, running a few hundred yards from the airport to East Harbour (identified on maps as the town of Utila), and two to three cars have been occasionally reported on it. Other settlements are on Pigeon Cay and Suc-Suc Cay, offshore to the southwest, connected to each other by an over-water walkway; and at West End. Most of the patch coral reef near the island is between these two places — the small offshore cays are surrounded by coral, making for good diving. There are some good walls and slanting reefs, though most dive sites are farther from shore than those off Roatan.

ARRIVALS AND DEPARTURES

Arriving by Boat

Boats run irregularly from La Ceiba on the mainland to Utila and to the other islands, and you can inquire for captains at the San Carlos bar in La Ceiba or at the tourist information office. But as I have said elsewhere, it is more certain to take the plane.

Arriving by Air

Isleña (tel. 430179) schedules flights to Utila daily except Sunday at 6 a.m. and 4 p.m. from La Ceiba, in Canadian-built Twin Otter short takeoff craft, or in DC3s, for a fare of $15 each way. Return flights are at 6:30 a.m. and 4:30 p.m. When demand warrants, Isleña operates an air bridge, ferrying passengers to Utila as the plane fills up.

Passengers on diving packages will be met at the airport. A truck meets incoming planes and will take you into town for $2 or so, or you can walk in — it's under a mile.

Departing by Boat

Boats can be hired to continue to Roatán; there is no current scheduled service. Otherwise, fly back to La Ceiba.

WHERE TO STAY

TRUDY'S, East Harbour, tel. 453195. 20 rooms, $30 double. Owned and operated by Miss Trudy herself. Don't expect luxury, but this is a clean, pleasant, homey place, within walking distance of the airport, with views of the water. You can eat here, too, and make arrangements for diving and snorkeling.

SONNY'S VILLA, 6 rooms. $10 per person. A little place right by the water. Meals are served, and you can also arrange fishing and diving here.

CAPTAIN SPENCER'S HOTEL, tel. 453161. 8 rooms, $8 per room. Clean rooms, but no special features, and no views.

PALM VILLA has individual plain cottages for about $20 for up to four persons, with a cooktop.

UTILA LODGE. 8 rooms. U.S. reservations: 800-282-8932. Week-long dive package $650 per person including airport pickup, three daily boat dives and two night dives per week, tanks, weights, belts; non-diving $600. Single supplement $300. Week-long fishing package with five days of fishing from $995 in the flats to $1195 offshore. Heavy tackle included for offshore fishing; bring your own light tackle.

A new lodge in the village, built right over the water on two levels. Each air-conditioned room has a ceiling fan, front and rear porch entry, a single and double bed, and equipment closet. The bar has inexpensive local drinks. Personal gear is *not* available for rent — bring your own, or make arrangements beforehand for rental through a local dive shop.

Utila Lodge is one of the few hotels in the Bay Islands ready, willing and able to receive sport fishermen. There are two fully equipped diesel-powered boats, and the specialties are marlin in the deeps, tarpon and permit and snook closer in, and bonefish in the flats. For an occasional fishing day, the rate is $118.50 for a single fisherman on a skiff, about $150 per fisherman offshore. Marina facilities are available, with 14 slips on a 130-foot dock.

Other Lodging

You can also ask around for rooms in private homes.

Rooms and houses can also be found on Pigeon Cay and the Cayes nearby; camping is permitted on Water Cay, reached by boat from Pigeon Caye. There is an inexpensive lodging place at Blue Lagoon, at the end of the peninsula to the southwest of East Harbour; boat operators can tell you if it's currently open.

WHERE TO EAT AND DRINK

Food is served in any number of small eateries in East Harbour. Fish, of course, is your best, fresh but always either fried or in a soup. And you'll find Caribbean-style pastries and spice cakes and coconut bread. Call the fare wholesome at best.

Of numerous bars, the **Bucket of Blood** is one popular gathering spot. The **Bahía del Mar** has a dock.

PRACTICAL INFORMATION

Services in East Harbour include a couple of **banks**; several Protestant **churches**; and **shops** with items fashioned from coral. You should not purchase the latter under any circumstances. Coral jewelry could be confiscated when you return to the United States.

THINGS TO DO

There are now a few **dive shops** on Utila. Try **Utila Dive Centre** or **Cross Creek Divers** (tel. 453134). Prices at Cross Creek are somewhat lower than if you book through a dive resort: about $35 for two one-tank dives, and beginners are welcome. They have an introductory course over four days for about $200, including basic lodging.

Or ask around for other dive operators. But check the condition of the equipment before going out. Diving is an unregulated business in Honduras, and unless you go through a hotel that offers dive packages, you can't be sure of what you're getting.

You can also **visit a cay**. At **Miss Trudy's**, for example, you can arrange to be dropped off for a day for snorkeling, and picked up, box lunch included, for $10 per person or less. It's like having your own private island for the day. Make arrangements a day in advance. **Water Cay**, off the southwest of the main island, is said to have good **snorkeling** off the south shore. Or, from town, walk out and snorkel off the airstrip.

Also found, without too much difficulty, are caves both over water (especially on **Pumpkin Hill**) and under water, **Blue Lagoon** along the south side of the island, waterways through the mangroves to explore by canoe, and trails across the island's interior.

ROATÁN

Roatán is the largest of the Bay Islands, roughly Cuba-shaped, stretching about 40 kilometers, and usually no more than three kilometers wide. Separated by a passage almost narrow enough to step across, at the eastern end, is the island of **Helene** (or Santa Elena), and slightly beyond are **Morat** and **Barbaret** (Barbareta).

If you like sun, beaches, swimming, a nice island away from it all, genial people, you'll find all that on Roatán. It is everything that you might hope for from a perfect Caribbean island, and it is not yet too commercial.

If you like diving, you might as well call it paradise.

And that's not the end of it. If you're a birder, you can see a wealth of tropical birds. And to round things out, there is even a lot of barely touched forest, for seafaring, rather than agriculture, has been the heritage of the islanders.

Landscape and Seascape

There is a long, irregular mountain ridge inland on Roatán, with hilltops reaching up to 235 meters, but these are just the peaks of the mountains that lie below the waters. Beaches and cliffs punctuate the north shore. It was the inlets and bays on the south, some with deep water, all protected by reefs, that attracted the first European pirates and loggers, and, in modern times, divers.

Reefs line the north coast, a few hundred meters from shore; along the south, coral formations are, in many places, within just steps of the beach. With easy diving, hotels, frequent air service, towns, and even a small road network, Roatán is what most people think of when they think of a vacation in the Bay Islands.

With the exception of a couple of "Spanish" settlements inland at **Corozal** and **Juticalpa**, the people of Roatán live right along the coast — many in white clapboard tin-roofed stilt houses set right above the water that is their highway and disposal system. Most are English-speaking blacks, though Black Caribs inhabit the village of Punta Gorda on the north side of the island. Inland, much of the hardwood forest in the hills has been virtually untouched since English woodcutters and their slaves took timber more than 150 years ago. Hikers occasionally find pieces of pottery made by the Paya Indians who lived here in pre-Columbian times. Versions differ, but the name of the island might be a corruption of "rattan," from the vines of the island's forests, or a derivative of the Nahuatl expression for "place of women."

ARRIVALS AND DEPARTURES
By Air
Sahsa Airlines (tel. 451093 in Coxen's Hole) provides service from La Ceiba on the mainland to Roatán. Departures are currently at 6 a.m. and 12:30 p.m. daily; at 7 a.m. only on Sunday. The fare is $40 each way.

There are also daily flights from San Pedro Sula and Tegucigalpa in the afternoon. From Tegucigalpa, the fare is about $75.

Return flights on Sahsa are at 6:30 a.m. to La Ceiba, San Pedro Sula and Tegucigalpa, and in the afternoon for La Ceiba.

Some of the flights are in 737s, which I recommend. Others are in DC-3s, which are a trip not only in space, but back into time. They remind me of the plane in the final scene of *Casablanca*.

Sahsa operates a through flight to Roatán on Sunday from Miami, and on Friday and Sunday from New Orleans. On other days, you can reach Roatán from any U.S. gateway after a quick change of plane in La Ceiba or San Pedro Sula.

Isleña Airlines (tel. 451088 in Coxen's Hole) operates Canadian-built Twin-Otter short takeoff craft, as well as DC3s. Five flights are scheduled most days from La Ceiba, (currently at 6:30 a.m. (except Sunday), 8 a.m., 10 a.m., 2 p.m. and 4:30 p.m.) but if there's a demand beyond the schedule, they'll simply fly back and forth until everyone has been accommodated. The flight takes about 20 minutes, the fare is about $20.

Aerolíneas Sosa, tel. 451154 in Coxen's Hole, has operated flights from La Ceiba.

From October through December, expect some delays from bad weather and darkness. Airports are sometimes closed because of strong winds, as well as rain. But everything passes. Don't expect a delay of more than one day.

If you are connecting to the Bay Islands from an international flight, there's always a chance that you'll have to spend the night in La Ceiba if the international leg of your flight is delayed. They won't hold the domestic flight for too long.

The airport (or airstrip) is located two kilometers from Coxen's Hole. Facilities include a snack bar, gift shop, and a tourist office, the latter forever closed. If you have reservations, you'll be picked up and carted off

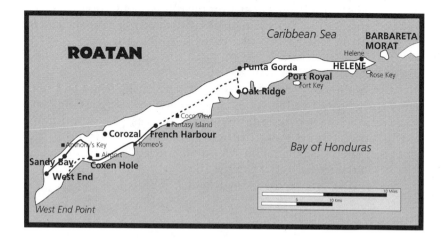

to your lodgings. Taxis at the airport are plentiful, and high-priced. Bargain hard. If you walk, it's just ten minutes to Coxen's Hole.

By Boat

Boats also operate from the single pier in La Ceiba to the islands, and irregularly between the islands (see page 162). To return to La Ceiba by boat, ask around in Coxen's Hole. There's usually a boat in the afternoon.

GETTING AROUND

Unlike the other islands, Roatán has some significant roads, generally in excellent condition.

A single paved road runs northward across the island from Coxen's Hole to West End; and eastward from Coxen's Hole to French Harbour.

An unpaved road runs from Coxen's Hole west to Flowers Bay. From French Harbour, a dirt road continues inland through the hills, with branches to Oak Ridge and Punta Gorda.

If you absolutely *must* drive, **Roatán Rent a Car**, tel. 451097, rents vans, cars, pickup trucks and motorcycles. **Amigo Renta A Car** has a desk at the airport, and at Fantasy Island. Call 451128. **Toyota Rent A Car** has a desk at the airport, tel. 451166.

By Bus or Boat

Buses operating on the island are small, with 15 to 30 seats. All start from Coxen's Hole and go in either direction, departing about every 30 minutes, or more frequently between 7 and 9 a.m. and 3 and 6 p.m. The friendly driver knows everybody along the way.

To get around, you flag down a bus (or other passing vehicle if no bus arrives) and pay the driver's helper for the ride — about a dollar on most routes during the day, more at night. On Sundays, you have to take taxi. Or else you're fetched to wherever you're going by boat.

DIVING AND FISHING BOATS

Most of the resorts mentioned below have diving boats, and some have fishing boats. In addition, the *Bay Island Aggressor*, a cruising boat designed to accommodate 20 divers, is based at Roatán, as are the *Isla Mia* and the *Maid'en Desert*. You arrive by plane, and off you go from one dive spot to another, sleeping on board. Another live-aboard that regularly operates in the Bay Islands is the Isla Mia.

See "Diving," above, for more details.

Towns and Accommodations

As I mentioned earlier in the book, there are hotels on Roatán that price everything in U.S. dollars, though Lempiras will be accepted if you insist. Generally, these are the resorts outside of towns, though there are exceptions, which are noted.

COXEN'S HOLE

From La Ceiba or anywhere on the mainland, you buy a ticket for Roatán, but once you arrive at the town's airstrip and are talking to locals, you better ask for **Coxen's Hole**, the local name, which recalls Captain John Coxen, a pirate of past days.

Coxen's Hole has an attractive, small central plaza, and clapboard houses and small general stores and lumber depots and outboard motor repair shops, and one or two larger general stores that style themselves "supermarkets." The wharf can be lively, with the landing of the catch, and processing and re-loading for export to the United States. If you like fish, it's enough to whet your appetite. Coxen's Hole is the capital of the islands, but, with just a few thousand inhabitants, effectively conceals any self-importance.

WHERE TO STAY

HOTEL CAY VIEW RESORT, tel. 451202, fax 451179. 15 rooms. $30 single/$40 double.

This is the best hotel in Coxen's Hole, good and clean, and the location is advantageous. Yes, they have a terrace with a view of a cay, as well as a bar and restaurant, and they'll make arrangements for diving and fishing. They sell nice black coral figurines, but then, if you have any conservation conscientiousness, you shouldn't be buying black coral. The Cay View is where groups from cruise ships land about once a week, for a half-day stay in the Bay Islands.

HOTEL EL PASO, Coxen's Hole, tel. 451059. $10 single or double. On Coxen's Hole's main street, with restaurant.

ALLAN'S, tel. 451243, is clean and simple. $5 single/$10 double. Under the bridge.

HOTEL AIRPORT VIEW, tel. 451167, about a five minute walk from the airport, has eight basic rooms. Look for the owner at the *"supermarket"* (large convenience store) next door. $12 for a room with a fan, $20 with air conditioning, or $25 for the two-room *suite* with air conditioning.

HOTEL BRISAS DEL MAR is a small hotel just beside the Cay View, with eatery. About $6 per person.

Similarly inexpensive is the **HOTEL CORAL**, tel. 451080. The basic but clean **HOTEL SHILA**, tel. 451015, has rooms for about $10 single/$15 double, serves meals, and arranges diving, fishing and horseback riding.

WHERE TO EAT

There's a **Burger Hut**, with imitation American hamburgers. The **Restaurant Brisas del Mar** serves more local cuisine, just opposite the Hotel Cay View, and most of the hotels have eating rooms in which you can consume fried fish, coconut bread, boiled bananas, and lots of Port Royal beer.

PRACTICAL INFORMATION

Banks

Banks include **Bancahsa**, **Banco Atlántida**, **Banffaa**, **Banco Sogerin** in the Cay View Hotel.

Dive Shops

Various dive shops rent equipment (which you should look over carefully) and offer diving trips, though the offerings may be better at West End (see below).

Gift and Book Shops

Being the island metropolis, Coxen's Hole has more amenities, shops, and services than are found elsewhere in the islands, including several souvenir shops. One, the **Traveller's Rest Gift Shop**, in the Bay Islands Company building (across from the airline offices) sells **maps and books,** and has a Xerox machine.

Other Services

There is a **post office**, and a Hondutel office for international **phone calls.**

Near Sandy Bay

This area is known for good scuba diving and snorkeling, and several dive resorts are located nearby:

ROATAN BEACH RESORT, tel. and fax 451425. 10 rooms. $125 per person with daily diving, $90 non-diving. U.S. reservations tel. 800-395-5688 or 708-537-2381, fax 708-520-3908. Week-long diving package: $695, including three daily boat dives, meals, transfers, and one night dive. Non-diving package, $595.

A new, intimate resort, said to offer excellent diving at north shore sites. Rooms are either individual or two to a cottage, fairly soundproof, air-conditioned, with sea views. Good for getting away from the crowd.

ANTHONY'S KEY RESORT, Sandy Bay, tel. 451003, fax 451329. 50 units. U.S. office: 1385 Coral Way, Suite 401, Miami, FL 33145, tel. 800-227-3483 or 305-858-3483, fax 305-858-5020.

Weekly dive packages from $775 to $975 per person, including three one-tank boat dives daily and two night dives per week, dolphin encounter and dolphin dive, and all activities. Additional nights $132 to $139 single/ $220 to $234 double with meals and diving.

Non-diving rate, $140 single/$240 double. Children 3 to 11, $45. About 15% lower in summer.

Everything about Anthony's Key can be described in superlatives. The landscaping alone makes it a paradise. The resort flows down a slope, and across to a small cay. Structures, plantings and terrain are all integrated, and there is a great respect for the environment. There are units in the lodge on a hill, bungalows set into the foliage on the slope, and slat houses along the edge of the cay, on stilts in the water, reached by a 60-second boat ride. Macaws and hummingbirds flap and gyre about. Rooms are clean and somewhat sparse, but easy on the senses. Meals are simply prepared, and hearty. The bar is quite expensive.

The emphasis is on diving, as elsewhere on the island, with many boats and good instructors and equipment. Numerous groups come here. The location near the west end of the island allows easy access to diving spots on both shores. (Northers might churn up the sea in front of Anthony's Key, while the south shore remains calm.) Rates are higher than elsewhere, but Anthony's Key has a lot more: horseback riding, weekly beach picnic, swimming with dolphins, a dinner party on the key, island-style entertainment, crab races, tennis, and use of canoes, kayaks, pedal boats and small sailboats are included in the daily rate (non-guests can use the sailboats for a fee).

There are also a **wildlife sanctuary** with trails on nearby **Bailey's Key**, the **Museum of Roatán**, a decompression chamber, a doctor on-site, and secluded beaches. Fishing can be arranged, and snorkeling equipment is available for rent. Also available: resort diving courses, PADI instruction, underwater photo courses, and videos in which you can star. The souvenir shop has a good assortment of trinkets, and a photography shop offers processing, and rentals of cameras and underwater equipment. There's even the Casino Royal, if you're interested in gambling between dives. Anthony's Key is one of the best resorts on the island, and highly recommended.

OCEANSIDE INN, Sandy Bay, tel. 451552, fax 451532. 8 rooms. $25 single/$40 double. U.S. reservations, tel. 800-241-5271.

Package price from $331 per person for seven days, including airport pickup, meals, picnic, and night out in French Harbour. Dives cost an additional $20 each, $22 with equipment, even less (!) for a package of ten dives.

Located alongside Anthony's Key (and right next to their dolphin pen), Oceanside Inn has good-sized hardwood-panelled rooms, all upstairs with sea view, steady breeze, and ceiling fans. The louver style of building is quite similar to that used in the cottages at Anthony's Key, though the facility is brand-new, and more modest and homey. Food is said to be quite good, emphasizing seafood prepared American-style— lobster, shrimp, pan-fried grouper, etc., served in a breezy dining room. The hotel also has two sun decks, a patio bar, and gift shop. A dolphin show can be included, optionally, with a package stay, for $75. Other excursions and options are dive certification ($260), horseback riding ($12) and rafting on the mainland ($89, including air transport and lunch).

The owners of Oceanside are Hondurans who have returned after successful business careers in the States, so they know the worlds of both the islands and their guests.

There are assorted other small places that rent rooms in the area. **THE BAMBOO INN,** with seven rooms, charges about $18 per person for the night, and you become part of Dora and J.J.'s family.

Gardens, Institutes, and Museums

Carambola Botanical Garden, across the road from Anthony's Key Resort, has plantings of native and exotic species, including spices, elephant ear, hibiscus, bird of paradise, and many, many others. The locale is excellent for birding. The hilltop, reached via a 20-minute hike, offers good sea view.

The **Institute for Marine Sciences** (IMS) at Sandy Bay uses the facilities of Anthony's Key to care for, train and investigate a dozen or so bottle-nosed dolphins. Visitors are invited to swim with the dolphins in limited numbers. IMS is also a sanctuary and rehabilitation center for ailing marine mammals, sea turtles and birds.

IMS offers classes on marine mammals and coral reef biology, and, of course, the reef surrounding Roatan makes for a superb field laboratory. Students, according to their resources, stay at Anthony's Key Resort or at the Institute's dormitory. Degree credits may be available in cooperation with various universities. For information, contact the Anthony's Key office in the States, or Anthony's Key directly (see above).

The **Roatán Museum**, in the same building as the Institute for Marine Sciences, houses exhibits on the ethnology of the Bay Islands. Displays include Paya and Mayan artifacts, and a video presentation on the islands' past and prospects.

WEST END

West End is a quiet town on the north coast of Roatán, opposite and west of Coxen's Hole, about ten kilometers away. There are beaches and palm trees, and for the visitor, things are cheap. Rooms may be rented by asking around of locals. The going rate is $10 per person per night, or less. You can always find a place, except at Easter week.

Restaurants are really simple. Many are tiny affairs run by housewives. Chino's has Chinese food, and also rooms to rent. Vivian and Foster's Restaurant is located on pillars in the water, not far from the Lost Paradise, serving an honest and unpretentious soda-shop menu of hamburgers and sandwiches. Mr. Foster really exists. He has a lot of muscles, but he is a friendly giant. They also have rooms at West End Point for about $25 double, including the boat ride out.

The reef off West End is protected as part of the **West End Marine Sanctuary**.

Access to West End is by island bus from Coxen's Hole. A taxi from the airport should cost under $10.

WHERE TO STAY

(Aside from generic rooms in town)

ROBERTS HILL HOTEL, tel 451176. 8 rooms. $20 double. These are individual units opposite the beach.

LOST PARADISE INN, tel. 451306, fax 451388. 34 rooms, $40 per person, including three meals and airport transfer.

This is a simple motel, at the end of the road . . . you'll feel that you've finally found the Lost Paradise. Simply furnished rooms have showers, but nothing extra and nothing fancy. You pay an honest price and get honest accommodations, with helpful owner and employees. There are no diving facilities on site, but there are several dive shops in West End Town, five minutes away on foot. Free boat rides are given to nearby beaches. The motel is near the beach on a bay, but not all rooms have sea views.

SUEÑO DEL MAR, tel. 451498. 8 rooms. $75 single/$110 double/ $145 triple with meals ($50/$60/$70 without meals), plus 10 percent service and tax. Children 2 to 12 half price. U.S. reservations, P. O. Box 5240, Sierra Vista, AZ 85636, tel. 800-377-9525 or 602-378-6055, fax 602-378-6155.

Dive packages from approximately $90 per person per day, including three boat dives, unlimited beach diving, meals, and one night dive per week.

The newest accommodation at West End, right on the beach at the end of the road, near the Lost Paradise Inn. The lodge is built in sedate plantation style, two-storied, L-shaped and hugging the beach, of varnished wood, with generous porches. Rooms are large, with walk-in closets, private bath, and two queen-sized beds. Guests on a diving package can take their meals at any time in the restaurant, which is open to the public.

Sueño del Mar, like a couple of other resorts in the vicinity, is *small*. There could be some drawbacks, but on the plus side, everyone is on a first-name basis, one of the owners is always on site, and diving is scheduled and locations are selected according to the wishes of guests. There are three dive boats. Call the toll-free number, and chances are you can talk with one of the owners in Arizona and get detailed answers to your questions.

FOSTER'S COVE are two-bedroom palm-shaded beach houses, built of pine and raised well above sandfly level on high stilts, owned by Mr. Foster and his American partner, Robert Beels. Each has an ample deck, wicker furniture, and one king and two twin beds, solar electricity, and a gas stove. The rate is about $500 per week for a unit that sleeps four persons. Maid service is extra, and a cook can be hired. Children and pets are welcome. Access is by boat from West End village.

Packages with diving and meals can also be arranged from about $800 per person. For information in the U.S. or Canada, call Maya World Travel, tel. 800-392-6292.

SEAGRAPE PLANTATION, tel. 451428. 16 rooms. U.S. reservations, 9846 Highway 441, Leesburg, FL 34788, tel. 800-392-6292.

Weekly package with meals, two boat dives daily, one night dive and unlimited shore dives, from $500.

These are rooms with private bath, two each in eight individual bungalows built over coral on an expansive 11-acre site about a half mile from West End village. Though it's set well back from the sea, they have a good dive shop.

GETTING AROUND

The beach at West End Town is okay, but the best beaches are three kilometers away, at West End Point, the very tip of the island. Just ask for a boat near Foster's Restaurant. You can also walk along the beach. Or take a glass-bottom boat trip over the reefs — inquire at Foster's.

Bargain Diving
At last count, there were four or five dive shops at West End, either independent or attached to lodging places, such as Seagrape Plantation, with compressors, well-maintained equipment, knowledgeable divemasters — and a willingness to strike a deal, especially during slow periods. I've heard of five- or six-dive packages for something like $100. You can't expect to walk into a steal like this on just any day, and diving is reasonable enough in any case on a package basis in the Bay Islands. But if you find yourself with extra time but no extra funds, and an unrequited passion for diving, check out West End.

You'll also find **wind surfing** gear available, and, most likely, **sea kayaks**.

WEST END POINT

Some of the best beaches on the island are here. White sand, palm trees, crystal clear waters — a tropical fantasy come true. But be on guard for sunburn! The snorkeling is excellent 100 meters from the beach, where the water is only five feet deep. There are coral and fish in all sorts and varieties, and when the weather is good, there are no currents at all.

East of Coxen's Hole
ROMEO'S RESORT, Brick Bay, tel. 451127, fax 451594. 30 rooms. About $96 per person daily with meals and diving, $88 non-diving. U.S. reservations: tel. 800-535-DIVE or 305-633-1221, fax 305-633-1102.

Weekly dive package from $670 to $840 per person, lower in summer, including three daily boat dives and two night dives per week.

This is a quiet place off the road between French Harbour and Coxen's Hole, in a sheltered cove, run by the same Romeo who managed Romeo's Restaurant in French Harbour. Most rooms are in a long concrete building, the central section of which (with terrace restaurant, front desk and gathering areas) has a soaring roof that suggests the South Seas. The whole place is pleasant enough, with luxuriant vegetation all around and views everywhere to the mangrove-lined waters. And Brick Bay (English Harbour) is a good place to anchor: Romeo's is the closest hotel to Mary's Place, one of the most famed dive spots in the islands.

Standard rooms have two double beds, ceiling fans, balconies, and lagoon views. Deluxe rooms on the lower level are air conditioned. A hillside house, Casa Pepe, can be reserved for groups. Facilities include a pool with wooden deck, pavilion dining area, bar, sea kayaks, dockside gear storage, slide film processing, and several dive boats. Onshore amusements include volleyball, Ping Pong, and island trips. The current management, the Silvestri family, has worked hard to develop this hotel (which formerly was a yacht club) as a complete dive and vacation center, and they personally look after the needs of guests in the best innkeepers' tradition.

FRENCH HARBOUR YACHT CLUB, 16 rooms, tel. 451478, fax 451459. $35 single/$45 double.

Whence the hotel's name derives, I know not. It's near the harbor, but not on the water, though the hotel has docks and motor boats and dinghies, and a bar, a short walk away. Maybe it's for yachties who want to sleep ashore. You have good views in any case, in a hilltop, remodelled, traditional, tin-roofed island house, with verandas, and a six-acre buffer zone. And it's clean. Rooms come with hot showers and fans, each with one double and two twin beds, air conditioning, and a television. The location is on the main road, eight kilometers from the airport, a half-kilometer from town.

FRENCH HARBOUR

French Harbour is about ten kilometers up the south coast to the east of Coxen's Hole. Nobody here speaks French (I was disappointed to learn my first time out). The bay is quite big, and you will find a large processing and packing operation for shrimp and lobster traveling on to the States. The town itself is a small concentration of houses built on pillars over the water, which serves as transport route and disposal system. I wouldn't go out of my way to visit the place, but you'll pass through getting to some of the resorts nearby. Bus service is frequent from Coxen's Hole.

WHERE TO STAY

HOTEL DIXON'S PLAZA, French Harbour, tel. 451317. $25 double. Air-conditioned rooms, t.v. room, even parking, if you've brought your car.

BUCCANEER HOTEL, tel. 451032, fax 451036. 30 rooms. $100 single/$160 double with meals and airport transfer. Weekly diving rate approximately $550.

In French Harbor along the sea. This is an attractive, modern hotel built of wood, with soaring ceilings and screened and glassed walls that let in plenty of light. Guest rooms, facing the water, extend along an elevated deck.

The beach is not as attractive as at some other resorts, but rooms are comfortable, wood-panelled and carpeted, and the place is easy-going and cozy, without any pretense. Diving and boat tours for swimming are available — you can't swim in the shallows right in front. Amenities include a restaurant, cable t.v., and hot water in some of the rooms. A gazebo set out in the water is fitted with lights to allow night views of tropical fish. The value here is quite good.

In French Harbour, if you don't have the money to stay at the Buccaneer Inn, the **CORAL REEF INN** next door will give you shelter from predators at $15 per person, and there are smaller places where you can find a room for $10.

WHERE TO EAT AND DRINK

Romeo's Restaurant, the predecessor of Romeo's Resort, is one of the top eating places on Roatán, specializing in crab. Or, you can stop just for drinks, over piers lapped by Caribbean waters.

NIGHTLIFE

Celebrity, in French Harbour, is currently the disco of note on the island of Roatan, and if you stay anywhere for a few days, you're likely to spend at least a few hours here one night for reggae and salsa.

PRACTICAL INFORMATION

Banks

Bank agencies include **Banco Atlántida**, **Banco Sogerín**, and **Banffaa**.

Tour Information

Bay Islands Tour and Travel Center, tel. 451184.

Near French Harbour

FANTASY ISLAND, tel. 451222, fax 451268. 75 rooms. $100 single/ $130 double/$150 triple; $40 per child. Daily diving (3 dives), $50. Visa, Master Card, American Express. Package rates with three meals per day, $150 to $170 single/$228 to $250 double/$414 triple. Week-long dive packages $1300 single/$2100 double/$2900 triple, including three boat dives daily and one night dive per week.

U.S. reservations: 304 Plant Avenue, Tampa, FL 33606, tel. 800-676-2826, fax 813-251-0301.

This is a one of the newer resorts in the Bay Islands, opened in 1989, a marina-diving-beach complex with some of the most comprehensive facilities. From a distance, it looks like condominiums in ski country, two stories of attached clapboard units with peaked roofs. Up close, you'll espy the palm-shaded verandas, and a dining area with soaring roof and cupola.

Rooms come with ceiling fans, air conditioning, carpeting, refrigerator, shower and tub, artificial plants, satellite t.v., and private balconies.

There are three bars, and plenty of loud music to accompany your time at the crushed-shell beach (if that's what you're looking for).

The resort is located two kilometers east of French Harbour on a small (15-acre) cay, about 500 feet offshore. The last stretch of road is unpaved.

As at some of the other Bay Islands resorts, they try hard at Fantasy island, though in a country without a strong resort tradition, some things still don't come together perfectly at meal time, or in room furnishings.

For diving, Fantasy Island offers the most modern facilities on the island, with a dive gazebo, camera rentals, film processing, a fleet of custom dive boats, and easy access to both sides of the island.

There is good snorkeling, and canoes and windsurfers are provided. And Fantasy Island also has tennis courts and a marina.

Less expensive packages are available during the slow season, from September 15 to December 15.

COCO VIEW RESORT, French Cay, tel. 451013, fax 451011. 25 rooms (9 beach rooms, 4 luxury bungalows, 12 over-water cabanas). About $130 per person daily with diving and meals, $110 for non-divers ($110 diver, $90 non-diver after one week). U.S. address: Box 877, San Antonio, FL 33576, tel. 800-282-8932, fax 904-588-4158.

Weekly dive packages from $725 per person with all meals, transfer from airport, two daily boat dives and unlimited beach and night diving; non-diver packages from $625.

This is considered by some knowledgeable folks to be *the* place for divers. Located on a peninsula on the south shore, it was a wild, remote place, when you could only reach it by boat from French Harbour. Now, it's just beside Fantasy Island, more accessible, but still quite nice. You don't sleep in an aquarium, but aside from that, everything is diving.

Units, all with overhead fans (no air conditioning) and hot showers, are in two guest houses, and in individual roundhouse bungalows (extra charge $50 per person on a weekly package) and cabanas built on stilts over the water. It's not luxurious, and the price is appropriate, a good balance between budget and comfort. The resort is ten minutes by boat from Old French Harbour (just east of French Harbour), and transportation from the airport is included in the rate.

Wall Diving and Other Diversions at Coco View

There is spectacular wall diving 100 yards out, and there are reefs and channels nearby, accessible on two dive boats. The wreck of the *Prince Albert*, a 140-foot freighter, deliberately sunk in 1985, is directly in front of the resort, in 65 feet of water. Tanks, backpacks and weights are provided and stored at dockside, and other equipment can be rented. Processing for E-6 slide film is available.

Instruction capabilities include resort, certification and specialty courses.

Landside diversions include kayaks, board games, Ping Pong and picnics on a private islet. Sailing and fishing can be arranged. Also available are rental houses at **PLAYA MIGUEL**, the development adjacent to the hotel, at about $800 per week. These have two or three bedrooms, full kitchen and sundecks. For four persons, the rate is $2700 to $2800 with diving and meals, or $1785 to $2000 for non-divers; and live-aboard boats with air-conditioned quarters, at about $650 per person per week. Children are not encouraged to come except during a specific family week in July.

OAK RIDGE

Oak Ridge is 22 kilometers up the coast from Coxen's Hole, an hour's drive away, mostly over a dirt road that takes you to the most wild part of the island. Officially, the town is called José Santos Guardiola, after the national hero/dictator/president of Honduras at the time the Bay Islands were recovered by Honduras; but nobody in the islands calls it by anything but its real name. A tongue of land wraps around a bay here, and most of the houses sit on stilts in a semicircle above the water.

Meals and snacks can be purchased at watering holes in the village, as well as at the hotels in the vicinity of the town that specialize in diving. **BJ's Backyard** is one. Or take a break from diving to explore the mangroves by boat and listen to and look for birds.

WHERE TO STAY

HENRY'S COVE RESORT, tel. 452180 and **HOTEL SAN JOSÉ** have rooms for under $15 per person.

REEF HOUSE RESORT, Oak Ridge, tel. 4552297, fax 452142. 3 bungalows, 12 other rooms. $120 single/$200 double per day with diving and three meals, $90 single/$160 double without diving, including meals. U.S. address: P O Box 40331, San Antonio TX 78229, tel. 800-328-8897, fax 210-341-7942. American Express, Visa, Master Card.

Week-long diving package $625 to $750 per person, including two boat dives daily, meals, one night dive per week, unlimited shore diving. Fishing packages run $200 per day single, $225 per day double with meals and boat.

This is a nice resort, with serious dive packages. A wide, sea-view passageway connects the large rooms, each with louvers, sea breeze and overhead fans for cooling. The long, shallow sea area in front of the hotel is perfect for swimming, and there are beaches nearby. Food is usually served buffet-style, with an emphasis on fish, and there are an open-air bar and terrace, and an indoor dining and reading area.

Reef House has one main diving boat, the 37-foot diesel-powered *Henry Morgan*, and several smaller boats for fishing and cruising. There's a wall diving site right in front of the hotel. Of the many, many dive sites nearby, some of the most notable are Calvin's Crack, a cleft in the reef; Crab Wall, encrusted with sponges; and Church Wall. A diving trip to Barbareta Island, with beach picnic, is often included with weekly packages. Resort and certification courses are available.

Snorkeling equipment is provided for guests at no additional charge, and you can snorkel right from the hotel—the reef is just outside your door. Windsurfers, sailboats, kayaks, and a water bicycle are available to guests.

Fishing packages provide a 14-foot skiff for every three to four persons. Bring your own tackle.

The detailed price list for extras for diving equipment rentals, and for persons not on dive packages, includes: $25 per single tank dive, $35 per two-tank dive, $30 per night dive, $75 for a resort scuba course, $350 for full certification. Daily tank rental $7; regulator $10; buoyancy compensator, $8; masks, fins and snorkel, $7; dive light, $5.

PUNTA GORDA

On the north shore of Roatán, opposite Oak Ridge, **Punta Gorda** is a Black Carib village. Unlike Creole Bay Islanders, Caribs build their houses right on the ground, and use traditional, locally available palm thatch for floors and roofs. Superficially, Black Caribs look like other islanders. But you see just from their bearing and dress that they are different, more relaxed. They do not look as if they are ready to help you or to cater to you, but they are perfectly okay.

OLD PORT ROYAL

Old Port Royal is not a town at all in modern times, but it was the site of pirate encampments in the seventeenth century, and English fortifications in the eighteenth century. The last great battle here was fought offshore at Fort George in 1782. The English were ousted after a two-day battle, though not for the last time.

The remains of four different forts still exist, two on Roatán, and two on Fort Cay offshore, and there are some vacation houses in the area, which is otherwise uninhabited. Wood from wrecks found offshore has been dated to before the arrival of Columbus, suggesting that Europeans visited this area earlier than is generally acknowledged.

Boats on diving and fishing excursions will sometimes stop to let visitors walk around the old fortifications; or you can hire a boat for a trip out from Oak Ridge. A trail reaches Port Royal from the end of the island road east of Punta Gorda — it's a hike through the hills to reach the site.

Port Royal Park and Wildlife Reserve protects Roatán's water supply, and not incidentally, is a haven for birds and small mammals, such as the opossum and agouti.

BARBARETA

Barbareta, three kilometers from Helene (the island that adjoins Roatán), is a five- by two-kilometer island covered with forests and fringed with coconut palms. Spring water is abundant, and a hotel has sometimes operated here.

Barbareta Marine National Park, covering Barbareta, Morat, and the eastern part of Roatán, protects Diamond Rock forest, the last remnant of tropical rain forest on the island, as well as coral reef and the largest mangrove area.

GUANAJA

Columbus called Guanaja the Island of Pines (he landed at El Soldado beach on the north shore), and there are still some pine and oak trees left, though logging and fires have considerably changed the landscape over the years. The island measures about 18 by 6 kilometers, and most of it is green and hilly — the highest point on the Bay Islands, 1400 feet, is here. There are more Spanish-speaking people on Guanaja than elsewhere in the Bay Islands.

If you like Roatán, you'll love Guanaja. It's like an earlier version of Roatán — no real roads, only a few resorts, but of the best type. And the people are genuinely friendly and glad to have you around.

The dive spots are excellent, with clear water and spectacular formations — walls, caves, channels, ridges, tunnels — certainly as good as Roatán's, or, according to local enthusiasts, better. The main diving is off the reef and cays that border the southern shore, and the walls that drop in the depths of the Bartlett Trough.

ARRIVALS AND DEPARTURES
By Air

Sahsa has operates flights to Guanaja daily except Saturday from La Ceiba at 6 a.m., 12:30 p.m. and 4 p.m. The fare is $23. Return flights are at 6:45 a.m., 1:15 a.m. and 4:45 p.m.

Isleña Airlines (tel. 454208 in Guanaja, 430179 in La Ceiba) also has flights.

The airstrip is right next to the canal that cuts across Guanaja about a third of the way across the island, from its southwest tip. If you have a reservation, you'll be fetched and taken to your hotel. Otherwise, you can take a boat to Bonacca town for about a dollar, along with the locals.

BONACCA

Officially, this is the town of Guanaja, though locals call it **Bonacca**, or El Cayo. Bonacca is also known as the Venice of Honduras, and the similarity is genuine not only in the presence of canals, but also in their aroma. The architecture of Bonacca is not quite as grand as that of its Italian cousin.

Bonacca sits on Hog Cay and Sheen Cay, half a kilometer offshore, where Cayman Islanders settled and constructed stilt houses over the water. With time, new houses were added in outlying sections, and connected by walkways on stilts. Eventually, fill was dumped around the houses, dry land was built up, trees were planted, and some of the canals were closed off. Today, Bonacca is a labyrinth of zigzagging pathways and walkways, its houses built close one upon another.

SEEING THE SIGHTS

Guanaja Marine National Park covers 90 percent of the island and surrounding reefs. Sea Cave, along the south of the island, is a rock that rises 80 feet from the Caribbean, and is said to have been a headquarters for William Walker when that American adventurer was trying to take over Honduras more than a hundred years ago.

The *Jado Trader* is a wreck deliberately sunk off southern Guanaja in 1987, to form an artificial reef. The 260-foot ship remains intact in 90 feet of water, making for the premier wreck dive in the Bay Islands.

WHERE TO STAY

The **HOTEL ALEXANDER** on Hog Cay (tel. 454326, fax 454179) has 12 seafront rooms with private baths, and, unexpectedly, 24-hour satellite television. At about $30 double facing the sea, less inside, it's probably the closest to a vacation hotel that you'll find right in Bonacca. There's a slightly higher charge for air conditioning.

The **HOTEL MILLER**, with 20 rooms (tel. 454327 or 454240) charges about $30 per person. The **CARTER** charges about $10 a person. The **HOTEL ROSARIO** has rooms at about $15 double, more if you require a television and air conditioning. None of these, given the congested surroundings, can really be called a resort destination.

WHERE TO EAT

Bonacca has various eating places where locals gather for drinks and snacks, the **Ca Fé Coral** and **Glenda's** among them.

SPORTS AND RECREATION

Snorkeling trips to offshore cays and points around the island are organized on an ad-hoc basis from most of the hotels, usually at $10 per person or so. For **diving**, if you're not staying at one of the hotels that offer packages, inquire at Dive Inn at the Ca Fé Coral eatery (but look over the equipment). **Fishing** can be arranged with various skippers in Bonacca Town, if your hotel doesn't have the capability.

NIGHTLIFE

There's a disco, or juke joint, called **Mountain View**, which, while a basic sort of place with a large dance hall, such as you will find in any Central American village, affords unusual views of water and boats on three sides, and mountains on the other.

PRACTICAL INFORMATION

Bonacca has a bank branch (**Banco Atlántida**), several general stores, pharmacy, and a cable television system!

WHERE TO STAY AROUND THE ISLAND

BAYMAN BAY CLUB, tel. 454191, 454179 (430457 in La Ceiba). 16 cottages, $125 per day including diving and meals, $115 non-diving. U.S. address: 10097 Cleary Blvd., Suite 287, Plantation, FL 33324, tel. 800-524-1823, 305-370-2120, fax 305-370-2276. American Express.

Week-long dive package, from $675 per person, including meals, two daily boat dives, and shore dives; non-diver, from $625, including meals.

This is one of the best resorts in the islands, located on the northwest side of Guanaja, an elegant club in the jungle. Individual varnished hardwood cottages are sited in the dense foliage of the hillside; all have balconies and ceiling fans, louvers on three sides, and views down to the beach and out to sea. The location is isolated, and the atmosphere is quiet. The reef comes almost to shore, and a 300-foot-long dock provides easy walking access for diving or just observing the fish from topside.

The rate includes two daily boat dives, unlimited shore dives, one night dive, and a round of activities including buffet meals (good food here), picnics, cruises, excursions to Bonacca Town, and hikes. There is a three-level clubhouse, the center of all action, including a bar, game area with billiards, a collection of books, and observation deck. Dockside facilities include a dive shop and compressors. Uniquely, Bayman Bay Club has dive kayaks to take guests to diving and snorkeling sites.

POSADA DEL SOL (Inn of the Sun). 23 rooms, tel. 454311. $134 to $145 daily per person for divers, $112 to 129 for non-divers (based on double occupancy), children under 12 half diver rate. U.S. Reservations address: 1201 U.S. Highway 1, Suite 220, North Palm Beach, FL 33408, tel. 800-642-DIVE, 407-642-3483, fax 407-627-0225. American Express, Master Card, Visa.

Weekly dive package, $910 to $1150 per person, including three daily boat dives, unlimited shore diving, and two night dives per week; non-diver, $700-$750. Off-season specials from $1400, *including* air fare(!).

Posada del Sol is a classy, tan-colored, palm-shaded villa on a good-sized estate at the base of the hills on Guanaja's south side. Rooms have beamed ceilings, sea views, and tiled floors — in solid Spanish genre, rather than the usual island stilt style. There are also four detached hillside units, each with two rooms. The owners are former commercial divers. The site is very nice and relaxing. There are lots of good diving places in the area and on the eastern side of the island, and the resort owns its own beach on the north side where picnics are staged. Aside from the usual compressors and the three diving boats with water-level platforms and instruction facilities, Posada del Sol has a hillside pool with hardwood deck and adjacent bar, tennis court, gift shop, exercise equipment, processing for E-6 film, underwater video camera rental, water skiing, Hobie Cat, and windsurfing. Deep sea fishing can be arranged (bonefish, permit and snook can be caught in the flats right in front of the hotel) and guest boats can be accommodated.

Posada del Sol is in a class with Anthony's Key and Fantasy Island as one of the Bay Islands' top resorts—well designed, attentively staffed, with very good food, and recommended.

CLUB GUANAJA ESTE, 14 rooms. About $120 double with meals. U.S. address: P.O. Box 40541, Cincinnati, Ohio 45240, tel. 513-825-0878.

More modest than the other resorts on the island, the Club Guanaja accommodates guests in seven cottages built on stilts, on grassy plots just a few feet from the coconut-palm-shaded beach. All face the water, and have private bath and porch. Amusements are limited to a bar, taped music and radio, and a VCR. Diving is right from the dock, sailing and fishing are arranged, and fishing guides are available. Near the northeastern tip of Guanaja, twenty minutes by boat from the airport.

CASA SOBRE EL MAR, tel. 454269. U.S. tel. 800-869-7295 or 615-443-1254.

On Pond Key, off the main island, a private house with three guest rooms, built on concrete piles directly over the water and the coral reef (ideal for snorkeling right from the door). Each room has private bath. Spring water is piped from the mainland. Casa Sobre el Mar has its own compressor, and supplies tanks, boat, and guide for diving. There's a wreck right off the dock, 80-feet down, which is recommended for night diving.

The package rate, with meals and dives, is $600 per person per week. A small extra charge is made for fishing, to cover fuel.

NAUTILUS RESORT, tel. 454135. 6 rooms. U.S. reservations: P. O. Box 1472, Marble Falls, TX 78654, tel. 800-535-7063 or 512-863-9079. Tel. 370397 in Tegucigalpa. $80 single/$130 double with meals, $105 single/

$180 double/$240 triple with diving. One-week diving package with two daily boat dives, one night dive, unlimited shore dives, meals and airport transfers from $600 per person; non diving from $450.

On Guanaja's south shore, within view of Bonacca Town, Nautilus resort is a former private retreat totally renovated in 1992. The concrete guest house, with generous balconies and overhangs, is set well back from the beach, with just three guest rooms on each level, furnished and decorated with Mexican and Central American crafts. Two rooms are air conditioned. Extras include a television and video, and the balcony has commanding sea views.

Set on 60 hillside acres and reached by boat, the hotel has a thousand feet of beachfront, and a fast dive boat to reach the best spots quickly, along with a compressor, ample tanks, and rental equipment. Courses from certification to rescue diving are available. There are also trails through the forest nearby, and horseback riding, fishing and sailing can be arranged. The wind is steady, and is said to help control the sand flies on the beach.

CAYOS COCHINOS (HOG CAYS)

The **Hog Cays** are off the coast of Honduras, 20 kilometers to the northeast of La Ceiba, and 30 kilometers south of Roatán. Consisting of two main islands and thirteen smaller cays, they have coral reefs, coconut palms, small mountains, and hardly any inhabitants but for a few Garífuna (Black Carib) fishermen. The entire mini-archipelago is a marine reserve, **Santuario Marino Cayos Cochinos**.

Big Hog (Cayo Grande) and **Little Hog** (Cayo Pequeño) are the two major islands, the former U-shaped, providing a sheltered anchorage, and covered with hardwoods, palm, and cactus.

ARRIVALS AND DEPARTURES
By Air

Transport to the island is by air taxi from La Ceiba or San Pedro Sula to a landing strip on Cochino Pequeño Cay just across the water from the hotel, at $100 to $150 per person (sometimes included with off-season packages).

By Boat

There is also informal and irregular boat service to some of the Hog Cays from the Garífuna fishing villages east of La Ceiba. Ask in Nueva Armenia. If you go on your own, take a hammock and all your food and plenty of time; but what you will have to pay for camping and how you will return are unpredictable.

Moorings off the reef are available at Plantation Beach (see below) for visiting yachts.

WHERE TO STAY

PLANTATION BEACH RESORT. 10 rooms. U.S. address: 8582 Katy Freeway, Suite 118, Houston, TX 77024, tel. 800-628-3723, fax 713-973-8585. In Honduras, call or fax 420974. Weekly dive package $750 to $900 per person, including three daily boat dives and night dives; non-diver $700. To *really* get away from it all, you'll book a week at Plantation Beach on privately owned Cayo Grande, the largest island in the group — all of a mile across, and once a pineapple plantation. Guests stay in mahogany-and-stone cottages, with hammocks and decks, four rooms with sleeping lofts to each. There are also two small separate houses.

In addition to diving at some of the less-visited (and even unexplored) sites in the islands, there are hiking trails, a beach, snorkeling, windsurfing, and sailboats available for charter.

14. WESTERN HONDURAS

INTRODUCTION

We've gone from Tegucigalpa to the north, along the coast, and out to the Bay Islands. Now we'll head back south along the western edge of the country.

Western Honduras is mountainous, curving along the borders of Guatemala and El Salvador. It is fairly densely populated for Honduras (though it doesn't seem so), with the highest concentration of Indian inhabitants, some living in villages virtually isolated from modern life. There are few roads, most of them are unpaved, rutted, and little traveled.

The Road to Copán

Copán, site of the most important pre-Columbian ruins in Honduras, is just 225 kilometers by air from Tegucigalpa. But there are no scheduled flights, and the roads that meander out this way in a roughly direct route from Tegucigalpa are so poor, that most travelers go all the way to San Pedro Sula from the capital, then cut back to the south — a trip of close to 500 kilometers — or else charter a small plane.

The road to Copán from San Pedro Sula follows the **Chamelecón River**, twisting and turning, and gradually gaining altitude. The banana fields of the lowest of the lowlands fade out, gradually replaced by pasture, corn fields, and tobacco. Much of the route has been resurfaced in the last couple of years, and the 185 kilometers can be driven at a moderate pace in three hours or less.

La Entrada, 135 kilometers from San Pedro Sula, is a hot, dusty junction, a transit point for visitors heading to the Copán ruins. Most traffic continues to Santa Rosa de Copán. (When getting directions, always specify **Copán Ruinas**, *not* Santa Rosa de Copán.) There's a small archeological museum. If you have to stay the night, you can find rooms at the **HOTEL CENTRAL** or the **HOTEL TEGUCIGALPA** for less than $5 per person.

Past La Entrada, you'll notice tall, single-story buildings. These are used for curing tobacco grown locally. They're painted black to absorb the maximum amount of solar heat.

La Jigua, a few kilometers out of La Entrada, contains a colonial church, recently restored. From Florida, farther along the road, a branch track leads for 10 kilometers to **Cerro Azul National Park**, covering 150 square kilometers along the Guatemalan border (only nine square kilometers are an absolute reserve – the rest is farmed with some restrictions). The protected area includes caves, cloud forest and recovering forest. The lake atop Cerro Azul mountain, known as **Laguna de los Pinares**, is frequented by migrating birds. Its outlet is a waterfall.

COPÁN RUINAS

This town, also known at times in its history as San José de Copán, is quaint and small, with a population of under 5000. It's in a lovely valley surrounded by gentle mountains, not too cold, and not too warm, at an altitude of about 600 meters. The streets are cobblestoned, many buildings have tile roofs, and the plaza has a colonial air – all in all, a pleasant place just for resting and walking around. The ruins that give the town its name are a kilometer away.

ARRIVALS AND DEPARTURES
By Bus

From San Pedro Sula, the Etumi bus company has at least two direct buses daily to Copán Ruinas, recently at 10 a.m. and 1 p.m., from 6 Calle, 6/7 Avenidas SW.

Empresa de Transportes Torito, 5 Avenida SW No. 34, tel. 534930, has buses departing hourly (or more frequently) to Santa Rosa de Copán. To reach the ruins of Copán, take this bus as far as La Entrada (two hours), then catch the bus for Copán Ruinas at the Texaco station, departing about every 40 minutes until 4:30 p.m. It's still a ride of another two hours or so from this point. The road is tortuous in both the back-and-forth and up-and-down senses, but not in bad enough shape to slow vehicles to a crawl, a combination that can lead to unpleasant consequences for passengers. Take a travel sickness pill if you're subject to that malady. Copán Ruinas is 64 kilometers onward.

Travel Tips

Information for bus travel from San Pedro Sula is given above. I recommend taking the bus only if you are going to stay for a few days (which is not a bad idea). It is ruinous to try to arrive, visit the ruins, and leave in one day by public transportation. Even a drive on the winding roads will be quite tiring.

To return to San Pedro Sula, take one of the two direct buses in the morning, or else one of the buses that leave for La Entrada at least every hour. From La Entrada, there are frequent buses to San Pedro Sula.

Most Honduran tours depart from San Pedro Sula, rather than from Tegucigalpa (see pages 111-112 for names of agencies), at prices ranging upward from $130 for an overnight stay.

From the Bay Islands, one-day trips operate to Copán for about $125 per person, overnight trips for about $165 per person. Arrangements can be made through most hotels, or when booking a dive package in the Bay Islands.

The quickest way to reach Copán, if your time is short and you have some money to spare, is by air taxi from Tegucigalpa, San Pedro Sula, or from the Bay Islands. The landing strip is right beside the visitors' center at the ruins.

To Guatemala

Guatemala is just 11 kilometers away from Copán, but anyplace interesting in Guatemala is farther removed, and transport from the border area is poor.

Vans leave Copán Ruinas for the border at El Florido every hour, starting at 7 a.m. Leave town by noon to make onward connections. Buses leave from the border at 8 a.m., 10 a.m. and 12:30 p.m. for Chiquimula, the first major town in Guatemala. Intermittent transport in pickup trucks is sometimes available at other hours. For more details, see *Guatemala Guide*, by Paul Glassman (Open Road Publishing/Passport Press).

THINGS TO DO

Archaeology Museum

The Regional Museum, on the town square, is well done, and gives a good presentation of the Maya. Not only jade and shell and bone jewelry are housed here, but also some of the more valuable altars and monuments from both the main ceremonial center and outlying areas. You can see the reconstruction of a tomb, the jewels of a governor, the dried blood of an ancient sacrifice, a skull with jade filling in a tooth, a very male bat from Temple 22, an expressive sculpture called "the melancholy woman," and clay figurines.

The museum is well worth a visit. Hours are 8 a.m. to noon and 1 to 4 p.m., and there is a small charge.

Panoramic Views

For a panorama of the town of Copán Ruinas and the valley stretching beyond, walk up to the **Cuartel**, also known as Fuerte José Trinidad Cabañas, the remains of an old army outpost, on the hill four blocks directly north of the square — follow the road that passes the museum. Though of centenary appearance, with massive walls and corner towers, and empty inside but for a grassy expanse, it only dates from 1946.

WHERE TO STAY

Comfortable rooms are rather limited in number in Copán Ruinas, and if there's a tour group in town, facilities will be quickly overwhelmed. It's best to arrive with reservations, or in a rented vehicle so that you can backtrack to San Pedro Sula or continue to Guatemala if everything desirable is full.

Phone service to Copán Ruinas is limited. If you can't call a hotel directly, dial 983010 and ask for the hotel you want. If this doesn't work, send a telegram (which is inexpensive within Honduras).

These hotels are all on the main square, or just a few blocks away:

HOTEL MARINA, tel. 983070, 983071, fax 983072 (tel. 390956, fax 390957 in Tegucigalpa). 40 rooms. $64 single/ $75 double/$90 in suite, $11 per extra person, less in older rooms. Visa, Master Card, American Express. Add $25 for three meals.

This gracious establishment, located on one side of the main square, is the best place to stay, a complex that has grown from a traditional town home to a resort complex, the only one in this part of Honduras with pool, air-conditioned rooms, sauna, tennis courts, and meeting facilities. The wings of the new section, built in traditional ranch style with covered outdoor passageways, barrel-tile roofs and red-tile floors, surround quiet interior gardens. Rooms have televisions and modern bathrooms.

The older part of the hotel is dark and shady, with screened terraces, and tropical birds in the gardens. Rooms in this part go for about $20 double. There's also an annex with plainer rooms with shared baths, for about $5 per person.

Since the Marina is the only resort-class hotel in Copán Ruinas, it's often filled with visitors on package trips from San Pedro Sula or the Bay Islands; and a tour could well be your only option for getting a comfortable room in Copán Ruinas during the dry season. An overnight trip from San Pedro Sula generally costs $130 or more per person, including bus, meals, and guide service at the ruins.

The **HOTEL MAYA COPAN**, near the museum, with a courtyard covered with flowers and tropical plants, is attractive on the surface, though rooms are bare and rustic and just adequate, with little light. The rate is about $10 per person. Horseback rides and fishing can be arranged.

Inexpensive hotels are clustered along the road from the square out toward the ruins. The **BRISAS DE COPÁN** has simple, clean rooms — some have private baths. The **MINI-HOTEL PATY** has a few rooms behind the restaurant, sharing bath.

In the same area are **LOS GEMELOS** and the **HOTEL HERNÁNDEZ**. None of these are as atmospheric as the hotels on the square, where most rooms open onto a patio, but they'll do, especially with prices of $5 or so per person, or $10 with private bath. Take a look at what's available before you settle in.

WHERE TO EAT

Generally, you'll eat at the hotels. The **Glifos** ("glyphs") restaurant of the Hotel Marina offers the most extensive menu in the village, with everything from a club sandwich to Mexican-style chilaquiles (chicken, peppers and fixings served with sauce on tortillas) to steaks to chicken cordon bleu. Breakfast at the Marina costs about $4, lunch or dinner $10 or so for a complete meal.

La Llama del Bosque ("flame of the forest"), a block and a half from the museum, also has good food.

The **Tunkul**, a block south of the museum, is the local book exchange, gossip center, and not coincidentally, most popular spot for eating and imbibing. Bar food is served: sandwiches, salads, chicken, spaghetti and *baleadas* (Honduran burritos), all at $5 or less. Unusual for town eating places, pleasant North American music usually plays.

The **Mini-Hotel Paty** serves a set meal for $2, including a tiny main course but extensive garnishings of plantains, beans, and rice. And there are cheap eating stands in the market.

LEARN SPANISH

The **Escuela de Español Ixbalanque** ("Ish-ba-lan-keh" Spanish school) offers one-on-one instruction in Spanish for four hours a day, five days a week. Students board with local Spanish-speaking families, or have the option of staying at a hotel. The directors of the school are a Texan and a Honduran, and all teachers are government-certified.

Since Copán Ruinas is pretty much a backwater town without the hordes of resident foreigners present in other Spanish-language study centers (Antigua, Guatemala, or San José, Costa Rica), students have ample opportunity to experience the language in an extemporaneous manner. Which is to say, you can talk a lot in Spanish with real people in real-life situations.

Rates at Ixbalanque are modest, indeed — $125 a week, including room and board, if a room is taken with a local family. They'll even arrange pickup in San Pedro Sula for an additional charge.

To reserve class time and accommodations, contact Darla Brown, Escuela Ixbalanque, Copán Ruinas, Honduras, tel. 983432, fax 576215.

EXCURSIONS FROM COPÁN RUINAS

M.C. Tours, working out of the Hotel Marina, tel. 983453 and 983454, arranges package stays in Copán and excursions in the area. Offerings are a horseback tour of the coffee farm of the Welchez family, which owns the Hotel Marina; a visit to hot springs; a cloud forest hike; and a horseback visit to outlying ruins are available. Prices range from $25 to $30 per person. And, now that the phones are in, they can arrange package tours throughout the country.

Go Native Adventure Tours, working out of Ixbalanque Spanish School (tel. 983432, fax 576215), offers excursions to students and non-students alike. Destinations include Pico Bonito cloud forest, Cuero y Salado wildlife refuge, the forests, rivers and lagoons of Mosquitia, and a beach walk from Puerto Cortés to Tela. Rates vary accoriding to number of participants and the trip — about $150 to visit two reserves, including an overnight stay, $450 for a five-day trip through Mosquitia.

PRACTICAL INFORMATION
Exchanging Money
The free market for **currency exchange** is on the square. You can usually get rid of Guatemalan money here, or right at the border, if you're coming from that direction, but it will be hard to exchange Guatemalan currency anywhere else in Honduras. There's also a **bank** at one corner of the square.

Phone and Post
The Hondutel (**telephone**) office and **post office** are near the museum.

Laundry Service
Copán Ruinas is also the cleanup center for traveling grungy gringos. **Justo a Tiempo** ("Just in Time") laundry, just off the square alongside the church, offers same-day wash and dry. Arrive in the morning, drop off your clothes, see the ruins, and change for dinner. Open 7:30 a.m. to 5:30 p.m., Monday through Friday.

THE COPÁN RUINS
Beginnings
Copán was the Athens of the Mayan world, where art and astronomy flourished. There were larger Mayan cities to the north, in present-day Mexico and Guatemala, and the structures at Copán are relatively modest compared to those at Tikal and Palenque and Chichén-Itzá. But there are more carved monuments at Copán then elsewhere, and the intricate, swirling, decorative art surpasses not only that of other Mayan cities, but of any other civilization in the Western Hemisphere before the arrival of Europeans.

Copán might have been settled as early as 2000 B.C. The valley was fertile and well watered. Over time, harvests became more and more abundant, with the perfection of corn agriculture and of a calendar to guide planting. Gradually, more organized societies grew up in Copán and the neighboring areas, among the people that are today called the Maya.

Copán developed in much the same way as other Mayan cities. Simple thatched houses on foundations evolved into temples on substantial masonry platforms. Ironwood, or *chicozapote*, substituted for less sturdy materials in lintels. Relatively soft volcanic rock was dressed using harder rock, and later incised with obsidian tools. Household implements were made of wood and clay; as techniques improved, pottery became more complex, and beautiful, and was used for ceremonial purposes. Newer, more complicated, more beautiful buildings were erected right on top of older ones.

The custom developed of memorializing rulers and royal families and recording history on buildings and monuments and in tombs. Great stones were rolled down from nearby mountains, carved with glyph figures representing names and numbers and events, and erected in the plazas as stelae.

The Rise ...

None of this happened in isolation. The **Copán River**, which flows into the Motagua, in present-day Guatemala, probably served as a link to other Mayan centers, and as a route for trade in cacao and obsidian, and there were probably roads as well. There are some artistic similarities between Copán and Quiriguá in Guatemala, which could have been reached by water, and the same language was used for writing throughout the Mayan area.

The Classic Era at Copán spanned just a few hundred years, from 465 A.D., the first date inscribed on a monument, to 800 A.D. During this period of recorded history, construction and reconstruction and astronomical discoveries and artistic expression were most intense. Despite the general air of mystery that surrounds Copán, the names of some of its rulers are known, and some of its cultural history has even been uncovered: *Smoke Jaguar* lived to the ripe age of 82, and was succeeded by *18 Rabbit*, who broke the tradition of destroying monuments with each change in rulers and using the rubble as fill in new structures. 18 Rabbit's successor, *Squirrel*, commemorated rulers of old whose monuments had been destroyed, and rebuilt the ball court. Other rulers have been identified as *Leaf Jaguar*, *Smoke Monkey*, and *Dawn*.

... and Fall

But the creative impulse and energy of Copán were not to last forever. The city and its suburbs grew, perhaps to more than 15,000 inhabitants.

COPAN

Copán became no longer self-sufficient, and thus vulnerable. For some reason — perhaps war, disease, drought, famine, overuse of resources — building suddenly stopped, no more dates were inscribed, and maintenance came to a halt. Rain forest grew into the plazas and onto the temples, earthquakes tumbled temples, and the city was obscured. People still lived at and near Copán, but not as part of a great civilization.

Interest in Copán was lost, if not the city itself, for a thousand years. Then newly independent and newly opened Central America began to draw interest from potential trading partners. American diplomat John Lloyd Stephens visited Copán in 1839, and later published a description, accompanied by illustrations, in *Incidents of Travel in Central America, Chiapas and Yucatan.* He was so impressed that he bought the site — for fifty dollars.

Reviving Interest in Copán

Alfred P. Maudslay, arriving from England in 1881, was the first of a stream of archeologists to study Copán. For a time, the Carnegie Institution of Washington took charge of the ruins. The **Instituto Nacional de Antropología e Historia** assumed control in 1952. New excavations have been carried out in recent years. With ongoing work, interpretations of life at Copán, and of the Maya in general, are constantly being revised.

The main ceremonial center of Copán covers about 30 hectares, or

75 acres, but this is only a small part of the residential and administrative and ceremonial area that was built up by the Maya. Other areas which can be visited are called El Bosque ("the forest"), to the southwest, and Las Sepulturas ("the burials"), to the east. While the main temples and stelae are in the ceremonial center, important monuments, some with detailed chronologies, were placed up and down the slopes of the valley.

ORIENTATION

The ruins are a ten-minute walk from town, about a kilometer away. You can follow the road, or, more pleasantly, take the trail that runs just to the side of the road, right alongside some mounds and carved monuments, or stelae. The usual visiting hours at the site are from 8 a.m. to 4 p.m. An entry fee of several dollars is collected.

The **visitors' center** is well organized and well maintained. There are some exhibits, and a model of the site, photos, pottery (including pieces of Olmec and Teotihuacan origin), sculptured pieces of bone, and jade pendants. Time-line charts show the rise of the Maya relative to contemporary civilizations. Take a good look before you go out among the ruins. Several guide booklets are available for sale, including one in English published by the Instituto Hondureño de Antropología e Historia.

There are two **restaurants**, the official one in the visitor's center, with limited offerings; and one across the road, which is owned by one of the guides, is inexpensive, and serves decent, simple food. Both restaurants have gift shops attached. There are also picnic tables in a citrus grove toward the ruins.

Hiring a Guide

Guides can be hired on-site. They have a lot more information, especially in the way of local lore, than is provided in this book or in the booklets you can buy at the site; and though some of what they tell you may be strictly anecdotal, and may conflict with published descriptions and analyses, I strongly recommend that you hire one in order not to miss anything. Expect to pay a guide $10 or more for a two-hour walkaround.

Walking Around the Ceremonial Center

From the reception center, walk across the airstrip. You approach the ruins via a wide trail lined with towering tropical trees.

• **Caution 1**: You can be heavily fined if you destroy or damage anything at the site — stone, plant or animal — or if you try to take home any souvenirs. Or you can go to prison for several years. Or both.

• **Caution 2**: There are irritating plants, sometimes ten feet high, which can cause a severe reaction. They have pale-green leaves and small spines.

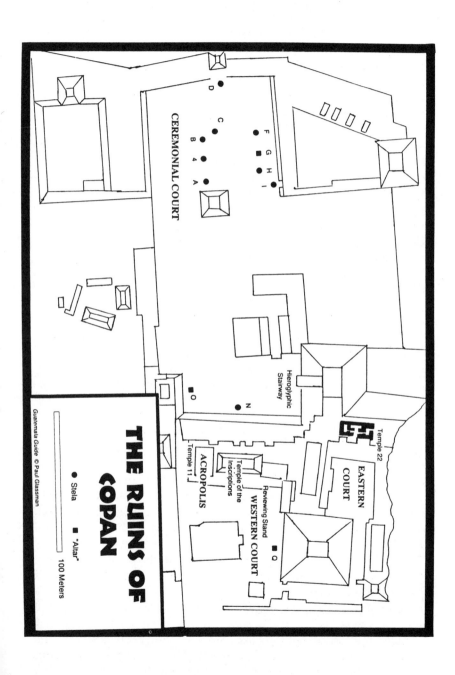

The **Ceremonial Court**, or **Great Plaza**, is the long, open area that you reach first, at the northern extreme of the ruins. There are stairways on three sides, and stelae, or large stones, reaching as high as four meters, carved with some of the most beautiful art created by the Maya. All of the exposed facing stones were once covered with stucco, and painted. In most cases, the stelae were erected to celebrate an important event, such as the coronation or accession of a ruler. The noble figure is depicted figuratively, with animals and fruits and trees as symbols of power and lineage and ruling forces. Elaborate glyphs depict dates and detail history. Everything is exaggerated, and interlaces in an Oriental manner, and indeed, some modern adventure-scholars have found notable similarities between Copán sculpture and art in Asia.

Most of the stelae show a noble, probably a king or other official of Copán, standing straight up with feet together, short arms crossed in front, holding a scepter, a flamboyant accoutrement upon his head. Additional figures and ornaments fill the front of the block, while glyphs on the sides and back relate the story of the ruler and his dynasty.

Stela A, dating from 731 A.D., at the south of the Ceremonial Court, includes the glyph symbols for Tikal and Palenque, indicating knowledge of and contact with those other Mayan cities. The chamber underneath this and other stelae held offerings of jewelry, ceramics, and sometimes animals. Stela 4, just north of Stela A, comes from late in the recorded history of Copán, and shows that art evolved toward more natural representation. A great round stone in front of Stela 4, looking like a four-foot-high Big Mac, was used to sacrifice captives and human offerings. The head of the victim was placed on a depression in the surface, and channels carried off the blood, making for a neat job.

Stela B, to the north of Stela 4, commemorates the accession of a ruler named 18 Rabbit. Symbols of power include the macaws' beaks at the top, miniature heads of previous rulers, and the detailed headdress. The beaks were once thought to be the trunks of elephants, imputing a direct knowledge by the Maya of things Asian. **Stela C**, unusually, has a figure carved on the back instead of glyphs, and shows traces of red paint, which might once have covered other monuments as well. Both an old and young figure are shown. A turtle-shaped stone lies alongside.

Stela D, next to the steps at the north end of the plaza, dating from 736 A.D., shows a double column of glyphs on the rear side. The short beard of the figure is an indication of youth. Sea shells and figures of gods appear on top. The figures on the altar before it are of Chac, the god of rain.

Along the east side of the plaza, **Stela F**, to the north, also with the remains of paint, shows a figure whose robes extend from the front around the sides to form a frame for the glyphs on the back. A representation of the sun is similar to those on stelae C and 4, and the same artist might well have carved all three. Next comes Altar G, a double-headed serpent with a glyph equivalent to 800 A.D., one of the latest dates written at Copán. **Stela H** shows an unusual figure in a skirt, who may be a representation of 18 Rabbit. A statue found underneath was made of gold that probably came from Colombia or Panama.

Stela I, inset in a stairway on the east side of the court, shows a masked figure, who may be Smoke Jaguar, who ruled from 628 to 695 A.D., and was the father of 18 Rabbit.

The **Central Court** is the area adjoining the ceremonial plaza, on the south. All the way at the eastern extreme is Stela J, covered completely by glyphs. The only similar Mayan stela known is at Quiriguá.

The **Ball Court** is just south of the Ceremonial Court, characteristically a narrow paved area with three sloped sides. Some glyphs along the platforms bear the Mayan equivalent of 775 A.D., and others represent royal macaws. The macaw was a sacred and symbolic bird for the Maya, and you'll see plenty of macaws around Copán today, especially on the fence at the entrance to the site. This court sits atop two earlier structures, the first built in the fifth century. The players probably had to hit markers along the side with a rubber ball. In ball games played elsewhere when the Spaniards arrived, the losers lost their heads.

The Ball Court is closed to foot traffic, and more and more areas of the site are being closed to casual visitors, as it becomes painfully clear that removing earth and debris, and exposing Mayan structures to the elements and to the footsteps of visitors, only hastens their deterioration.

To the south of the Ball Court is the most spectacular of Copán's treasures: the **Hieroglyphic Stairway**. More than a thousand glyphs set in the 63 steps — together constituting the longest known Mayan inscription — relate the history of Copán's rulers, up to 755 A.D., when the structure was dedicated under ruler *Smoke Shell*. Unfortunately, the glyphs can barely be read, since the stairway was rebuilt and the stones reset in random sequence.

Along the center of the stairway are four male sculptures that remain of the original five. An altar before the steps shows a head inside the jaws of a monster.

In 1989, archeologists excavating behind the hieroglyphic stairway stumbled upon a noble tomb, considered to be that of *Yax Cuc Mol*, King Quetzal-Macaw.

Along the south of the stairway plaza, **Stela N** is an especially beautiful work of art, dated at 761 A.D. The human faces on each side extend to the edges, almost as a precursor to a statue. Serpents and indications of the cardinal points can be seen on top. One glyph on the back represents Mars; the Maya also had symbols for Jupiter and Venus.

Altar O, opposite the Hieroglyphic Stairway, is a stone block with a depression that might have served as a seat. **Altar 41**, nearby, has a jaguar face and a snake at the north and south ends, respectively, of its front face, possibly representing a mythical struggle. "Altar" is a generic term, used in the absence of any real knowledge of what purposes these blocks served.

The group of structures to the south of the Hieroglyphic Stairway is called the **Acropolis**. Overlooking the Western Court of the Acropolis is **Temple 11**, with its staircase called the Reviewing Stand. Huge snails and grotesque gods, one of them *Ik*, the rain god, adorn the way up the steps to the Temple of the Inscriptions, with its glyph panels. "El Viejo" (The Old Man), the gap-toothed sculpture at the southwest corner of the superstructure, stares right at a stela on a distant mountainside. Temple 11 was built during the reign of *Yax Pac* ("King Dawn," also known as "rising sun"), who ruled from 763 A.D. until his death in 820, and oversaw the last major construction at Copán.

In 1993, a tomb was discovered under Acropolis, apparently that of *Yax Kuk Mo*, the fifth-century ruler who founded Copán's royal dynasty.

Along the eastern edge of the Western Court, **Altar Q** depicts the royal lineage of Yax Pac. Four royal figures are shown on each side of the rectangular block; together, they are Yax Pac, and his 15 ancestors.

The last major area of central Copán is the **Eastern Court** of the Acropolis. Like other open areas, this plaza was slightly sloped, and a Mayan drain still carries off rain water. **Temple 22**, on the north side, built under the reign of *18 Rabbit*, who ruled from 695 to 738 A.D., is another spectacular example of Mayan architecture as spectacle. The doorway to the structure at the top is flanked by sculpture that turns it into monstrous serpents' jaws. At the corners are figures of *Chac*, the long-nosed god of rain. These motifs are indications of influence from Mayan areas farther to the north. The inner doorway shows themes from Mayan cosmology, including death's heads at the base. Along the sides, figures called *Bacabs*, looking like caricatures of modern-day Maya, hold up heaven, with a two-headed serpent above.

A model of Temple 22 may be seen in the visitors' center.

On the west side of the Eastern Court is the **Jaguar Stairway**. Stone jaguars flank the steps. Their eye sockets, now empty, were once filled with polished obsidian.

Temple 20, largely sliced away by the shifting Copán River below, is on the eastern side of the court. The river was re-routed in 1935 to forestall further damage. Some protective work is still going on. The layers visible on the damaged side of the temple neatly illustrate how new buildings were erected directly atop older ones.

Nature Trail

Adjacent to the ceremonial center is a trail through a section of tropical forest that has been protected from agricultural development. A Spanish-language guide booklet is available on site. The trail runs for about a kilometer, ending at **Ball Court B**.

Copán's protected forest is a sample of leafy mid-level rain forest, with its vegetation determined by elevation, rainfall and temperature. It's considered a seasonally dry forest, since rain falls mostly from May to November, and the trees shed their leaves during dry periods to conserve energy.

Much of the relatively dense forest seen today has grown back only over the last 50 years; many centuries are required for full regeneration of the original diversity and complexity of the forest, and even that may never happen, since agriculture has taken away the habitat of many of the original species. In the process of recovery, the forest penetrates the mounds of stone built by the Maya, and deliberately, steadily and inevitably demolishes their work — unless held back by consolidation teams.

The nature trail is low-lying, and can be waterlogged during the rainy season.

Nineteen numbered stopping points indicate particular features of the forest, such as Mayan mounds, humus, and secondary growth.

Species of interest include:
• *Matapioja* ("lice-killer"): the root of which forms a shampoo effective in treating lice.
• *chichicaste*: a thorny plant often seen on roadsides
• *anona* (custard apple): one of many trees with edible fruits. Others are the *ramón* or *masica* (breadnut), still occasionally used as a food source, with shiny leaves similar to those on coffee bushes; and the *guanacaste*, or earpod, with its brush-like leaves.
• *ceiba* (silk-cotton): one of the massive trees of the tropical forest, with great buttress roots to support its weight in the shallow soil
• *guarumo* (cecropia): a tree swarming with ants that feed on its sap and lay their eggs in its trunk.
• *matapalo* (strangler fig): which climbs, entangles, penetrates, overwhelms, and eventually murders many a tropical tree that provides its initial support.

Once you get to know many of the trees along the nature trail, you'll be able to identify them among the ruins. The ceiba in particular grows on many temples, able to support its massive trunk with buttresses and roots that penetrate the cracks between stones.

Significant animals that frequent or occasionally enter the nature reserve and ruins include:
• The jaguar, which figures widely in Mayan ceramics and stone carving
• White-tailed deer
• Monkeys
• Bats.

Las Sepulturas

About two kilometers east of the ceremonial center, this ancient residential area has been studied intensively only in the last decade. Some of the houses were modest, but others had multiple rooms and sculptured façades, and some of the tombs have yielded magnificent vases.

It is thought that the residents included foreigners, such as *Lencas*, who traded with or otherwise served the purposes of the Maya. Jade found in Las Sepulturas and elsewhere in Copán evidences trade with the Motagua valley area of Guatemala. Some of the most notable pieces of sculpture from Las Sepulturas, including one known as El Brujo, are on exhibit at the museum in town.

Tickets for Las Sepulturas are sold at the visitors' center near the central part of Copán. Hours here are also from 8 a.m. to 4 p.m.

After Copán?

After visiting the ruins of Copán, the choices for most travelers are to continue to Guatemala (see page 210), or to return to San Pedro Sula. The adventurer's route, however, is around the bend of Honduras north of the Salvadoran border, through the mountains, and back toward Comayagua and Tegucigalpa.

Side Trips

Aguascalientes are hot springs about 45 minutes by car from Copán Ruinas. Some tours stop at the springs going to or from Copán Ruinas.

South toward Santa Rosa de Copán

From La Entrada, where the branch road forks toward Copán Ruinas, the main highway of the west continues toward the regional center of **Santa Rosa de Copán**. Along the way, at **San Nicolás**, are ponds formed by the Chorro de Carrizal and the Chorro del Callejón, artesian geysers.

At **Trinidad** are some partially explored caves, in the hill of the same name, and **Zapotal Lake**.

SANTA ROSA DE COPÁN

Santa Rosa de Copán is 170 kilometers from San Pedro Sula, at the near-perfect tropical altitude of 1100 meters. With a church nearly 200 years old, cobblestoned streets and tile-roofed houses, Santa Rosa has a pleasant colonial air, though it was founded only in 1802, not long before independence. Tobacco has long been a major crop in the area, and cigars are made in town.

ARRIVALS AND DEPARTURES
By Bus
Connections to north, south and west are very good from Santa Rosa de Copán. There are buses about every hour to Nueva Ocotepeque, to the south, connecting with small shuttle buses for the Guatemalan border at Agua Caliente. Trade and religious pilgrims follow this route to Esquipulas, just inside Guatemala. Buses for San Pedro Sula also depart at least every hour, passing the junction for Copán Ruinas at La Entrada. The bus station is on the highway outside of town, a short ride by local bus or taxi.

From Tegucigalpa, Santa Rosa de Copán is served by Transportes Catrachos. About five buses operate daily.

WHERE TO STAY
As a stopping point on the main route to Guatemala, Santa Rosa de Copán, has a good supply of rooms, mostly no-frills traveling salesmen's accommodations. Almost all of the hotels will feed their clients as well.

HOTEL CONTINENTAL, tel. 620802. 20 rooms, $15 per person. Modern hotel, with bar, restaurant, parking, and cable television.

HOTEL ELVIR, Calle Centenario, tel. 620103. 35 rooms. $15 single/ $22 double. Also fairly new, with a good, plain restaurant, televisions in rooms, private bathrooms.

HOTEL MAYALAND, tel. 620147. 30 rooms, $10 single, $15 double. Large hotel with coffee shop and bar, near bus terminal.

Cheaper rooms, for $6 per person or less, are available at the **HOTEL ERICK** and the **HOTEL MAYA**, and, less desirably, at the **HOTEL COPÁN**.

PRACTICAL INFORMATION
Banks
Santa Rosa de Copán's facilities include several banks (**Banco Atlántida**, **Banco Central** on the main square, **Banco de Occidente** on Calle Centenario).

NUEVA OCOTEPEQUE
Nueva Ocotepeque is just 15 kilometers away from both Guatemala and El Salvador, in piney highlands along the **Lempa River**. The Lempa rises in Guatemala, and forms part of the still-disputed border with El Salvador. The original town of Ocotepeque was founded in 1830 — its

Nahuatl name means "pine hill" — and destroyed by floods on the Marchala River in 1934. Nueva ("new") Ocotepeque was founded the following year, on the site of the village of Sinuapa.

In the short, bitter war of 1969, the army of El Salvador quickly captured Nueva Ocotepeque, but was obliged to retire soon after, under diplomatic pressure.

Montecristo-Trifinio National Park, near Ocotepeque, extends into Guatemala and El Salvador, including the border-marking peak of Montecristo (2419 meters) covering 54 square kilometers of regenerating forest. The absolute reserve above 1800 meters covers 20 square kilometers, most of which is regenerating forest. The park is currently in a state of development.

ARRIVALS AND DEPARTURES
By Bus

Buses leave frequently for the Guatemalan border, and it's also possible to cross to El Salvador and continue to San Salvador, 100 kilometers distant, if you have reason to go that way, but inquire first about conditions along the route. Guatemala has a consulate in Nueva Ocotepeque.

GRACIAS

Gracias, high in the pine country of southwest Honduras, was founded in 1536 by Gonzalo de Alvarado, brother of the conqueror of Guatemala, and for a time was the base from which the valley of Comayagua was subdued. The name of the town is a shortened form of the phrase of thanksgiving, "*gracias a Dios.*"

Gracias saw its moment of glory several hundred years ago. In 1544, the Audiencia de los Confines, then the governing council for all of Central America, was briefly based here. But Gracias soon lost all importance. The trade route from Guatemala passed to the west. The silver mines were in Tegucigalpa to the southeast. And the regional capital settled in Comayagua, to the northeast, once the rebellious chief Lempira was subdued.

This early loss of face, though, had the effect of preserving some of the town's colonial heritage. Three colonial churches survive, along with the Casa de los Leones, one of the first buildings in Gracias, named for the heraldic lions that decorate its doorway. Old fortifications above the town can be visited as well, and there are some **hot springs** nearby. And overlooking Gracias from the west is the peak of **Celaque** ("cold water" in Nahuatl, the language of the Indian allies of the conquistadors), at 2849 meters (9350 feet) the highest mountain in Honduras.

ARRIVALS AND DEPARTURES

By Bus

At least five buses run daily between Santa Rosa de Copán and Gracias, a two-hour ride. While Gracias is reached most easily from Santa Rosa de Copá, the road from Tegucigalpa via La Esperanza is being improved.

WHERE TO STAY

Accommodations are available at the **HOTEL ERICK** near the square and the **HOTEL IRIS**, by the **San Sebastián church**, as well as at several other basic, family-run establishments.

Nearby Celaque National Park

Celaque National Park takes in the largest cloud forest in Honduras on Celaque mountain, and also the richest, its diversity protected by the steep slopes that have resisted cut-and-burn agriculture over the centuries. Among endangered mammals that inhabit the park are ocelots, peccaries, pumas and jaguars. Quetzals and linnets are among resident bird species. There is even wild cattle.

The park is currently being developed for visitors. Trails, dormitories and campsites are being prepared, and some may be available at the time of your visit. Inquire for information at the COHDEFOR (forestry) office in Gracias, opposite the southeast corner of the square.

The most direct access route to the park is from Gracias along the road to the hydroelectric station; there is also a trail to the peak from Belén Gualcho, to the west. The ascent to the peak takes two to three days.

LA ESPERANZA AND INTIBUCA

La Esperanza is the administrative center of the department of Intibucá. Adjacent is the town of **Intibucá**, for the most part populated by Lenca Indians who still maintain their traditional ways: communal land ownership, and *guancascos,* exchange visits of saints at town fiesta times, among other customs.

La Esperanza and Intibucá are located at over 1600 meters, on a plateau that is still partly forested, and timber is one of the main products of the region. The cool climate and old adobe houses with thick walls lend a remote, old-time air. Sunday is the traditional market day, when country people come to town to sell their wares, much in the manner of Indian villages in Guatemala.

La Gruta, once a penal colony, contains an altar to the Virgin of Lourdes. Nearby are public swimming areas. A few kilometers out, at **La Posona**, is a dam with fishing, and boats for rent.

ARRIVALS AND DEPARTURES

By Bus

La Esperanza is 86 kilometers by gravel road from the main Tegucigalpa-San Pedro Sula highway at Siguatepeque. There is usually one daily bus from the capital (4 Calle, 8/9 Avenidas, Comayagüela), and one from San Pedro Sula. Buses leave at the break of day for Tegucigalpa, San Pedro Sula and Comayagua.

WHERE TO STAY

There is inexpensive lodging, including the **HOTEL GÓMEZ**.

MARCALA

Marcala, southeast of La Esperanza on the way to El Salvador, is one of the centers of coffee growing in Honduras. It's a pleasant center with a main square shaded by full-grown trees. The ridge of mountains to the east shelters several communities of indigenous Lenca who have maintained their traditional ways over the centuries.

15. SOUTHERN & EASTERN HONDURAS

INTRODUCTION

South to the Coast

You leave Tegucigalpa on a road through hilly country, climbing to **Sabana Grande**. There are good views of high plateaus. The vegetation changes to pines, and it is fresh and windy as you gain altitude. From the heights, before long, you can see the Gulf of Fonseca in the distance, as you begin to wind down through hilly and broken terrain toward the Pacific Ocean.

Once in the low country, you follow the course of the Nacaome River. At **Pespire**, right along the river, there is a church with silver domes, impressive and unexpected. Pespire ("pyrite river") is an old town, founded in 1640.

You reach the Pan American Highway at **Jicaro Galán**. Here you can stay at the **TURICENTRO OASIS,** 25 rooms, tel. 812220. $25 single/$30 double, $40 for four persons. A full-fledged motel and highway resort, getting on in years but well maintained, with air-conditioning, pool, restaurant, and cable television. Arrangements can be made for horseback riding, and fishing in the Gulf of Fonseca. The restaurant here serves a range of seafood and steak main courses, as well as sandwiches and salads, at a top price of about $7. If you're driving through the area, you can stop and use the pool at a charge of a dollar or so a person; or for free, if you order something in the restaurant.

A right turn there takes you to **Nacaome** ("double flesh," signifying two founding Indian nations), six kilometers onward on the way to El Salvador. Nacaome officially dates from 1535 as a town, though it was a major indigenous settlement long before. Nacaome is on a strategic invasion route: in 1844, the Honduran army defeated the Nicaraguans here. There is a colonial church in Nacaome, and there are two hot springs within walking distance.

Goascoran is the town near the border of El Salvador — El Amatillo lies on the other side. Silver was once mined nearby. Goascarán has the most basic of accommodations. Buses run frequently to the border from the Belén market in Comayagüela.

THE GULF OF FONSECA

Five kilometers onward from Jícaro Galán toward the east is the intersection for **Tigre Island**. Three volcanoes are visible, one each in Nicaragua and El Salvador, and one on Tigre Island itself (see below).

Namasique, near the gulf, was a field of battle in the 1907 war with Nicaragua, and saw the first use of machine guns in Central America.

The Gulf of Fonseca is the huge inlet of the Pacific Ocean bordered by El Salvador, Nicaragua and Honduras. Of 288 islands in the gulf – most of them Honduran, some awarded to El Salvador in a recent border arbitration – **Zacate Grande** ("tall grass") is the largest, adjacent to the mainland and reached by bridge. **Isla de Pájaros**, "bird island," has what you would expect: lots of birds. And the treasures of Sir Francis Drake and other pirates are buried along the many beaches in the gulf, if you believe what people say.

The area under and around the gulf seethes with volcanic activity, and the great Central American volcanic ridge marches right across the water. Cosigüina Volcano, nearby in Nicaragua, 859 meters high, erupted spectacularly in 1838. On the Salvadoran side is Conchagua Volcano, 1243 meters high. **El Tigre Island**, between the two, is a volcano.

AMAPALA

Amapala, on El Tigre Island, reached by ferry from the end of the road, was for most of the history of Honduras the major Pacific port of the country, and once the locale of major intrigue. Britain occupied El Tigre Island in 1849 to make a point about debts owed by Honduras, an action that stirred the ire of the United States, not to mention that of the locals.

Now that modern container facilities have been built near San Lorenzo, off the Pan American Highway, Amapala is on the way to becoming a ghost town, with some of the lost-in-time atmosphere that clings to the old mining towns near Tegucigalpa. The ascent of the island-volcano is relatively easy as volcano-climbing goes. Amapala's **beaches** are sticky, dark volcanic sand, and little-frequented, except at holiday times.

ARRIVALS AND DEPARTURES

To reach Amapala, take a bus from Tegucigalpa toward Choluteca, and get off at the road junction before San Lorenzo. Pickup-taxis take passengers to the strait at El Coyolito, where skiffs can be hired for the short trip across to the island.

WHERE TO STAY

The **PENSIÓN INTERNACIONAL** offers meals and inexpensive beds. Otherwise, accommodations are limited.

Moving East

Continuing east from Jícaro Galán, you pass **San Lorenzo**, the processing center for Honduras' recently developed (and thriving) shrimp farming industry – shrimp are now the third leading export. Nearby are port and container facilities at **Henecán**; and the junction for **Balneario Cedeño**, a beach on the Gulf of Fonseca (see below). Oxcarts appear from the fields. Huts are primitive. It all seems out of the Middle Ages, until suddenly you are at the impressive suspension bridge at the entrance to Choluteca over a muddy river.

CHOLUTECA

Choluteca is the major city of the south, 142 kilometers from Tegucigalpa, with a population of over 50,000. The Cholula Indians of Mexico might have known or settled the area, lending their name to the city. Spanish dispatches mention Choluteca as early as 1522, for the wealth of its mines. The city was renamed in 1585 as Jérez de la Frontera de Choluteca, after a city in Spain, and had nicknames that referred to tamarind-sized gold nuggets mined nearby. It was also an indigo-producing center around the time of independence, until that market collapsed with the development of synthetic dyes.

Choluteca lies on a vast alluvial plain guarded by mountains, which, like few other parts of southern Honduras, is suitable for large-scale agriculture. You'll see herds of cattle guided by cowboys. Sugar cane is also evident. The relatively dry and sometimes hot area also produces excellent melons. The rainy season here is mainly from May to September.

Though there are no particular activities in town for visitors, Choluteca is clean and pleasant enough, a transit point with good accommodations. It's also a base for dove hunting. The season runs from November 1 to March 15.

ARRIVALS AND DEPARTURES

By Bus

Service is very efficient between Tegucigalpa and Choluteca. There are hourly buses throughout the day, until 6 p.m. Some buses continue to San Marcos de Colón, to the east. From there, you can pick up another bus to the Nicaraguan border, and continue to Managua, if you happen to be headed that way.

From Tegucigalpa, buses leave from the Mi Esperanza station, 6

Avenida, 24/25 Calles, Comayagüela (tel. 382863). Service is every hour from 6 a.m. The ride takes about three hours, the ticket costs less than $2.

There are several other companies as well that serve this route, including Transportes Dandy, 20 Calle, 6/7 Avenidas, Comayagüela, with departures every two hours. In Choluteca, the Mi Esperanza station, one block from the Pan American Highway, has a restaurant and hotel, neither especially recommendable.

These buses will also drop you at the turn for Cedeño beach.

WHERE TO STAY

HOTEL PIERRE, Avenida Valle, Barrio El Centro, tel. 820676, 29 rooms. $12 single/$17 double with fan, $20 single/$25 double with air conditioning. Centrally located, very clean, opposite the market downtown. Friendly personnel, well-maintained and recommended. Protected parking.

HOTEL LA FUENTE, Pan American Highway, tel. 820263 or 820253, fax 820273. 45 rooms, $29 single/$42 double. American Express, Master Card, Visa. This is the best-known hotel in Choluteca, with a nice interior garden with pool. Rooms are air-conditioned and clean, and there are a bar and restaurant, but facilities and furniture are getting on in years, with doubtful maintenance. If you stay elsewhere in town, you can use the pool and garden here for a minimal fee. Some rooms get the noise of the Restaurant Charley, a popular local hangout.

HOTEL PACÍFICO, tel. 820838. $6 per person ($14 with air conditioning). This is the perfect budget hotel, clean and simple and quiet, with a nice interior courtyard. A block from the highway, and two blocks from the bus station.

The three-story **HOTEL IMPERIO MAYA** (35 rooms, tel. 822625, fax 820273) is on the Pan American Highway next to the Shell gasoline station. It's just so-so, but rooms are clean and the price is only about $18 double with private bath, and air conditioning that might work.

HOTEL CAMINO REAL, Guasaule road (P. O. Box 13), tel. 820610, fax 822860. 23 rooms, $22 single/$28 to $35 double. Master Card, Visa. Located a kilometer east of town on the Pan American Highway. Simple rooms, pool, nice garden. You can take a taxi to the hotel from the bus station for less than a dollar.

HOTEL BRASSAVOLA, Barrio Cabañas, tel. 822534, fax 822555. $12 single/$20 double. A downtown hotel with air-conditioned rooms with televisions; coffee shop; parking; *and*, quite unusually, self-service washing machines and dryers.

WHERE TO EAT

There aren't too many places to eat here. At the **Hotel Pierre**, the coffee shop is clean, and provides honest meals for $4 and less. Nearby is **Pizza Taste**, run by the owner of the Pierre. The restaurant in the **Hotel La Fuente** is somewhat more elaborate. And the **Charley Restaurant**, next to Hotel La Fuente, a beer garden (*jardín cervecero*) serving grilled meats accompanied by music, is the in place in town, open only from 7 p.m. to 11 p.m.

The **Camino Real** hotel on the eastern outskirts is a favorite meal stop for drivers. There's a sheltered dining patio, as well as an air-conditioned restaurant. Seafood and sandwiches are served, with most dishes priced under $4 — a good deal, indeed. And the fruit drinks are refreshing in the local heat.

PRACTICAL INFORMATION

There are branches of the **Banco Central de Honduras**, **Banco Atlántida** and **Banco de Occidente**, and taxi drivers who double as money changers. A **Hondutel** office can handle long-distance calls. The **post office** is in the same building. Several **pharmacies** include **Los Indios**, opposite the Banco de Occidente. The **Viajes Mundiales travel agency** is located in the Centro Comercial (shopping center) at Calle Real 205.

I mention all these because in most country towns in Honduras, you can expect to find very little in the way of facilities. A **landing strip** accommodates small planes, though a larger commercial jetport is planned for a site north of the city.

SEEING THE SIGHTS

Newly restored is the house of **José Cecilio del Valle**, one of authors of the declaration of independence of Central America, near the Cathedral opposite Valle Park. There's a cultural center in the colonial church of La Merced, which dates from 1643, with some exhibits, usually by local artists. Construction of the suspension bridge over the Choluteca River was started in 1935 and completed in 1937. And there is also a correspondence university in town.

Directly east of Choluteca, at **El Corpus**, about 15 kilometers down a dirt road, is the **Poza de Ocampo**, a noted local swimming hole.

CEDEÑO

Cedeño is located along the Gulf of Fonseca about 35 kilometers from Choluteca. The gulf has unlimited beaches, the waves are not too big, and the water is warm. And there are no dangerous currents, as at the more exposed beaches elsewhere on this coast. The village and beach are crowded on weekends, especially on Sundays.

Cedeño is more a fishing village than the beach resort ("*balneario*") that it is claimed to be. There are some hotels, but all are dirty. If you want to stay here, you'd do better to camp outside of the village. Ask permission of the owner of any desirable site.

Many small eateries serve fresh fish and shrimp. It's really pleasant to enjoy your meal and look out to the fishermen landing the catch in narrow boats. People around here are obviously of more Indian descent than others in the interior of the country. Houses along the beach are on stilts, and everything looks ready to fall down.

ARRIVALS AND DEPARTURES
By Bus or Taxi
Buses run from the Choluteca market to Cedeño about every hour, and the trip takes about 90 minutes. Or, you can go in a taxi for about $15 for as many passengers as will fit in. From Tegucigalpa, there are direct buses from the Mercado Mayoreo (wholesale market) at 3:30 a.m. and 1:30 p.m. These take about three and a half hours.

By Car
By car, Cedeño is about 33 kilometers off the Pan American Highway, via a paved, flat road. Along the way you get a view of oxcarts, melon and sugarcane fields, sugar processing plants, and salt pans, where sea water is evaporated.

PUNTA RATÓN WILDLIFE RESERVE
Up the gulf, reached by a road that branches from the road to Cedeño, is the **Punta Ratón Wildlife Reserve**, just south of the village of Punta Ratón. Giant sea turtles nest here from August into November.

Other wildlife reliably sighted in the dense forest and along the narrow strip of beach and overhead includes sea birds, parrots, doves, pelicans, and iguanas.

GUASAULE
Guasaule is the town on the Pan American Highway at the border with Nicaragua. There are no accommodations of note. Local buses run from Choluteca. Arrive by 3 p.m. if planning to continue into Nicaragua.

San Marcos de Colon, to the northeast of Choluteca, is higher up, at an elevation of almost 900 meters. About ten kilometers to the east is **El Espino**, on the border of Nicaragua.

From Tegucigalpa, buses for San Marcos leave from the Mi Esperanza station, 6 Avenida, 24/25 Calles, Comayagüela, about every two hours.

East of Tegucigalpa
What with *Contra* training camps and border skirmishes, the road to **Danlí**, 108 kilometers east of Tegucigalpa, was little traveled in recent

years, except by those with a military stake in the area, and foreign journalists. With the outbreak of peace in Nicaragua and along the border, there is now no reason for others to stay away.

The road to Danlí passes **San Antonio de Oriente** (see page 116) and **El Zamorano** (see page *****), both easily reached on day excursions from Tegucigalpa.

Yuscaran, "place of the house of flowers" (in Nahuatl), off the Danlí highway to the south, is an ex-mining town, picturesque like other, similar towns that have been left behind economically. Founded around 1730 as a base for exploiting the Quemazones and Guayabillas mines, it retains some old buildings, including the Fortín house, a nineteenth-century residence open daily to the public. **Güinope**, to the southwest of Yuscarán, is known for its orange groves.

DANLÍ

Danlí ("sandy stream" in Nahuatl), founded in 1667, is the major town of the area directly east of Tegucigalpa, where sugar, tobacco and coffee are produced. Located at an altitude of 700 meters, about four hours from the capital by bus, it offers fair accommodations, and surroundings of piney hills. Danlí's corn festival is celebrated the last week of August to honor the staff of life in Central America, with corn stew (p*ozole*), corn beverages (*atol*), corn hooch (*chicha*), corn tortillas, and corn cakes, along with rodeos and bullfights.

The road south from Danlí heads toward Estelí in Nicaragua.

ARRIVALS AND DEPARTURES

Buses of the Discua Litena company (tel. 327939) serve Danlí from the Jacaleapa market in Tegucigalpa, on the road to Colonia Kennedy, about five kilometers from downtown. Also Emtraoriente, 6 Calle, 6/7 Avenida, Comayagüela, tel. 378965, 6 departures from 6:30 a.m. to 4:30 p.m. for Danlí and Paraíso, farther south.

Transportation is available several times an hour to the Nicaraguan border at Las Manos, about 30 kilometers to the south.

Facilities in Danlí include several **banks** (Banco Atlántida, Banco Central de Honduras, Banco Sogerin).

WHERE TO STAY

GRAN HOTEL GRANADA, tel. 932499, fax 932774. 36 rooms, $12 per person. A motel on the way out toward Tegucigalpa. Bar and restaurant, air-conditioned rooms, pool.

Also: **HOTEL LA ESPERANZA**, Calle Gabriela Mistral, next to the Esso station, tel. 932106; and **HOTEL EBENEZER**, tel. 932655. Each about $8 per person.

Northeast of Tegucigalpa

The Olancho Highway runs north from Tegucigalpa through mountains, and then northeast through hills in the vast grasslands of Olancho department.

Cedros, 85 kilometers from Tegucigalpa, on a spur from the Olancho road, is a mining town where the first constitutional congress of Honduras was held in 1824.

JUTICALPA

Juticalpa ("place of snails" in Nahuatl) is the major town of Olancho department. The first Spanish settlement in this part of Honduras, it was founded by refugees from the original settlement of San Jorge de Olancho, which was destroyed by a volcanic eruption in 1611 (other refugees founded Olanchito, farther to the north).

Juticalpa and environs are the Wild West of Honduras, a sparsely settled frontier area with its own traditions. Horseback riders use a peculiar saddle with heavy, shoe-like stirrups to which a lasso is tied. Gold has been mined since colonial times, and panned along the Guayape River. In addition to cattle ranches, sugar and grains are planted.

ARRIVALS AND DEPARTURES

Juticalpa is about five hours by bus from Tegucigalpa. Empresa Aurora buses depart about every hour from 8 Calle, 6/7 Avenidas, Comayagüela. The main road continues northeast from Juticalpa to Catacamas and Dulce Nombre de Culmí, and up to the Caribbean lowlands, reaching the coast at Iriona. Another road heads to the northwest, then runs almost parallel with the former road, before turning to the northwest to terminate in Trujillo.

At least one bus runs daily along this route — a full day's journey away. Another track runs to the northwest, over wild, sparsely inhabited mountains and down toward Olanchito and the department of Yoro.

WHERE TO STAY

HOTEL EL PASO, tel. 952311, has parking. HOTEL ANTÚNEZ, tel 952250, is quite large, with 45 rather plain rooms. About $10 per person at either, nothing better is available.

Catacamas

Catacamas, site of a government agricultural school, has a few plain hotels, among them the JUAN CARLOS (tel. 954212), the CENTRAL, tel. 954276, and the CATACAMAS, tel. 954085. Some buses from Tegucigalpa for Juticalpa continue to Catacamas.

Further East

Sierra de Agalta National Park lies 50 kilometers northeast of Juticalpa and about 20 kilometers north of Catacamas. Included in the park's boundaries are the Agalta Ridge, with peaks as high as 2500 meters, one of the largest expanses of dwarf forest in Honduras, and numerous caves. Unique to the park is the *choloepus hoffmanni*, a species of two-toed sloth.

Dormitories, trails and campsites are being readied. For information on the current state of facilities, inquire at COHDEFOR, the forestry department, in Juticalpa.

The **Talgua Cave**, undeveloped for visitors, lies five kilometers from Catacamas along the main highway.

Dulce Nombre de Culmi, on the edge of the northeastern wilderness of Honduras, was a colonial settlement, from which the Spanish attempted to raid the English trading post at Black River on the Caribbean.

HONDURAS MISCELLANY

In this section you'll find assorted information, observations, and facts and figures – useful and otherwise.

BILLIARDS

This can seem to be the national entertainment. There are *billares* in every city and town. Billiards is a men's game, and only a certain type of woman is tolerated in pool halls.

COKE BOTTLES

These have replaced the cross on many a hilltop, in enlarged size, though you should make no mistake, the Catholic church remains quite strong in Honduras.

FIESTAS

In addition to national holidays, every town has its own local celebration day, usually in honor of its patron saint. In some Indian towns of the west, fiestas are rich in religious tradition. Elsewhere, they are revelry with no excuses, a break from humdrum existence, with beauty contests, dances, and always lots of drinking. Itinerant purveyors of mechanical games, cotton candy and religious trinkets eke out a living by following the fiesta route from town to town.

Here's a compiled list of town fiestas, usually giving the main day, though festivities can last for up to a week. Many of these towns are not mentioned elsewhere in this book. The department (*departamento*, or province) is listed to help you find each place.

January

1: Dulce Nombre de Culmí, Olanchi. 6: La Unión, Copán; Fraternidad, Ocotepeque. 14: San Juan, La Paz; San Antonio de Oriente, Francisco Morazán; 15: Cedros, Francisco Morazán; Esquías, Comayagua; El Triunfo, Choluteca; Liure, El Paraíso; San Lucas, Paraíso; Intibucá, Intibucá; San Juan, Intibucá; Opatorio, La Paz; San Juan, La Paz; San Manuel Colohete, Lempira; Esquipulas del Norte, Olancho; Guayape, Olancho; Gualala,

Santa Bárbara; Langue, Valle; Jocón, Yoro; Victoria, Yoro. 18: Morocelí, Paraíso. 20: San Sebastián, Comayagua; Pespire, Choluteca; Alauca, Paraíso; Danlí, Paraíso; Marale, Francisco Morazán; Ojojona, Francisco Morazán; Reitoca, Francisco Morazán; Colomoncagua, Intibucá; Erandique, Lempira; San Sebastián, Lempira; Aramecina, Valle; Olanchito, Yoro. 20: Santa Lucía, Francisco Morazán; 21: Jesús de Otoro, Intibucá. 25: Cedeño, Choluteca; Siguatepeque, Comayagua; Soledad, Paraíso; Ceguaca, Santa Bárbara.

February
2: Tegucigalpa: Virgin of Suyapa, Patron Saint of Honduras; Duyure, Choluteca; Comayagua, Comayagua (Virgin of Candelaria); Humuya, Comayagua; El Corpus, Choluteca; Jacaleapa, Paraíso; Sabanagrande, Francisco Morazán; Villa de San Francisco, Francisco Morazán; San Antonio, La Paz; Yarula, La Paz; Candelaria, Lempira; Cololaca, Lempira; Sesenti, Ocotepeque; Salamá, Olancho; Santa María del Real, Olancho; San Francisco de Ojuera, Santa Bárbara; Sensentí, Ocotepeque; Goascarán, Valle. 9: Concepción del Sur, Santa Bárbara. 11: Veracruz, Copán; Choloma, Cortés; Ilama, Santa Bárbara. 14: San Matías, Paraíso; La Campa, Lempira. 24: San Jerónimo, Copán. 28: Santa Fé, Ocotepeque; Concordia, Olancho.
Third Saturday: Paraíso, Paraíso (coffee festival).

March
4: La Unión, Lempira. 7: Concepción del Sur, Santa Bárbara. 8: Mapulaca, Lempira. 19: San José de Comayagua; Copán Ruinas; Florida, Copán; Morolica, Choluteca; San José, Choluteca; Oropolí, Paraíso; San José, La Paz; Piraera, Lempira; Ocotepeque, Ocotepeque; Lucerna, Ocotepeque; San José de Colinas, Santa Bárbara; Nacaome, Valle; Alianza, Valle; Barrio Buenos Aires, Tegucigalpa. 25: San Elena, La Paz (Dance of Los Negritos). 25-April 2: Intibucá (provincial fair).
Moveable: Holy Week

April
18-23: French Harbour, Bay Islands. 23: San Jorge, Ocotepeque. 25: San Jerónimo, Copán; San Marcos de la Sierra, Intibucá; Dolores Merendón, Ocotepeque; San Marcos, Ocotepeque; San Marcos, Santa Bárbara; Taulabé, Comayagua.

May
3: Tela and Triunfo de la Cruz, Atlántida (Holy Cross); Trinidad, Copán; Santa Cruz de Yojoa; San Miguel Guancapla, Intibucá; San Pedro Tutule, La Paz; Guarita, Lempira; Santa Cruz, Lempira; Sinuapa,

Ocotepeque; El Rosario, Olancho; Manto, Olancho; Atima, Santa Bárbara; Gualala, Santa Bárbara; Amapala, Valle. 8: Macuelizo, Santa Bárbara. 13: San Francisco de la Paz, Olancho. 15: La Ceiba, Atlántida (May 8-23) (major Carnival celebrations, with fireworks, music, and general mischief); Concepción de María, Choluteca; Tocoa, Colón; San Isidro, Choluteca; Güinope, Paraíso; Lepaterique, Francisco Morazán; San Isidro, Intibucá. 20: Concepción del Norte, Santa Bárbara; 22: Sabá, Colón; Santa Rita, Copán; Santa Rita, Santa Bárbara; Morazán, Yoro; Santa Rita, Yoro. 28: La Trinidad, Comayagua; Ojos de Agua, Comayagua; Trinidad, Copán; Trinidad, Santa Bárbara. 25: El Corpus, Choluteca. 30: San Fernando, Ocotepeque; Omoa, Cortés. Yuscarán, Paraíso (mango fair);

June
3: Nueva Armenia, Francisco Morazán; San Isidro, Choluteca. 6: Fraternidad, Ocotepeque. 13: Tela, Atlántida; Minas de Oro, Comayagua; Villa de San Antonio, Comayagua; Cabañas, Copán; San Antonio, Copán; San Pedro, Copán; Veracruz, Copán; San Antonio de Cortés; San Antonio de Flores, Choluteca; San Antonio de Flores, Paraíso; La Venta, Francisco Morazán; Maraita, Francisco Morazán; San Antonio de Oriente, Francisco Morazán; Masaguara, Intibucá; San Antonio, Intibucá; Erandique, Lempira; Vallodolid, Lempira; Ocotepeque, Ocotepeque; El Níspero, Santa Bárbara. 21: Balfate, Colón (Garífuna); San Luis, Comayagua. 24: El Porvenir, Atlántida; La Entrada, Copán; Trujillo, Colón (Garífuna); La Unión, Copán; Nueva Arcadia, Copán; San Juan de Opoa, Copán; Yuscarán, Paraíso; Paraíso, Paraíso; San Juan de Flores, Francisco Morazán; San Marcos de la Sierra, Intibucá; La Paz, La Paz; San Juan, La Paz; San Juan Garita, Lempira; La Labor, Ocotepeque; Juticalpa, Olancho; Guarizama, Olancho; Quimistán, Santa Bárbara. 29: San Pedro, Copán; San Pedro Sula, Cortés; Apacilagua, Choluteca; Nuevo Celilac, Santa Bárbara; Yorito, Yoro.

July
15: San Buenaventura, Francisco Morazán; 16: Santa Fé , Colón; La Virtud, Lempira; San Francisco, Lempira; El Negrito, Yoro. 20: Magdalena, Intibucá. 22: Oak Ridge (José Santos Guardiola), Bay Islands, discovery of America. 22-29: La Esperanza, Intibucá (potato festival). 25: La Jigua, Copán; Camasca, Intibucá; Santa Elena, La Paz; San José, Ocotepeque; Lepaterique, Francisco Morazán; Santiago Puringla, La Paz; Lepaera, Lempira; Piraera, Lempira; Yoro, Yoro. 26: La Ceiba, Atlántida (milk festival); La Libertad, Comayagua; Meambar, Comayagua; San Marcos de Colón, Choluteca; Santa Ana de Yusguare, Choluteca; Yauyupe, Paraíso; Santa Ana, Francisco Morazán; Santa Ana, La Paz; Campamento, Olancho; Guata, Olancho. 31: Roatán (Coxen's Hole), Bay Islands.

Third Sunday: Yuscarán (mango and zapote festival)

August
2: San Ignacio, Francisco Morazán. 10: Alubaren, Francisco Morazán; San Lorenzo, Valle. 15: Esparta, Atlántida; Jutiapa, Atlántida; Sonaguera, Colón; Corquán, Copán; Santa Rita, Copán; Pimienta, Cortés; Puerto Cortés, Cortés; Marcovia, Choluteca; El Porvenir, Francisco Morazán; Utila, Bay Islands; Opatoro, La Paz; Santa María, La Paz. 21: La Iguala, Lempira; Arada, Santa Bárbara; Chinda, Santa Bárbara; Naranjito, Santa Bárbara. 24: Namasigüe, Choluteca; Talgua, Lempira; Villanueva, Cortés. 28: San Agustín, Copán. 30: La Masica, Atlántida; Santa Rosa de Aguán; El Triunfo, Choluteca; Santa Rosa de Copán; La Lima, Cortés; Guaimica, Francisco Morazán.
Last Saturday of August: Danlí, Paraíso (Corn festival);

September
8: San José del Potrero, Comayagua; Erandique, Lempira. 10: San Nicolás, Copán; El Progreso, Yoro. 11-17: Olanchito, Yoro. 12: Dulce Nombre de Culmí, Olancho; Dulce Nombre, Copán. 24: Veracruz, Copán; Aguanqueterique, La Paz; Mercedes, Ocotepeque; San Esteban, Olancho; Arenal, Yoro. 16: San Manuel, Cortés; 28: San Jerónimo, Comayagua. 29: Tegucigalpa, Francisco Morazán; Potrerillos, Cortés; San Miguelito, Francisco Morazán; Dolores, Intibucá; San Miguel Guancapla, Intibucá; Marcala, La Paz; San Rafael, Lempira; Macuelizo, Santa Bárbara.

October
4: San Francisco, Atlántida; Dolores, Copán; Texiguat, Paraíso; Orica, Francisco Morazán; Reitoca, Francisco Morazán; Cabañas, La Paz; Cane, La Paz; Chinacla, La Paz; San Francisco, Lempira; Santa Cruz, Lempira; Tambla, Lempira; San Francisco del Valle, Ocotepeque; La Unión, Olancho; San Francisco de Becerra, Olancho; Azacualpa, Santa Bárbara; San Francisco de Yojoa; Tatumbla, Francisco Morazán; Valle de Angeles, Francisco Morazán; Catacamas, Olancho. 8: El Rosario, Comayagua; El Rosario, Olancho; Belén, Lempira. 17: Amapala, Valle (fish festival) 18: San Lucas, Paraíso. 19: Piraera, Lempira.

November
4: Paraíso, Paraíso; La Paz, La Paz. 24: La Libertad, Francisco Morazán; 24; Mercedes, La Paz. 30: Orocuina, Choluteca.

December
4: Las Flores, Lempira; La Virtud, Lempira; Santa Bárbara, Santa Bárbara. 8: Limón, Colón; Lamaní, Comayagua; Teupasenti, Paraíso;

Concepción, Copán; Cucuyagua, Copán; Concepción de María, Choluteca; Choluteca, Choluteca; Yuscarán, Paraíso; Potrerillos, Paraíso; La Esperanza, Intibucá; Concepción, Intibucá; Gracias, Lempira; Gualcince, Lempira; San Manuel Colohete, Lempira; Tambla, Lempira; Concepción, Ocotepeque; Juticalpa, Olancho; Santa Bárbara, Santa Bárbara; Yoro, Yoro; El Progreso, Yoro; Sulaco, Yoro. 12: Comayagua, Comayagua; Comayagüela (Virgin of Guadalupe); La Labor, Ocotepeque. 13: Gracias, Lempira; Santa Lucía, Francisco Morazán; Santa Lucía, Intibucá; Yamaranguila, Intibucá; Virginia, Lempira. 18: Lejamaní, Comayagua; Tomala, Lempira. 19: Caridad, Valle. 25: Lamaní, Comayagua; Puerto Lempira, Gracias a Dios; Brus Laguna, Gracias a Dios; Belén Gualcho, Ocotepeque; 25-28, Minas de Oro, Comayagua.

FIREWORKS

Fireworks are great toys in Honduras for children of all ages. They're sold to kids to play with, and some devices are as big as dynamite sticks, with equivalent sounds. You don't want to be around when one explodes, but sometimes it's hard to avoid. You'll hear explosions at night and think that a bank robbery or revolution is going on, but it's only play or a celebration. For me, the scariest occurrence is when kids set off explosions near a bank guard armed with a tommy gun and dressed in a bullet-proof vest.

HUNTING

The Choluteca area (Pacific coast) is famous for the hunting of white-winged doves. The season runs from November 1 to March 15. Other quarry, around Danlí, are quail, pigeons, deer, wild turkey, and boar.

Hunting arrangements are generally made in advance through tour operators, who need details of guns and two passport photos to obtain a licence. Ammunition must be purchased locally.

MILITARY AND SECURITY

Security is everywhere in Honduras. There are guards at every hotel of any pretension, at stores, at banks, at restaurants and parking lots. In the countryside, army encampments and barracks dot the landscape.

Is all this a problem? Don't forget that there have been wars in recent years on either side of Honduras, and some concern about invasion is inevitable. But in my travels through Honduras, by plane and bus and on bicycle, I have never felt afraid, or exposed to any untoward danger.

Of course, you don't want to go looking for trouble. Display appropriate deference to people in uniform, don't take pictures of military installations (at least not openly), and cooperate if you're asked for identification or stopped for some other reason.

MOVIES

At movie theaters in Tegucigalpa and San Pedro Sula, what you pay depends on where you sit — up in the balcony, out of popcorn range, costs more, but never over a dollar. You'll usually get a double bill, the print may be old, the projector is creaky, but seeing a movie in Honduras is great fun. I recently saw a bat at a movie house.

In small villages, video halls, usually located in back of small restaurants, have replaced itinerant projectionists. Up to 30 persons are seated in front of a t.v., and the latest Mexican thrillers are shown at a charge of a few cents per person.

SALARIES

A laborer on a coffee or banana plantation might make up to ten lempiras a day — just under $3 at the official exchange rate. That income goes to support not only himself, but, usually, several dependents as well. A secretary in Tegucigalpa might make double that amount.

SEXUAL ROLES

"Nice" women — I'm talking from the local point of view — don't smoke or drink in public, and those who do are considered to be of doubtful virtue.

But despite some old-fashioned ideas about morality, legal marriage is not always the rule in Honduras. A church wedding costs money that many do not have, or would rather spend on other priorities. So many working-class couples, and even solid middle-class couples, simply live together without legal blessing, and without the support of liberal and liberated ideology.

WEIGHTS AND MEASURES

Mostly, Honduras follow the metric system: kilometers (equivalent to .62 miles), kilograms (2.2 pounds), and liters (1.05 U.S. quarts). However, you'll also find some U.S. measures in use, especially gallons, along with old Spanish measures. The q*uintal* is equal to 100 pounds, the *arroba* is 25 pounds, the *vara* is about nine-tenths of a yard, and the *manzana* is a square measurement equal to about 1.72 acres or .7 hectare.

INDEX

TRAVEL NOTES

TRAVEL NOTES

TRAVEL NOTES

TRAVEL NOTES

TRAVEL NOTES

TRAVEL NOTES

HELLO!!!

DEAR READER,

By this point, you know that I speak my mind. Now it's your turn.

If you've discovered a hotel or restaurant and would like to share it with others, drop me a line. If you've had a bad experience with any service used by visitors — whether I've mentioned it or not — I want to know about that, too.

Thanks for writing.

Sincerely,   Paul Glassman

OPEN ROAD PUBLISHING
P.O.Box11249, Cleveland Park Station, Washington, DC 20008

COME TO HONDURAS

OPEN ROAD PUBLISHING

YOUR PASSPORT TO GREAT TRAVEL

COSTA RICA GUIDE by Paul Glassman, 5th Ed. Glassman's classic travel guide to Costa Rica remains the standard against which all others must be judged. Discover great accommodations, reliable restaurants, pristine beaches, and incredible diving, fishing, and other water sports. Revised and updated. **$14.95**

BELIZE GUIDE by Paul Glassman, 6th Ed. Glassman's new BELIZE GUIDE has quickly become the guide of choice for Belize travelers. Perhaps the finest spot for Caribbean scuba diving and sport fishing, Belize's picture-perfect palm trees, Mayan ruins, tropical forests, uncrowded beaches, and fantastic water sports have made it one of the most popular Caribbean travel destinations. **$13.95**

HONDURAS GUIDE by J.P.Panet with Leah Hart and Paul Glassman, 2nd Ed. Glassman's superior series of Central America travel guides continues with the revised edition of his fascinating look at Honduras and the Bay Islands. **$13.95**

GUATEMALA GUIDE by Paul Glassman, 8th Ed. Glassman's first travel guide to Central America, it remains the single best source for visiting Guatemela. **$16.95**

FLORIDA GOLF GUIDE by Jimmy Shacky. The most comprehensive and detailed guide yet to Florida's 1,000-plus golf courses. **$14.95**

LAS VEGAS GUIDE by Ed Kranmar and Avery Cardoza. Find out about the great hotels, restaurants, shops, and excursions – plus more pages of gambling tips and strategies than any other Vegas guide. **$5.95**

THE WASHINGTON, DC, ETHNIC RESTAURANT GUIDE by Jonathan Stein. This book is the only available ethnic dining guide for the entire Washington area. Includes over 150 terrific ethnic restaurants. **$9.95**

CHINA GUIDE by Ruth Lor Malloy, 8th Ed. The first guide to modern China and still the best, Malloy has shown you the real China since 1975, now with new sections on Beijing, Shanghai, and other top Western destinations, plus detailed information on hundreds of beautiful but more distant areas. **$17.95**

DISNEY WORLD AND ORLANDO THEME PARKS: THE COMPLETE GUIDE by Jay Fenster. Easily the most comprehensive and most enjoyable travel guide to the Magic Kingdom and Orlando's other great theme parks. **$12.95**

Ask for Open Road's travel publications from your favorite bookstore, or order directly by writing to:

OPEN ROAD PUBLISHING
P.O. Box 11249, Cleveland Park Station, Washington, D.C., 20008.
Please include $3.00 for first book, $1.00 thereafter for postage and handling.
Discounts available for special order or bulk purchases.